Workshop on Computational Approaches to Linguistic Creativity 2009

(CALC 2009)

Held at NAACL HLT 2009

Boulder, Colorado, USA
4 June 2009

ISBN: 978-1-61738-566-7

Printed from e-media with permission by:

Curran Associates, Inc.
57 Morehouse Lane
Red Hook, NY 12571

Some format issues inherent in the e-media version may also appear in this print version.

Printed by Curran Associates, Inc. (2010)

For permission requests, please contact the Association for Computational Linguistics at the address below.

Association for Computational Linguistics
209 N. Eighth Street
Stroudsburg, Pennsylvania 18360

Phone: 1-570-476-8006
Fax: 1-570-476-0860

acl@aclweb.org

Additional copies of this publication are available from:

Curran Associates, Inc.
57 Morehouse Lane
Red Hook, NY 12571 USA
Phone: 845-758-0400
Fax: 845-758-2634
Email: curran@proceedings.com
Web: www.proceedings.com

Introduction

It is generally agreed upon that linguistic creativity is a unique property of human language. Some claim that linguistic creativity is expressed in our ability to combine known words in a new sentence, others refer to our skill to express thoughts in figurative language, and yet others talk about syntactic recursion and lexical creativity. Computational systems incorporating models of linguistic creativity operate on different types of data, including written text, audio/speech/sound, and video/images/gestures. Creativity-aware systems will improve the contribution Computational Linguistics has to offer to many practical areas, including education, entertainment, and engineering.

The idea behind the 2009 workshop on Computational Approaches to Linguistic Creativity (CALC) originated in our own previous activities, including the organization of the 2007 NAACL-HLT workshop on Figurative Language Processing and work within the Story Generator Algorithms project (German Research Foundation grant ME-1546/2-1). We are well aware of the fact that each single linguistic creativity phenomenon is challenging to describe, detect, or generate on its own. Consequently, the main goal of the present workshop is to provide a venue for researchers to inform each other and the NLP community at large of the state of the art of current systems.

Yet, linguistic creativity phenomena are intertwined with others, and with each other. To illustrate, metaphorical concepts are related to their lexical and syntactical surface realization; the events of a story are expressed by narrator and character speech; and humor involves semantic, situational, and cultural knowledge. With twelve peer-reviewed contributions covering a wide range of phenomena related to linguistic creativity, the workshop will thus strengthen research and foster collaboration in the field. At the same time, it will contribute to a better understanding of the new issues and challenges that need to be tackled.

For CALC 2009, we received a total of 19 submissions coming from 13 different countries. Eight papers were accepted for oral presentation and four were selected for a poster session. We are especially grateful to the authors who submitted excellent papers and to our hard working program committee. We would like to express our enormous gratitude to the U.S. National Science Foundation (IIS award #: 0906244) for the generous support of the workshop which allowed many participants from three continents to attend the workshop and present their work. Particular thanks go to the invited speaker, Nick Montfort (MIT), who kindly agreed to give a talk on Interactive Fiction, and whose paper is included in this volume. Last but not least, we want to thank Christy Doran and Eric Ringger, the publication chairs.

Anna Feldman and Birte Lönneker-Rodman

Organizers:

Anna Feldman, Montclair State University, USA
Birte Lönneker-Rodman, University of Hamburg, Germany

Program Committee:

Shlomo Argamon, Illinois Institute of Technology, USA
Roberto Basili, University of Roma, Italy
Amilcar Cardoso, University of Coimbra, Portugal
Afsaneh Fazly, University of Toronto, Canada
Eileen Fitzpatrick, Montclair State University, USA
Pablo Gervas, Universidad Complutense de Madrid, Spain
Sam Glucksberg, Princeton University, USA
Jerry Hobbs, ISI, Marina del Rey, USA
Sid Horton, Northwestern University, USA
Diana Inkpen, University of Ottawa, Canada
Mark Lee, University of Birmingham, UK
Hugo Liu, MIT, USA
Xiaofei Lu, Penn State University, USA
Ruli Manurung, University of Indonesia, Indonesia
Katja Markert, University of Leeds, UK
Rada Mihalcea, University of North Texas, USA
Anton Nijholt, University of Twente, The Netherlands
Andrew Ortony, Northwestern University, USA
Vasile Rus, The University of Memphis, USA
Richard Sproat, Oregon Health and Science University, USA
Gerard Steen, Vrije Universiteit, Amsterdam, The Netherlands
Carlo Strapparava, Istituto per la Ricerca Scientifica e Tecnologica, Trento, Italy
Juergen Trouvain, Saarland University, Germany

Additional Reviewers:

Carmen Banea, University of North Texas, USA
Alessandro Valitutti, Istituto per la Ricerca Scientifica e Tecnologica, Trento, Italy

Invited Speaker:

Nick Montfort, Massachusetts Institute of Technology, USA

Table of Contents

Conference Program

Thursday, June 4, 2009

8:30–9:15	Coffee Session
9:15–9:20	Welcome and Introduction to CALC-09
	Session 1: Metaphors and Eggcorns
9:20–9:45	*Discourse Topics and Metaphors* Beata Beigman Klebanov, Eyal Beigman and Daniel Diermeier
9:45–10:10	*Topic Model Analysis of Metaphor Frequency for Psycholinguistic Stimuli* Steven Bethard, Vicky Tzuyin Lai and James H. Martin
10:10–10:35	*Understanding Eggcorns* Sravana Reddy
10:35–11:00	Morning break
	Session 2: Generating Creative Texts
11:05–11:30	*Automatically Extracting Word Relationships as Templates for Pun Generation* Bryan Anthony Hong and Ethel Ong
11:30–11:55	*Gaiku : Generating Haiku with Word Associations Norms* Yael Netzer, David Gabay, Yoav Goldberg and Michael Elhadad

Thursday, June 4, 2009 (continued)

Poster Session 1

12:00–12:15 *Automatic Generation of Tamil Lyrics for Melodies*
Ananth Ramakrishnan A., Sankar Kuppan and Sobha Lalitha Devi

12:15–12:30 *Quantifying Constructional Productivity with Unseen Slot Members*
Amir Zeldes

12:30–14:00 Lunch

Invited Talk

14:00–15:00 *Curveship: An Interactive Fiction System for Interactive Narrating*
Nick Montfort

Poster Session 2

15:00–15:15 *Planning Author and Character Goals for Story Generation*
Candice Solis, Joan Tiffany Siy, Emerald Tabirao and Ethel Ong

15:15–15:30 *An Unsupervised Model for Text Message Normalization*
Paul Cook and Suzanne Stevenson

15:30–16:00 Afternoon Break

Session 3: From Morphology to Pragmatics to Text

16:00–16:25 *Morphological Productivity Rankings of Complex Adjectives*
Stefano Vegnaduzzo

16:25–16:50 *How Creative is Your Writing?*
Xiaojin Zhu, Zhiting Xu and Tushar Khot

16:50–17:15 *'Sorry' is the hardest word*
Allan Ramsay and Debora Field

17:15–17:30 Summary and General Discussion

Discourse Topics and Metaphors

Beata Beigman Klebanov
Northwestern University
beata@northwestern.edu

Eyal Beigman
Washington University in St. Louis
beigman@wustl.edu

Daniel Diermeier
Northwestern University
d-diermeier@northwestern.edu

Abstract

Using metaphor-annotated material that is sufficiently representative of the topical composition of a similar-length document in a large background corpus, we show that words expressing a discourse-wide topic of discussion are less likely to be metaphorical than other words in a document. Our results suggest that to harvest metaphors more effectively, one is advised to consider words that do not represent a discourse topic.

Traditionally, metaphor detectors use the observation that a metaphorically used item creates a local incongruity because there is a violation of a selectional restriction, such as providing a non-vehicle object to the verb *derail* in *Protesters derailed the conference*. Current state of art in metaphor detection therefore tends to be "localistic" – the distributional profile of the target word in its immediate grammatical or collocational context in a background corpus or a database like WordNet is used to determine metaphoricity (Mason, 2004; Krishnakumaran and Zhu, 2007; Birke and Sarkar, 2006; Gedigian et al., 2006; Fass, 1991).

However, some theories of metaphor postulate certain features of metaphors that connect it to the surrounding text beyond the small grammatical or proximal locality. For example, for Kittay (1987) metaphor is a discourse phenomenon; although the minimal metaphoric unit is a clause, often much larger chunks of text constitute a metaphor. Consider, for example, the TRAIN metaphor in the following excerpt from a Sunday Times article on 20 September 1992:

> Thatcher warned EC leaders to stop their endless round of summits and take notice of their own people. "There is a fear that the European train will thunder forward, laden with its customary cargo of gravy, towards a destination neither wished for nor understood by electorates. But the train can be stopped," she said.

In the example above, the quotation is not in itself a metaphor, as there is no indication that something other than the actual train is being discussed (and so no local incongruities exist). Only when situated in the context prepared by the first sentence (and indeed the rest of the article), the train imagery becomes a metaphor.

According to Kittay, a metaphor occurs when a semantic field is used to discuss a *different* content domain. The theory therefore predicts that a metaphorically used semantic domain would be off-topic in the given document.

Although a single document can have singular, idiosyncratic topics, it is likelier to discuss a mix of topics that are typical of the discourse of which it is part. We therefore derive the following hypothesis: Words in a given document that represent a common topic of discussion in a corpus of relevant documents would be predominantly non-metaphorical. That is, a smaller share of metaphorically used words in a document would fall in such topical words than the share of topical words in the document.

We test this hypothesis in the current article.

Proceedings of the NAACL HLT Workshop on Computational Approaches to Linguistic Creativity, pages 1–8,
Boulder, Colorado, June 2009.

Using a large background corpus, we estimate the topical composition of the target documents (section 1) that were annotated for metaphors (section 2). We then report the results of the experiment (section 3) that strongly support the hypothesis, and discuss the findings (section 4). The concluding section provides a summary and outlines the significance of the results for the practice of metaphor detection.

1 Topic identification

1.1 EUI corpus

Our aim was to create a large corpus of British media discourse regarding the emerging European Union institutions, with both Euro-phile and Euro-sceptic camps represented. Our corpus consists of 12,814 articles drawn from three British newspapers: *The Guardian* (34%), *The Times* (38%), and *The Independent* (28%), dating from 1990 to 2000. We used LexisNexis Academic[1] to search for the Subject index term *European Union Institutions* (henceforth, *EUI*).[2] After results are retrieved, we further narrow them down to only documents on the subject *European Union Institutions* in the detailed subject index of the retrieved results.[3,4]

1.2 Identification of discourse topics

We converted all 12,858 documents[5] (henceforth, **EUI+M** corpus) into plain text format and removed words from a list of 153 common function words. We then constructed an indexing vocabulary **V** that included all and only words that (a) contained only letters; and (b) appeared at least 6 times in the collection. All documents were indexed using this 21,046 word vocabulary. We will designate all the indexed words in document i as $\mathbf{D}_i$.

To identify the main discourse topics in the EUI+M corpus, we submitted the indexed documents to an unsupervised clustering method Latent Dirichlet Allocation (Blei et al., 2003) (henceforth, **LDA**).[6] The designation of the clusters as topics is supported by findings reported in Blei et al. (2003) that the clusters contain information relevant for topic discrimination. Additionally, Chanen and Patrick (2007) show that LDA achieves significant correlations with humans on a topic characterization task, where humans produced not just a topic classification but also identified phrases they believed were indicative of each class.

Using the default settings of LDA implementation,[7] we analyzed the corpus into 100 topics. Table 1 exemplifies some of the emergent topics.

1.3 Topical words in a text

LDA is a generative model of text. According to its outlook, every text is about a small (typically 5-7) number of topics, and each indexed word in the text belongs to one of these topics. However, in many cases, the relationship between the word and the topic is quite tentative, as the word is not particularly likely given the topic. We therefore use parameter k to control topic assignments – we only take LDA's assignment of word to topic if the word is in the top k most likely words for that topic. For k=25, about 15% of in-vocabulary words in a document are assigned to a topic; for k=400, about half the in-vocabulary words are assigned to some topic. We designate by $\mathbf{T}_i^k$ all indexed words in document i that are assigned to some topic for the given value of k. The ratio $\frac{|T_i^k|}{|D_i|}$ describes the proportion of discourse topical words in the indexed words for the given document.

[1] http://academic.lexisnexis.com/online-services/academic-features.aspx

[2] In LexisNexis subject index hierarchy: Government and Public Administration/International Organization and Bodies/International Governmental Organizations/European Union Institutions.

[3] In the initial search, an article that scores 72% on the subject would be retrieved, but it would not be classified as being on this subject, and so would not be included in the final dataset. Articles in the final dataset tend to score about 90% on the subject, according to LexisNexis index.

[4] There is a gap in LexisNexis' index coverage of *The Times* during 1996-7 and of *The Independent* during 2000. To avoid under-representation of the newspaper and of the relevant years in the sample, we added articles returned for the search SECTION(Home news) AND (European Union OR Brussels) on *The Times* 01/1996 through 04/1998, and SECTION(News AND NOT Foreign) AND (European Union OR Brussels) on *The Independent* throughout 2000.

[5] 12,814 EUI corpus plus 44 documents annotated for metaphors, to be described in section 2.

[6] No stemming was performed.

[7] downloaded from http://www.cs.princeton.edu/~blei/lda-c/

Table 1: Examples of topics identified by LDA in the EUI+M corpus. All words are taken from top 25 most likely words given the topic. We boldface one word per cluster, that could provide, in our view, an appropriate label for the cluster.

foreign nato military war russian **defence** soviet piece un kosovo sanctions bosnia moscow
rail tunnel **transport** train pounds channel eurostar ferry trains passengers services paris eurotunnel
countries europe **enlargement** new membership members eastern conference reform voting summit commission foreign join poland negotiations
parliament mep party socialist strasbourg christian vote leader labour conservative right political green democrat elections epp
television commission satellite tv broadcasting tickets film broadcasters bbc programmes **media** industry channel public directive
court article justice member directive treaty question provisions case law regulation judgment interpretation rules order proceedings
social workers **employment** working hours jobs week employers legislation unions employees chapter rights health minimum
bank central euro **monetary** rates currency interest bundesbank markets economic exchange finance inflation dollar german
players **football** clubs uefa league fifa game cup
fishing fish fishermen fisheries quota vessels boats waters sea fleet
racism racist ethnic xenophobia black minorities jury discrimination white relations
drugs patent research human companies genetic scientists health medical **biotechnology** disease
children parents punishment school rights family **childcare** corporal education law father mother
controls **immigration** border asylum checks passport police citizens crime europol
energy nuclear emissions oil electricity gas environment carbon tax pollution fuel global cut
commission fraud commissioners brussels report allegations officials inquiry meps **corruption** mismanagement staff santer

2 Metaphor annotation

Ideally, we should have sampled a small sub-corpus from the EUI corpus for metaphor annotation; however, the choice of the data for annotation predated the construction of the EUI corpus.

Our interest being in the way metaphors used in public discourse help shape attitudes towards a complex, ongoing and fateful political reality, we came across Musolff's (2000) work on the British discourse on the European integration process throughout the 1990s. Working in the corpus linguistics tradition, Musolff (2000) studied a number of metaphors recurrent in this discourse, making available a selection of materials he used, marked with the metaphors.[8]

One caveat to directly using the database is the lack of clarity regarding the metaphor annotation procedure. In particular, the author does not report how many people participated, or any inter-annotator agreement figures. We therefore chose 4 out of Musolff's list of source domains, took all articles corresponding to them (128 documents), along with 23 articles from other source domains, and submitted them to a group of 8 undergraduate annotators, on top of Musolff's original markup that is treated as another annotator.

Annotators received the following instructions, reflecting our focus on the persuasive use of metaphor, as part of an argument:

> Generally speaking, a metaphor is a linguistic expression whereby something is compared to something else that it is clearly *literally* not, in order to make a point. Thus, in Tony Blair's famous "I haven't got a reverse gear", Tony Blair is compared to a car in order to stress his unwillingness/inability to retract his statements or actions. We would say in this case that a metaphor from a VEHICLE domain is used. In this study we will consider metaphors from 4 domains.

For the 4 chosen domains we provided the following descriptions, along with 2 examples for each:

[8] available from http://www.dur.ac.uk/andreas.musolff/Arcindex.htm

AUTHORITY Metaphors that have to do with discipline and authority, like school, religion, royalty, asylum, prison, etc.

LOVE Metaphors from love/romance and family.

BUILD Metaphors that have to do with building (the process) and houses and other buildings or constructions, their parts and uses.

VEHICLE Metaphors that have to do with land-borne vehicles, their parts, operation and maintenance.

People were instructed to mark every paragraph where a metaphor from a given domain occurs. They were also asked to provide a comment that briefly summarizes the ground for their decision, saying what is being compared to what.[9]

Table 2 shows the inter-annotator agreement figures.

Table 2: Inter-annotator agreement, measured on 2364 paragraphs (151 documents).[11]

Source Domain of Metaphor	κ
LOVE	0.66
VEHICLE	0.66
AUTHORITY	0.39
BUILD	0.43

LOVE and VEHICLE are close to acceptable reliability, with the other two types scoring low. In order to understand the nature of disagreements, we submitted the annotated materials plus some random annotations to 7 out of the original 8 people for validation, 4-8 weeks after they completed the annotations, asking them to accept or reject metaphor markups. We found that metaphors initially marked by at least 4 people (out of 9) were accepted as valid by people who did not initially mark them in 91% of the cases, on average across the metaphor types. These are thus uncontroversial cases, with the missing annotations likely due to attention slips rather than to genuine differences of opinion. Metaphors initially marked by 1-3 people were more controversial, with the average validation rate of 41% (Beigman Klebanov et al., 2008).

Evidently, some of the metaphors are clearer-cut than others, yet even the more difficult cases got non-negligible support at validation time from people who did not initially mark them. We therefore decided to regard the whole of the annotated data as valid for the purpose of the current research. Our focus is on finding metaphors (recall), and less on making sure all candidate metaphors are acceptable to all annotators; it suffices to know that even the minority opinion often finds support.

In the second stage of the research, we expanded the repertoire of the metaphor types to include additional source domains, mainly from Musolff's list. The dataset has so far been subjected to non-expert annotations by a group of the total of 15 undergraduate students. Metaphors from the source domains of VEHICLE, LOVE, BUILDING, AUTHORITY, WAR, SHOW, SCHOOL, RELIGION, MEDICINE were annotated by different subsets of the students.

The outcome of the second stage of the project is not sufficient for addressing the issue of discourse topics vs metaphors, however, as there are instances of metaphors in the text that do not fall into any of the source domains singled out by Musolff as recurrent ones in the discourse under consideration. We are now at an early stage of the third phrase we call OpenMeta, where annotators are asked to mark all metaphors they can detect, not confining themselves to a given list of source domains. Only annotators who participated in the previous, type-constrained, version of the task participate in OpenMeta project. So far, we have 44 documents annotated by 3 people for open-domain metaphors. This subset features as full a coverage of all metaphors used in the documents as we were able to obtain so far, and it is going to serve as test data for the topics vs metaphors hypothesis.

[9]In the topics vs metaphors experiment, we test the hypothesis on words rather than paragraphs. For metaphors from a pre-specified domain, such as VEHICLE or LOVE, it was usually clear which words in the paragraph belong to the domain and are used metaphorically. People's comments often explicitly used words from the paragraph, or made it otherwise clear through their description. For OpenMeta phase (please see below), where people were asked to mark metaphors from any source domain, they were also asked to single out the words in the paragraph that witness the metaphor, and these are the words used in the current experiment.

[11]These are results for binary classification for each metaphor type rather than a multiclass classification, since some articles have more than one type and some have none.

Our test set is thus biased towards recurrent metaphorical domains (those named by Musolff), and towards metaphors that are relatively salient to a naive reader, from recurrent or other source domains. Metaphors marked in the test data are those afforded a high degree of rhetorical presence in the discourse – either quantitatively, because they are repeated and elaborated, or qualitatively, because they are striking enough to arrest the naive reader's attention. According to the Presence Theory in rhetoric (Perelman and Olbrechts-Tyteca, 1969; Gross and Dearin, 2003; Atkinson et al., 2008), elements afforded high presence are key to the rhetorical design of the argument. These are not so much metaphors we live by without even noticing, such as those often studied in Conceptual Metaphor literature, like VALUE AS SIZE or TIME AS SPACE; these are metaphors that are clearly a matter of the author's conscious choice, closest in the current theorizing to Steen's (2008) notion of *deliberate* metaphors.

2.1 Pseudo sampling

The annotated data is not really a sample of the corpus. In fact, it is not known to us exactly how the documents were chosen; although all 44 metaphor annotated documents are from the newspapers and dates participating in the EUI corpus, only 20% are actually in the EUI corpus. How can we establish that there is a fit between the EUI collection and the annotated texts? We check how well discourse topics cover the documents, in the corpus and in the annotated material. Specifically, for a fixed k, is there a difference in the $\frac{|T_i^k|}{|D_i|}$ for annotated documents as opposed to the corpus at large? Using a random sample of 50 documents from EUI corpus, a 2-tailed t-test yielded $p < 0.05$, for all k, the trend being towards a better coverage of the EUI documents than of the metaphor annotated ones.

We hypothesized that this was due to the large discrepancy in the lengths of the texts: An average text in the EUI sample is 432 words long, whereas the metaphor annotated texts are 775 words long on average, with the shortest having 343 words. Shorter texts tend to be less elaborate and more "to the point", with a higher percentage of topical words.

To neutralize the effect of length on topical coverage, we chose from the EUI sample only documents that were at least 343 words long, resulting in 31 documents. Comparing those to the 44 metaphor annotated documents, we found $p > 0.37$ for every k, i.e. the annotated documents are indistinguishable in topical coverage from similar-length documents in the EUI corpus.

3 Experiment

3.1 Summary of notation

V All and only non-stop words containing only letters that appeared in at least 6 documents in the collection.

$\mathbf{D}_i$ All words in document i that are in V.

$\mathbf{T}_i^k$ All words in document i that are in V and are in the top k words for some topic active in document i according to LDA output.

$\mathbf{M}_i$ All words in document i that are in V and are marked as metaphors in this document.

3.2 Hypothesis

We hypothesize that words in a given document that are high-ranking representatives of a common topic of discussion in a relevant corpus are less likely to be metaphorical than other words in the document. That is, such words would contain a smaller proportion of metaphors than their share in text. Using the definitions above: For an average document i and any k, $\frac{|T_i^k|}{|D_i|} > \frac{|M_i \cap T_i^k|}{|M_i|}$.

3.3 Results

As we hypothesized, metaphors are under-represented in topically used words. Thus, for k=25, about 15% of the indexed words in the document are deemed topical, containing about 3% of the metaphorically used indexed words in that document. For k=400, about 53% of the indexed words are topical, capturing only 22% of the metaphors.

4 Discussion

4.1 Metaphors from salient domains

A number of domains singled out by Musolff (2000) as being recurrent metaphors in the corpus, such

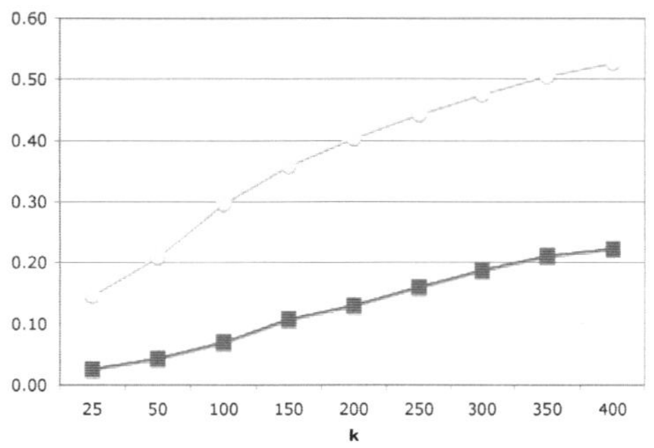

Figure 1: As hypothesized, $\frac{|T_i^k|}{|D_i|}$, shown in circles, is larger than $\frac{|M_i \cap T_i^k|}{|M_i|}$, shown in squares, for various k.

as VEHICLE or LOVE, are also things people care about politically, hence they also correspond to recurrent topics of discussion (see clusters titled *transport* and *childcare* in table 1). It has been shown experimentally that the subject's in-depth familiarity with the source domain is necessary for the metaphor to work as intended – see for example Gentner and Gentner (1983) work on using water flow metaphors for electricity. Our results suggest that participants in political discourse draw on domains not only familiar in general, but indeed highly salient in the specific discourse itself.

As a consequence, an extended metaphor from a discourse-topical domain can be easily mistaken by the topic detection software for a topical use of the relevant items. Consider, for example, an extract from a 19 December 1991 article in *Times*:

> Denis Healey, former Labour Chancellor of the Exchequer, urged the prime minister to stop playing Tory party politics with the negotiations over Europe and drew an image of Mr Major as a driver. He said: "I understand that if you are driving a car and sitting behind you is a lady with a handbag and a man with fangs, you may feel it wiser to drive in the slow lane. My own advice is that he should pull into a lay-by, turf the others out and then hand the wheel over to firmer and safer hands."

LDA considered $\{$*drive driving*$\}$ to belong to the topic that deals with safety and road accidents, including in its 200 most likely words $\{$*crash died accidents pedestrians traffic safety cars maps motorists*$\}$, although additional metaphorically used items from the same semantic domain, such as *lane* and *wheel*, were not among the top 200 representatives of this topic.

It is an intriguing direction for future research to compare the topical and metaphorical uses of such domains, in order to determine which aspects loom large indeed, being both matters of literal concern and prolific generators of metaphors, and how these are manipulated for persuasive effects. The example above suggests that in the British EU-related discourse in 1990s safety of driving is both a topic-of-discussion ("Cyclists and pedestrians are more vulnerable on British roads than anywhere else in the European Union", proclaims *The Times* on 18 February 2000) and a metaphorical axis, stressing the importance of care and control, the hallmark of the Euro-sceptic stance towards the European integration process.

4.2 Topical metaphors

Putting aside topic detector's mistakes on extended metaphors from certain domains such as discussed in the previous section, what do metaphors in the topical vocabulary look like? The last topic shown in table 1 has to do with criticism towards EU bureaucracy, reflecting extensive discussions in the British media in the late 1990s of alleged corruption and mismanagement in the European Commission. Together with the words cited in the table, this topic lists *root* as one of its 300 most likely words.

This word shows up as a metaphor in 3 of our test documents. In two of them it is used precisely in the context projected by the topic:

> In limpid language, whose meaning no bureaucrat can twist, these four wise men and one wise woman delivered, to their great credit, a coruscating indictment not just of individual commissioners, but of the entire management and corporate culture of the European Commission. They have made an incontestable case, in Tony Blair's words, for "**root** and branch reform".

Here, *root* is used in the *root and branch* idiom suggesting a complete change, a reform, which comes as part of a bundle with severe criticism. Yet the figurative nature of this expression as a metaphor from PLANT domain is apparent to naive readers, making it an instance of imagery routinely going together with criticism in this corpus. A related metaphorical sense of *root* is attested in similar contexts in the corpus, further explaining its connection to the topic:

> Not unless they insist on credible systems to hold commissioners and bureaucrats to account. And not unless they appoint a new team with a brief not just to **root** out malpractices but to shut down entire programmes, such as tourism and humanitarian aid, which the Commission is incompetent to manage and which should never have been added to its ever-expanding empire.

> A bloodied European Commission looks likely to cling on to power today after an eleventh-hour threat to quit by its President, Jacques Santer, called the bluff of the European Parliament ... All week MEPs had been talking up the "nuclear option" of sacking the full Commission body over a burgeoning fraud and nepotism scandal that dates from 1995 ... Early 1997: Finnish Commissioner Erkki Liikanen announces plan to **root** out nepotism in Commission and improve financial controls.

In the third document with *root* metaphor, *root* is used in a different environment, and is not considered topical by LDA:

> For at the **root** of this conflict lies the German denial that unemployment has anything to do with cyclical fluctuations in the economy.

Our quantitative results show that cases such as *root* are more an exception than a rule. Yet, from the perspective of the argumentative use of metaphors, such cases are instructive of the way certain metaphors get "attached" to certain topics of discussion. In this case, the majority of mentions of *root* in this critical context come from Tony Blair's expression that was cited and referenced widely enough to acquire a statistical association with the discussion of the Commission's failings in the corpus. Indeed, the political significance of Blair's successful appropriation of the issue was not lost on the media:

> Tony Blair has swiftly positioned himself as the champion of "**root** and branch" reform. Not to be outdone, William Hague unveiled a "10-point plan" for reform of the Commission, no doubt drawing on his extensive McKinsey management expertise.

In future work, we plan to look closely at the topical metaphors, as they potentially represent outcomes of leadership battles fought in the media, and can thus have political consequences.

5 Conclusion

Using metaphor-annotated material that is sufficiently representative of the topical composition of a similar-length document in a large background corpus, we showed that words expressing a discourse-wide topic of discussion are less likely to be metaphorical than other words in a document.

This is, to our knowledge, the first quantitative demonstration of the connection between metaphoricity of a given word and its role in the relevant background discourse. It complements the traditionally "localistic" outlook on metaphors that is based on the observation that a metaphorically used item creates a local incongruity because there is a violation of a selectional restrictions between verbs and their arguments (Fass, 1991; Mason, 2004; Gedigian et al., 2006; Birke and Sarkar, 2006) or in the adjective-noun pairs (Krishnakumaran and Zhu, 2007). Global discourse-level information can potentially be used to focus metaphor detectors operating at the local level on items with higher metaphoric potential.

Reining and Lönneker-Rodman (2007) use minimal topical information to focus their search for metaphors. Working with a French-language corpus discussing European politics, Reining and Lönneker-Rodman (2007) proposed harvesting salient collocates of the lemma *Europe*, that represents the main topic of discussion and is thus hypothesized to be the main target domain of metaphors in this corpus. Indeed, numerous instances of metaphors were collected using a 4-word window around the lemma in their corpus. Our work can be understood as developing a more nuanced approach to finding the likely target domains in the corpus – those words that represent a topic of discussion rather than the means to discuss a topic. Thus, it is not just Europe per se that is the target, but, more specifically, aspects such as monetary integration, employment, energy, immigration, transportation, and defense, among others. Our results suggest that to harvest deliberate metaphors more effectively, one is advised to consider words that do not represent a discourse topic.

References

Nathan Atkinson, David Kaufer, and Suguru Ishizaki. 2008. Presence and Global Presence in Genres of Self-Presentation: A Framework for Comparative Analysis. *Rhetoric Society Quarterly*, 38(3):1–27.

Beata Beigman Klebanov, Eyal Beigman, and Daniel Diermeier. 2008. Analyzing Disagreements. In *COLING 2008 Workshop on Human Judgments in Computational Linguistics*, pages 2–7, Manchester, UK.

Julia Birke and Anoop Sarkar. 2006. A clustering approach for nearly unsupervised recognition of nonliteral language. In *Proceedings of EACL*, pages 329–336.

David Blei, Andrew Ng, and Michael Jordan. 2003. Latent Dirichlet Allocation. *Journal of Machine Learning Resarch*, 3:993–1022.

Ari Chanen and Jon Patrick. 2007. Measuring correlation between linguists judgments and Latent Dirichlet Allocation topics. In *Proceedings of the Australasian Language Technology workshop*, pages 13–20, Melbourne, Australia.

Dan Fass. 1991. Met*: A method for discriminating metonymy and metaphor by computer. *Computational Linguistics*, 17(1):49–90.

Matt Gedigian, John Bryant, Srinivas Narayanan, and Branimir Ciric. 2006. Catching metaphors. In *Proceedings of NAACL Workshop on Scalable Natural Language Understanding*, pages 41–48.

Deidre Gentner and Donald Gentner. 1983. Flowing waters or teeming crowds: Mental models of electricity. In D. Gentner and A. Stevens, editors, *Mental models*. Hillsdale, NJ: Lawrence Erlbaum.

Alan Gross and Ray Dearin. 2003. *Chaim Perelman*. Albany: SUNY Press.

Eva Feder Kittay. 1987. *Metaphor: Its cognitive force and linguistic structure*. Oxford: Calderon Press.

Saisuresh Krishnakumaran and Xiaojin Zhu. 2007. Hunting elusive metaphors using lexical resources. In *Proceedings of the Workshop on Computational Approaches to Figurative Language*, pages 13–20, Rochester, New York.

Zachary J. Mason. 2004. CorMet: A computational, corpus-based conventional metaphor extraction system. *Computational Linguistics*, 30(1):23–44.

Andreas Musolff. 2000. *Mirror images of Europe: Metaphors in the public debate about Europe in Britain and Germany*. München: Iudicium. Annotated data is available at http://www.dur.ac.uk/andreas.musolff/Arcindex.htm.

Chaim Perelman and Lucie Olbrechts-Tyteca. 1969. *The New Rhetoric: A Treatise on Argumentation*. Wilkinson, J. and Weaver, P. (trans). Notre Dame, IN: University of Notre Dame Press.

Astrid Reining and Birte Lönneker-Rodman. 2007. Corpus-driven metaphor harvesting. In *Proceedings of the Workshop on Computational Approaches to Figurative Language*, pages 5–12, Rochester, New York.

Gerard Steen. 2008. The Paradox of Metaphor: Why We Need a Three-Dimensional Model of Metaphor. *Metaphor and Symbol*, 23(4):213–241.

Topic Model Analysis of Metaphor Frequency for Psycholinguistic Stimuli

Steven Bethard
Computer Science Department
Stanford University
Stanford, CA 94305
bethard@stanford.edu

Vicky Tzuyin Lai
Department of Linguistics
University of Colorado
295 UCB, Boulder CO 80309
vicky.lai@colorado.edu

James H. Martin
Department of Computer Science
University of Colorado
430 UCB, Boulder CO 80309
james.martin@colorado.edu

Abstract

Psycholinguistic studies of metaphor processing must control their stimuli not just for word frequency but also for the frequency with which a term is used metaphorically. Thus, we consider the task of *metaphor frequency estimation*, which predicts how often target words will be used metaphorically. We develop metaphor classifiers which represent metaphorical domains through Latent Dirichlet Allocation, and apply these classifiers to the target words, aggregating their decisions to estimate the metaphorical frequencies. Training on only 400 sentences, our models are able to achieve 61.3% accuracy on metaphor classification and 77.8% accuracy on HIGH vs. LOW metaphorical frequency estimation.

1 Introduction

Psycholinguistic studies of metaphor try to understand metaphorical language comprehension by presenting subjects with linguistic stimuli and observing their responses. Recent work has observed such responses at the electrophysiological level, measuring brain electrical activity as the stimuli are read (Coulson and Petten, 2002; Tartter et al., 2002; Iakimova et al., 2005; Arzouan et al., 2007; Lai et al., 2007). All these studies have attempted to make comparisons across different types of stimuli (e.g. literal vs. metaphorical) by holding the frequencies of the target words constant across experimental conditions. For example, Tartter et al. (2002) compared the metaphorical and literal sentences *his face was contorted by an angry cloud* and *his face was contorted by an angry frown*, where the two sentences end in different words, but where the final words *cloud* and *frown* had similar word frequencies. As another example, Lai et al. (2007) compared the metaphorical and literal sentences *Their theories have collapsed* and *The old building has collapsed*, where the two sentences end in exactly the same words, so the target word frequencies across conditions were perfectly matched. In both designs, controlling for word frequency allowed the researchers to attribute the differences in experimental conditions to interesting factors, like figurativity, rather than simple word frequency.

However, word frequency is not the only type of frequency relevant to such experiments. In particular, *metaphorical frequency*, that is, how inherently metaphorical one word is as compared to another, may also play an important role in explaining the psycholinguistic results. For example, if *collapsed* is usually used literally, a greater processing effort may be observed when a metaphorical instance of *collapsed* is presented. Likewise, if *collapsed* is usually used metaphorically, greater effort may be observed when a literal instance is presented. Psycholinguistic studies of metaphor have not, to date, controlled for such metaphorical frequency because there were no corpora or algorithms which could provide the needed metaphorical frequencies.

The present study aims to address this deficiency by producing models which can automatically estimate how often a word is used metaphorically. We build these models using only 50 examples each of a small number of target words (< 10), rather than requiring 50 or more examples of every target word

Proceedings of the NAACL HLT Workshop on Computational Approaches to Linguistic Creativity, pages 9–16,
Boulder, Colorado, June 2009.

(100+) in the stimuli, as would be required by standard corpus linguistics methods. Our approach is also novel in that it combines metaphor classification with statistical topic models. Topic models are intuitively promising for our task because they produce topics that seem to translate well to the theory of *conceptual domains*, which suggests that, for example, conceptual domains such as THEORIES and BUILDINGS are used to understand *Their theories have collapsed*. These topic models also show some promise for distinguishing conventional metaphors from novel metaphors.

2 Prior Work

Two types of prior research inform our current study: corpus analyses investigating metaphor frequency by hand, and machine learning models that classify text as either literal or metaphorical. The latter could be used to estimate metaphor frequencies by applying the classifier to a corpus and aggregating the classifications.

2.1 Metaphor Frequency

Researchers have manually estimated several different kinds of metaphor frequency. Pollio et al. (1990) looked at overall metaphorical frequency, performing an exhaustive analysis of a variety of texts, and concluding that there were about five metaphors for every 100 words of text. Martin (1994) looked at the frequency of different types of metaphor, using a sample of 600 sentences from the Wall Street Journal (WSJ), and concluded among other things that the most frequent type of WSJ metaphor was VALUE is LOCATION, e.g. *Spain Fund* ***tumbled*** *23%*. Martin (2006) looked at conditional probabilities of metaphor, for example noting that in 2400 WSJ sentences, the probability of seeing an instance of a metaphor was greatly increased after a first instance had already been observed. However, none of these studies provided the metaphorical frequencies of individual words needed for our research.

Sardinha (2008) performed what is probably closest to the type of analysis we are interested in. Using a corpus of Portuguese conference calls, Berber Sardinha identified 432 terms that were used metaphorically. He then took 100 instances of each of these terms in a general Brazilian corpus and manually annotated them as being either literal or metaphorical. Berber Sardinha found that on average these terms were used metaphorically 70% of the time, and provided analysis of the metaphorical frequencies of a number of individual terms. While it is exactly these kinds of individual term frequencies that we are after, we cannot use Berber Sardinha's data because his corpus was in Portuguese while we are interested in English. This brings out one of the main drawbacks of the corpus annotation approach: moving to a new language (or even a new genre) requires an extensive manual annotation project. Our goal is to avoid such costs by taking advantage of machine learning techniques for automatically identifying metaphorical text.

2.2 Metaphor Classification

Recent years have seen a rising interest in metaphor classification systems. Birke and Sarkar (2006) took a semi-supervised approach, collecting noisy examples of literal and non-literal sentences from both WordNet and metaphor dictionaries, and using a word-based measure of sentence similarity to group sentences into literal and non-literal clusters. They evaluated on hand-annotated sentences for 25 target words and reported an F-score of 0.538, a substantial improvement over the 0.294 majority class baseline.

Gedigian et al. (2006) approached metaphor identification as supervised classification, annotating around 4000 WSJ motion words as literal or metaphorical, and training a maximum entropy classifier using as features based on named entities, WordNet and semantic roles. They achieved an accuracy of 95.1%, a decent improvement over the very high majority class baseline of 93.8%.

Krishnakumaran and Zhu (2007) focused on three syntactically constrained sub-types of metaphors: nouns joined by *be*, nouns following verbs, and nouns following adjectives. They combined WordNet hypernym information with bigram statistics and a threshold, and evaluated their algorithm on the Berkeley Master Metaphor List (Lakoff, 1994), achieving an accuracy of around 46%.

All of these approaches produced models which could be applied to new text to identify metaphors, but each has some drawbacks for our task. The WSJ study of Gedigian et al. (2006) found 94% of their target words to be metaphorical, a vastly differ-

Target	L	M	M%
attacked	32	18	36%
born	45	5	10%
budding	16	34	68%
collapsed	10	40	80%
digest	7	43	86%
drifted	16	34	68%
floating	25	25	50%
sank	31	19	38%
spoke	47	3	6%
Total	229	221	49%

Table 1: Metaphorical (M) and literal (L) counts, and metaphorical percentage (M%), for the annotated verbs.

L	Aye, that's where I was *born* and reared.
M	VATman threatens our *budding* entrepreneurs.
M	Suddenly all her bravado *collapsed*.
L	This makes it easier for us to *digest* the wheat.
L	Gulls *drifted* lethargically on the swell.
M	My heart *sank* as I looked around.

Table 2: Examples of sentences with metaphorical (M) and literal (L) target words.

T#	Most frequent words
00	book (4%) write (2%) read (2%) english (2%)
17	record (3%) music (2%) band (2%) play (2%)
42	social (3%) history (2%) culture (1%) society (1%)
58	film (3%) play (2%) theatre (1%) women (1%)
82	dog (9%) rabbit (2%) ferret (1%) pet (1%)

Table 3: Example topics (T#) from the BNC and their most frequent words. Numbers in parentheses indicate the percent of the topic each word represents.

ent number from the 49% for our target words (see Section 3). Krishnakumaran and Zhu (2007) considered only a few different syntactic constructions, but we need to consider all the ways a metaphor may be expressed to evaulate overall metaphor frequency. Birke and Sarkar (2006) did consider a variety of target words in unrestricted text, but relied on large scale language resources like WordNet and metaphor dictionaries, while we are interested in approaches that are less resource intensive.

Thus, rather than basing our models on these prior systems, we develop a novel approach to metaphor frequency estimation based on using topic models to operationalize metaphorical domains.

3 Data

The first step in building models of metaphorical frequency is obtaining data for training and evaluation. In one of the post-hoc analyses of the Lai et al. (2007) experiment, 50 sentences from the British National Corpus (BNC, 2007) were gathered for each of nine of their target words. They annotated each instance as either literal or metaphorical, and then used these annotations to calculate metaphorical frequencies for analysis.

This data served as our starting point for exploring computational approaches to estimating metaphorical frequency. Table 1 shows the nine verbs and their metaphorical frequencies. Table 2 shows some examples. Some verbs, such as *digest*, are almost always used metaphorically (86% of the time), while other verbs, such as *spoke*, are almost always used literally (94% of the time). Annotation of just 50 instances of each of these nine verbs was time consuming, and yet to fully re-analyze the ERP results, metaphorical frequencies would be needed for all of the over 100 target words. Thus our goal was to automate this process.

4 Topic Models

Our approach to estimating metaphorical frequencies was first to classify words in unrestricted text as literal or metaphorical, and then to aggregate those decisions to estimate a frequency. Thus, we first needed to build a model which could identify metaphorical expressions. Our approach to this problem was based on the theory of conceptual domains, in which metaphors are seen as taking terms from one domain (e.g. *attacked*) and applying them to another domain (e.g. *argument*).

To operationalize these domains, we employed statistical topic models, in particular, Latent Dirichlet Allocation (LDA) (Blei et al., 2003). Intuitively, LDA looks at how words co-occur in the documents of a large corpus, and identifies *topics* or groups of words that are semantically similar. For example, Table 3 shows a few topics from the BNC. These topics can be thought of as grouping words by their semantic domains. For example, we might think of topic 00 as the *Book* domain and topic 42 as the *Society* domain. Because LDA generates topics that look much like the source and target domains associated with metaphors, we expect that LDA can provide a boost to metaphor identification models.

The LDA algorithm is usually presented as a generative model, that is, as an imagined process that someone might go through when writing a text. This generative process looks something like:

1. Decide what topics you want to write about.
2. Pick one of those topics.
3. Think of words used to discuss that topic.
4. Pick one of those words.
5. To generate the next word, go back to 2.

This is a somewhat unrealistic description of the writing process, but it gets at the idea that the words in a document are topically coherent. Formally, the process above can be described as:

1. For each document d select a topic distribution $\theta^d \sim Dir(\alpha)$
2. Select a topic $z \sim \theta^d$
3. For each topic select a word distribution $\phi^z \sim Dir(\beta)$
4. Select a word $w \sim \phi^z$

The goal of the LDA learning algorithm then is to maximize the likelihood of our documents, where for one document $p(d|\alpha, \beta) = \prod_{i=1}^{N} p(w_i|\alpha, \beta)$. Estimating these probabilities can be done in a few different ways, but in this paper we use Gibbs sampling as it has been widely implemented and was available in the LingPipe toolkit (Alias-i, 2008).

Gibbs sampling starts by randomly assigning topics to all words in the corpus. Then the word-topic distributions and document-topic distributions are estimated using the following equations:

$$P(z_i|z_{i-}, w_i, d_i, w_{i-}, d_{i-}, \alpha, \beta) = \frac{\phi_{ij}\theta_{jd}}{\sum_{t=1}^{T} \phi_{it}\theta_{td}}$$

$$\phi_{ij} = \frac{C_{word_{ij}} + \beta}{\sum_{k=1}^{W} C_{word_{kj}} + W\beta} \qquad \theta_{jd} = \frac{C_{doc_{dj}} + \alpha}{\sum_{k=1}^{T} C_{doc_{dk}} + T\alpha}$$

$C_{word_{ij}}$ is the number of times word i was assigned topic j, $C_{doc_{dj}}$ is the number of times topic j appears in document d, W is the total number of unique words in the corpus, and T is the number of topics requested. In essence, we count the number of times that a word is assigned a topic and the number of times a topic appears in a document, and we use these numbers to estimate word-topic and document-topic probabilities. Once topics have been assigned and distributions have been calculated, Gibbs sampling repeats the process, this time selecting a new topic for each word by looking at the calculated probabilities. The process is repeated until the distributions become stable or a set number of iterations is reached.

We ran LDA over the documents in the BNC, extracting 100 topics after 2000 iterations of Gibbs sampling. We left the α and β parameters at their LingPipe defaults of 0.1 and 0.01, respectively. Table 3 shows some of the resulting topics.

5 Metaphor Frequency

Our primary goal was to use the topics produced by LDA to help characterize words in terms of their metaphorical frequency. We approached this problem by first training metaphor classifiers based on LDA topics to identify target words in text as literal or metaphorical. Then we ran these classifiers over unseen data, and aggregated the individual decisions. The result is an approximate metaphorical frequency for each word. The following sections detail this process and discuss our preliminary results.

5.1 Metaphor Classification

Our data is composed of 50 sentences for each of nine target words, with each sentence annotated as either metaphorical or literal. We treated this as a classification task, where the classifier took as input a sentence containing a target word, and produced as output either LITERAL or METAPHORICAL.

We trained support vector machine (SVM) classifiers on this data, using LDA topics as features. For each of the sentences in our data, we used the LDA topic models to assign topic probability distributions to each of the words in the sentence. We then summed the topic distributions over all the words in the sentence to produce a sentence-wide topic distribution. The result was that for each sentence we could say something like "this sentence was composed of 5% topic 00, 2% topic 01, 8% topic 02, etc." We used these sentence-level topic probability distributions as features for an SVM classifier, in particular, SVM^{perf} (Joachims, 2005).

We compared this SVM-LDA model against two baselines. The first was the standard majority class classifier, which simply assigns all instances in the test data whichever label (metaphorical or literal) was most comon in the training data.

The second baseline was an SVM based on TF-IDF features, a well known document classification model (Joachims, 1998; Sebastiani, 2002; Lewis et al., 2004). Under this approach, there is a numeric feature for each of the 3000+ words in the training data, and each word feature is assigned the weight:

$$\frac{|\{w \in doc : w = word\}|}{|\{w \in doc\}|} \cdot \log \frac{|\{d \in docs\}|}{|\{d \in docs : w \in d\}|}$$

Essentially, this formula means that the weight increases with the number of times the word occurs in the document, and decreases with the number of documents in the corpus that contain that word. The vectors of TF-IDF features are then normalized to have Euclidean length 1.0, using the formula:

$$weight(word) = \frac{\text{tf-idf}(word)}{\sqrt{\sum_{word'} \text{tf-idf}(word')^2}}$$

To evaluate our model against both the majority class and the TF-IDF baselines, we ran nine-fold cross-validations, where each fold corresponded to a single target word. Note that this means that we trained our models on the sentences of eight target words, and tested on the sentences of the ninth target word. This is a harder evaluation than a stratified cross-validation where all target words would have been observed during training. But it is a much more realistic evaluation for our task, where we want to learn enough about metaphors from nine target words that we can automatically classify instances of the remaining 95.

Table 4 compares the performance of our SVM-LDA model and the baseline models[1]. The majority class classifier performs poorly, achieving only 26.4% accuracy[2]. The TF-IDF based model performs much better, at 50.7% accuracy. However, our SVM based on LDA features outperforms both baseline models, achieving 54.9% accuracy.

[1]For all models, hyper parameters (the cost parameter, the loss function, etc.) were set using only the training data of each fold by running an inner eight-fold cross validation.

[2]This might be initially surprising since our corpus was 49% metaphorical. Consider, however, that during cross validation, holding out a more metaphorical target word for testing means that our training data is more literal, and vice versa.

Model	Accuracy
Majority Class	26.4%
SVM + TF-IDF	50.7%
SVM + LDA topics	54.9%
SVM + LDA topics + LDA groups	61.3%

Table 4: Model performance on the literal vs. metaphorical classification task.

Type	Most frequent words
CONCRETE	book write read english novel
ABSTRACT	god church christian jesus spirit
MIXED	sleep dream earth theory moon
OTHER	many time only number large

Table 5: Examples of annotated topics.

5.2 Annotating Topics

The metaphor classification results showed the benefit of operationalizing metaphor domains as LDA topics. But metaphors are typically viewed as mapping a *concrete* source domain onto an *abstract* target domain, and our LDA topics had no direct notion of this concrete/abstract distinction. To try to represent this distinction, we manually annotated[3] the 100 LDA topics with one of four labels: CONCRETE, ABSTRACT, MIXED or OTHER. Table 5 shows examples of the annotated topics.

We then used the annotated topics to generate new features for our classifiers. In addition to the original 100 topic probability features, we provided four new probability features, one for each of our labels, calculated by taking the sum of the probabilities of the corresponding topics. For example, since topics 07, 13, 37 and 77 were identified as ABSTRACT topics, the probability of the new ABSTRACT feature was just the sum of the probabilities of the topic features 07, 13, 37 and 77. The last row of Table 4 shows the performance of the SVM model trained with the augmented feature set. This model outperforms all our other models, achieving an accuracy of 61.3% on the literal vs. metaphorical distinction.

These results are interesting because they show that human analysis of LDA topics can add substantial value for machine learning models at a low cost. Annotating the entire set of 100 topics took under

[3]All annotation was performed by a single annotator. Future work will measure inter-annotator agreement.

Model	Accuracy
Majority Class	0.0%
SVM + TF-IDF	22.2%
SVM + LDA topics	55.6%
SVM + LDA topics + LDA groups	77.8%

Table 6: Model performance on the HIGH vs. LOW metaphor frequency prediction task.

an hour, and yet provided a 6% gain in model accuracy. The speed of annotation suggests that LDA topics are conceptually accessible to humans, and the performance boost suggests that manual grouping of LDA topics may be a fruitful area for feature engineering.

5.3 Predicting Metaphorical Frequencies

Having constructed successful metaphor classification models, we return to our question of metaphorical frequency. Given a target word, can we predict the frequency with which that word will be used metaphorically? Our models are not accurate enough that we can expect the frequencies derived from them to be exact predictions of metaphorical frequency. But we may be able to distinguish, for example, words with high metaphorical frequency from words with low metaphorical frequency.

Thus, we evaluate our models on the binary task of assigning target words an overall metaporical frequency, either HIGH ($\geq 50\%$) or LOW ($< 50\%$). We can perform this evaluation using the same data and cross validation technique as before, this time examining each testing fold (which corresponds to a single target word) and aggregating the metaphor classifications to get a metaphorical frequency estimate of that target. Table 6 shows how the models fared on this task. The majority class model misclassified all the words, and the TF-IDF model managed to get only two of the nine correct. The LDA models performed better, with the model including the grouped topic features achieving 77.8% accuracy. This suggests that our model may already be good enough to use for analysis of the original Lai experimental data. Of course, this evaluation was carried out only over the nine available target words, so additional evaluation will be necessary to confirm these trends.

To further analyze our model performance, we looked at the metaphorical frequency estimates for each target word. Table 7 shows the estimates of our best model along with the true metaphorical frequencies. The three target words with the largest differences between true and predicted accuracies are *spoke*, *floating* and *digest*, with *spoke* and *floating* predicted to be much more metaphorical than they actually are, and *digest* predicted to be much less.

Word	True	Predicted	Difference
attacked	36%	24%	-12%
born	10%	2%	-8%
budding	68%	98%	+30%
collapsed	80%	98%	+18%
digest	86%	40%	-46%
drifted	68%	92%	+24%
floating	50%	100%	+50%
sank	38%	26%	-12%
spoke	6%	62%	+56%

Table 7: Model performance on the HIGH vs. LOW metaphor frequency prediction task.

We also performed some analysis of the model errors. In many cases it was difficult to judge why the model succeeded or failed in identifying a metaphor, but a couple of things stood out. First, 70% of the *digest* instances our model misclassified were *Digest* (capitalized), e.g. *Middle East Economic Digest*. Our topic models were trained on all lowercased words, so *Digest* and *digest* were not distinguished. Re-training the models without collapsing the case distinctions might address this problem. Second, *spoke* seems to be an inherently harder term to classify because it co-occurs with so many other topics. About 40% of the *spoke* instances occurred as *spoke of* or *spoke about*, where speaking about a metaphorical topic caused *spoke* to be interpreted metaphorically, and speaking about a literal topic caused *spoke* to be interpreted literally. Addressing this problem would probably require some understanding of argument structure, perhaps akin to what was done by Gedigian et al. (2006).

6 Metaphor Novelty

As a final exploration of topic models for metaphorical domains, we considered metaphorical novelty, as used in the original Lai experiment. In particular, we were interested in how LDA topics might reflect

Type	Stimulus Sentence
LIT	Every soldier in the frontline was attacked
CON	Every point in my argument was attacked
NOV	Every second of our time was attacked
ANOM	Every drop of rain was attacked
LIT	The old building has collapsed
CON	Their theories have collapsed
NOV	Their compromises have collapsed
ANOM	The apples have collapsed

Table 8: Example stimuli: literal (LIT), conventional metaphor (CON), novel metaphor (NOV) and anomalous (ANOM).

-0.19	like house old shop door look street room
-0.18	darlington programme club said durham hall
-0.15	film play theatre women actor work perform
-0.14	area local plan develop land house rural urban
-0.14	any sale good publish custom product price

Table 9: Top 5 topics correlated with conventionality.

0.20	freud sexual sophie male joanna people female
0.17	doctor leed rory dalek fergus date subject aug
0.13	book write read english novel publish reader
0.11	lorton kirov dougal jed manville vologski celia
0.09	war british france britain french nation europe

Table 10: Top 5 topics correlated with novelty.

more conventional or more novel metaphors. In the Lai experiment, conventional and novel metaphors for a particular target word shared the same source domain (e.g. WAR) but differed in the target domain (e.g. ARGUMENT vs. TIME). If LDA topics are a good operationalization of such domains, then it should be possible use LDA topics to distinguish between conventional and novel metaphors.

To explore this area, we employed the stimuli from the Lai experiment, and looked in particular at the conventional and novel conditions. The Lai experiment used 104 different target words, so these data included 104 conventional metaphors and 104 novel metaphors. Novel metaphors were generated for the Lai experiment by considering a conventional source-target mapping and selecting a new target domain. For example, the conventional metaphor *Every point in my argument was attacked* maps the source domain WAR to the target domain ARGUMENT, while the novel metaphor *Every second of our time was attacked* maps the source domain WAR to the target domain TIME. Table 8 shows example stimulus sentences from the Lai experiment. Though these experimental stimuli have the drawback of being manually constructed, not collected from a corpus, they have the advantage of being already annotated with a definition of novelty that clearly distinguishes the two types of metaphors.

We performed a simple correlational analysis using the conventional and novel metaphors from the Lai experiment. We produced topic distributions for each stimulus, using our topic models trained on the BNC. We then labeled conventional metaphors as -1 and novel metaphors as +1, and identified the topics that correlated best with this distinction. Table 9 shows the most negatively correlated (conventional) topics and Table 10 shows the most positively correlated (novel) topics.

Though even the best correlations are somewhat low, there seem to be some trends in this analysis. Conventional metaphors seem to correspond more to concrete terms, like *house*, *club*, *play* and *sale*. Novel metaphors have less of a coherent theme, including terms like *freud* and *sexual* as well as names like *Rory*, *Kirov* and *Britain*. This may reflect a real distinction in the use of conventional and novel metaphors, or it may be an artifact of how the experimental stimuli were created. A deeper investigation into the relations between LDA topics and metaphor novelty will probably require annotating sentences from some naturally occuring data.

7 Conclusions

We presented a novel two-phase approach to the task of *metaphorical frequency estimation*. First, examples of a target word were automatically classified as literal or metaphorical, and then these classifications were aggregated to estimate how often the target word was used metaphorically. Our classifiers operationalized metaphorical source and target domains using topics derived from Latent Dirichlet Allocation. Support vector machine classifiers took these topic probability distributions and learned to classify sentences as literal or metaphorical. These models achieved 61.3% accuracy on the classifiation task, and their aggregated classifications produced an accuracy of 77.8% on the task of distinguishing between target words with high and low metaphorical frequencies.

Future work will perform a larger scale evaluation, and will use our model's metaphorical frequency estimates to analyze psycholinguistic data. In particular, we will split the conventional metaphorical sentences of Lai et al. (2007) into low and high-frequency items. If the low and high frequency items display significantly different brainwave patterns, then this could suggest that metaphorical frequency of a given word plays a critical role in metaphor comprehension.

Future work will also explore frequency effects that consider the sentential context in the stimulus items. For example, a context like "*Their theories have* ____" probably gives a higher expectation of a metaphorical word filling in the blank than a context like "*The old building has* ____". Having a measure of how much the words in the preceding context predict an upcoming metaphor would provide another useful stimulus control.

References

Alias-i. 2008. LingPipe 3.7.0. http://alias-i.com/lingpipe/, October.

Yossi Arzouan, Abraham Goldstein, and Miriam Faust. 2007. Brainwaves are stethoscopes: ERP correlates of novel metaphor comprehension. *Brain Research*, 1160:69–81, July.

Julia Birke and Anoop Sarkar. 2006. A clustering approach for nearly unsupervised recognition of nonliteral language. In *European Chapter of the ACL (EACL)*.

David M. Blei, Andrew Y. Ng, and Michael I. Jordan. 2003. Latent dirichlet allocation. *Journal of Machine Learning Research*, 3:993–1022.

BNC. 2007. The british national corpus, version 3 (BNC XML edition). Distributed by Oxford University Computing Services on behalf of the BNC Consortium. http://www.natcorp.ox.ac.uk/.

Seana Coulson and Cyma Van Petten. 2002. Conceptual integration and metaphor: an event-related potential study. *Memory & Cognition*, 30(6):958–68, September. PMID: 12450098.

Matt Gedigian, John Bryant, Srini Narayanan, and Branimir Ciric. 2006. Catching metaphors. In *Workshop On Scalable Natural Language Understanding*.

Galina Iakimova, Christine Passerieux, Jean-Paul Laurent, and Marie-Christine Hardy-Bayle. 2005. ERPs of metaphoric, literal, and incongruous semantic processing in schizophrenia. *Psychophysiology*, 42(4):380–390.

Thorsten Joachims, 1998. *Text categorization with Support Vector Machines: Learning with many relevant features*, pages 137–142. Springer Berlin / Heidelberg.

Thorsten Joachims. 2005. A support vector method for multivariate performance measures. In *Proceedings of the 22nd international conference on Machine learning*, pages 377–384, Bonn, Germany. ACM.

Saisuresh Krishnakumaran and Xiaojin Zhu. 2007. Hunting elusive metaphors using lexical resources. In *Workshop on Computational Approaches to Figurative Language*.

Vicky Tzuyin Lai, Tim Curran, and Lise Menn. 2007. The comprehension of conventional and novel metaphors: An ERP study. In *13th Annual Conference on Architectures and Mechanisms for Language Processing*, August.

George Lakoff. 1994. Conceptual metaphor WWW server. http://cogsci.berkeley.edu/lakoff/.

David D. Lewis, Yiming Yang, Tony G. Rose, and Fan Li. 2004. RCV1: a new benchmark collection for text categorization research. *J. Mach. Learn. Res.*, 5:361–397.

James H. Martin. 1994. MetaBank: a Knowledge-Base of metaphoric language conventions. *Computational Intelligence*, 10(2):134–149.

James H. Martin. 2006. A rational analysis of the context effect on metaphor processing. In Stefan Th. Gries and Anatol Stefanowitsch, editors, *Corpus-Based Approaches to Metaphor and Metonymy*. Mouton de Gruyter.

Howard R. Pollio, Michael K. Smith, and Marilyn R. Pollio. 1990. Figurative language and cognitive psychology. *Language and Cognitive Processes*, 5:141–167.

Tony Berber Sardinha. 2008. Metaphor probabilities in corpora. In Mara Sofia Zanotto, Lynne Cameron, and Marilda do Couto Cavalcanti, editors, *Confronting Metaphor in Use*, pages 127–147. John Benjamins.

Fabrizio Sebastiani. 2002. Machine learning in automated text categorization. *ACM Computing Surveys (CSUR)*, 34(1):1–47.

Vivien C. Tartter, Hilary Gomes, Boris Dubrovsky, Sophie Molholm, and Rosemarie Vala Stewart. 2002. Novel metaphors appear anomalous at least momentarily: Evidence from N400. *Brain and Language*, 80(3):488–509, March.

Understanding Eggcorns

Sravana Reddy
Department of Computer Science
The University of Chicago
sravana@cs.uchicago.edu

Abstract

An eggcorn is a type of linguistic error where a word is substituted with one that is *semantically plausible* – that is, the substitution is a semantic reanalysis of what may be a rare, archaic, or otherwise opaque term. We build a system that, given the original word and its eggcorn form, finds a semantic path between the two. Based on these paths, we derive a typology that reflects the different classes of semantic reinterpretation underlying eggcorns.

1 Introduction

The term "eggcorn" was coined in 2003 by Geoffrey Pullum (Liberman, 2003) to refer to a certain type of linguistic error where a word or phrase is replaced with one that is phonetically similar *and* semantically justifiable. The eponymous example is *acorn* → *eggcorn*, the meaning of the latter form being derived from the acorn's *egg*-like shape and the fact that it is a seed (giving rise to *corn*). These errors are distinct from mere misspellings or mispronunciations in that the changed form is an alternate interpretation of the original.

The reinterpretation may be related to either the word's perceived meaning or etymology (as in the case of *acorn*), or some context in which the word is commonly used. In this sense, eggcorns are similar to *folk etymologies* – errors arising from the misinterpretation of borrowed or archaic words – with the difference being that the latter are adopted by an entire culture or linguistic community, while eggcorns are errors made by one or more individual speakers.

The formation of eggcorns and folk etymologies, mistakes though they are, involves a creative leap within phonetic and semantic constraints (much like what is required for puns or certain classes of jokes). Eggcorns range from simple reshapings of foreign words (*paprika* → *pepperika*) and substitutions from similar domains (*marshal* → *martial*), to the subtly clever (*integrate* → *intergrade*), the technological (*sound bite* → *sound byte*), or the funny (*stark-raving mad* → *star-craving mad*). The source of reinterpretation may be a weak imagined link (*wind turbine* → *wind turban*), or an invented myth (*give up the ghost* → *give up the goat*[1]). And often, it is not clear what the exact link is between the derived and the original forms, although it is usually obvious (to the human eye) that there is a connection.

This paper explores some ways of **automatically tracing the link** between a word and its eggcorn.

In reality, we are chiefly concerned with computing the connections between a *word and its reinterpreted form*. Such pairs may also occur as folk etymologies, puns, riddles, or get used as a poetic device. However, we use eggcorns as a testbed for three main reasons: there are a number of documented examples, the reanalyses are *accidental* (meaning the semantic links are more unpredictable and tenuous than in the cases of deliberate reshapings), and the errors are idiosyncratic and relatively modern – and hence have not been fossilized in the lexicon – making them transparent to analysis (as opposed to many folk etymologies and other historical errors). That said, much of the work described here can be potentially applied to other instances of semantic reinterpretation as well.

[1] `http://eggcorns.lascribe.net/english/714/goat/`

Proceedings of the NAACL HLT Workshop on Computational Approaches to Linguistic Creativity, pages 17–23,
Boulder, Colorado, June 2009.

The first part of the paper describes an algorithm (the "Cornalyzer") for finding a semantic path between the original and reinterpreted forms of an eggcorn pair. We then proceed to use the results of this algorithm to *cluster* the eggcorn examples into 5 classes, with a view to learning a typology of eggcorns.

2 Related Work

One work related to this area (Nelken and Yamangil, 2008) uses Wikipedia to automatically mine eggcorns by searching for pairs of phonemically similar words that occur in the same sentence context in different revisions. However, the mined examples are reported to contain many false positives since the algorithm does not include a notion of semantic similarity.

Folk etymologies, the closest cousin to eggcorns, have been studied from a linguistic point of view, including some of the same questions we tackle here (only, not from a computational side) – how is an new word derived from the original, and what are the different categories of folk etymologies? (Rundblad and Kronenfeld, 1998), (Scholfield, 1988). To the best of our knowledge, there has been no previous work in inducing or computationally understanding properties of neologisms and errors derived through misinterpretation. However, there is a substantial literature on algorithmic humor, some of which uses semantic relationships – (Stock and Strapparava, 2006), (Manurung et al., 2008), among others.

3 Data

The list of eggcorns is taken directly from the **Eggcorn Database**[2] as of the submission date. To assure soundness of the data, we include only those examples whose usage is attested and which are confirmed to be valid and contemporary reanalyses[3], giving a total of 509 instances. Table 1 shows a sample of the data.

Every example can be denoted by the tuple (w, e, c) where c is the list of obligatory *contexts* in which the reanalysis takes place, w is the original form, and e is the modified (eggcorned) form.

Table 1: A few eggcorns. 'X' can be replaced for w or e to give the original form in context, or the eggcorn in context respectively.

Original form w	Changed form e	Context c
bludgeon	bloodgeon	X
few	view	name a X
entree	ontray	X
praying	preying	X mantis
jaw	jar	X-dropping
dissonance	dissidence	cognitive X

The Cornalyzer uses WordNet (Fellbaum, 1998) version 3.0, including the built-in morphological tools for lemmatization and dictionary definitions[4].

4 Automated Understanding of Eggcorn Generation

Broadly speaking, there are two types of eggcorns:

1. Ones where e or a part of e is semantically related to the original word w (*lost* → *loss* in 'no love lost') or the context c (*pied* → *pipe* in 'pied-piper').

2. Eggcorns where e is related to an image or object that is *connected to* or evoked by the original (like 'song' in *lip-sync* → *lip-sing*).

For the first, a database of semantic relations between words (like WordNet) can be used to find a semantic connection between w and e. The second type is more difficult since external knowledge is needed to make the connection. To this end, we make use of the "glosses" – dictionary definitions of word senses – included in WordNet. For instance, the 'lip-sing' eggcorn is difficult to analyze using *only* semantic relations, since neither 'sync' nor 'lip' are connected closely to the word 'sing'. However, the presence of the word *song* in the gloss of *lip-sync*:

```
move the lips in synchronization
(with recorded speech or song)
```

[2] `http://eggcorns.lascribe.net/`

[3] In other words, all examples that are classified as 'questionable' (or otherwise indicated as being questionable), 'not an eggcorn', 'citational' or 'nearly-mainstream' are eliminated.

[4] From `http://wordnet.princeton.edu/`

makes the semantic connection fairly transparent.

The Cornalyzer first attempts to analyze an eggcorn tuple (w, e, c) using semantic relations (§4.1). If no sufficiently short semantic path is found, the eggcorn is presumed to be of the second type, and is analyzed using a combination of semantic relations and dictionary glosses (§4.2).

4.1 Analysis using Word Relations

4.1.1 Building the Semantic Graph

WordNet is a semantic dictionary of English, containing a list of *synsets*. Each synset consists of a set of synonymous words or collocations, and its relations (like hypernymy, antonymy, or meronymy) with other synsets. The dictionary also includes *lexical relations* – relations between words rather than synsets (for instance, a *pertainym* of a noun is an adjective that is derived from the noun).

WordNet relations have been used to quantify semantic similarity between words for a variety of applications (see Budanitsky and Hirst (2001) for a review of similarity measures). The Cornalyzer uses the same basic idea as most existing measures – finding the shortest path between the two words – with some modifications to fit our problem.

We adopt the convention that two words w_1 and w_2 have the relation R if they are in different synsets S_1 and S_2, and $R(S_1, S_2)$ is true. We also define two new lexical relations that are not directly indicated in the dictionary: w_1 and w_2 are *synonyms* if they are in the same synset, and *homographs* if they have identical orthographic forms and lexical categories but are in different synsets. [5]

This relational network can hence be used to define a graph G_s over words, where there is an edge of type t_R from w_1 to w_2 if $R(w_1, w_2)$ holds. Some of the relations in WordNet (like antonymy) are ignored, either because they invert semantic similarity, or are not sufficiently informative. Table 2 summarizes the relations used.

This graph can be used to find the semantic relationships between an original word w and its

Table 2: WordNet relations used to build the semantic graph.

Relation	Parts of Speech	Reflexive Relation	Example
Synonym	(N, N) (V, V) (Adj, Adj) (Adv, Adv)	Synonym	(forest, wood) (move, displace) (direct, lineal) (directly, at once)
Homograph	(All, All)	Homograph	(call [greet], call [order])
Hypernym	(V, V) (N, N)	Troponym/ Hyponym	(move, jump) (canine, fox)
Meronym	(N, N)	Holonym	(forest, tree)
Has Instance	(N, N)	Instance Of	(city, Dresden)
Cause	(V, V)	Caused by	(affect, feel)
Entails	(V, V)	not specified	(watch, look)
Similar To	(Adj, Adj)	Similar To	(lucid, clear)
Related	(V, V) (Adj, Ad)	Related	 (few, some)
Same Group	(V, V)	Same Group	(displace, travel)
Has Attribute	(Adj, N)	Attribute Of	(few, numerousness)
Derivational Relation	(N, V) (N, Adj) (V, Adj)	Derivational Relation	(movement, move) (movement, motional) (move, movable)
Pertainym	(Adj, N) (Adv, Adj)	not specified	(direct, directness) (directly, direct)

eggcorn form e, if both forms are in the dictionary, and there exists a path from w to e. However, it is often the case that e or w are not in the dictionary, or that a path does not exist. This could be because one of the forms is an inflected form or compound, or that some substring of e – rather than the whole word or collocation – is the reinterpreted segment. It is also essential to consider the strings in c, since many eggcorns result from semantic reinterpretation of the contexts.

Hence, three new non-semantic relations are defined: w_1 is a *substring* of w_2 if the orthographic form of w_1 is a substring of that of w_2, and w_1 and w_2 are *contextually linked* if they occur in the same collocation or compound. If w_2 can be derived from w_1 using WordNet's lemmatizer, w_2 is an *inflected* form of w_1.

A new graph G_e is constructed by adding edges of types $t_{substring}$, $t_{context}$, and $t_{inflect}$ to G_s. For all eggcorn tuples (w, e, c):

1. If e or w are not in the dictionary, add them to G_e as a vertex

2. Add edges of type *inflect* between e and its base form.

3. Add edges of type *substring* from e to every

[5] This paper uses 'word' to include sense – i.e, 'bank' as in *slope beside a body of water* and 'bank' as in *financial institution* are distinct. When required for disambiguation, the WordNet *sense number*, which is the index of the sense in the list of the word's senses, is added in parenthesis; e.g. bank (2) for the *financial institution* sense.

substring of length ≥ 3 that is in the dictionary (except those substrings which are base forms of e), and edges of type *supstring* in the other direction.

4. Extract a set of 'context words' from c by splitting it along spaces and hyphenation. Select those words which are in the dictionary.

5. Add edges of type *context* from w and e to each extracted context word.

For example, given the data in table 1, the following vertices and edges will be added to G_e:

Vertices bloodgeon, ontray, preying, praying

Substring edges (bloodgeon, blood), (bloodgeon, loo), (bloodgeon, eon), (view, vie), (entree, tree), (ontray, ray), (ontray, tray)

Superstring edges above edges in the other direction

Inflectional edges (preying, prey), (praying, pray). These edges are bidirectional.

Context edges (few, name), (view, name), (few, a), (view, a), (praying, mantis), (preying, mantis), (jaw, dropping), (jar, dropping), (dissonance, cognitive), (dissidence, cognitive). These edges are also bidirectional.

4.1.2 Tracing the Semantic Path

Given the semantic graph, our working assumption is that e is generated from w by following the shortest path from w to e (denoted by $P(w, e, c)$).

1. If w and e are both in the dictionary, find $P_1(w, e)$ = the shortest path from w to e in G_s

2. Find $P_2(w, e, c)$ = the shortest path using substrings of e and/or c in G_e

(Since the edges are unweighted, the shortest path from w to e is found simply by performing breadth-first search starting at w.)

$P(w, e, c)$ is simply the shorter of $P_1(w, e)$ (if it exists) and $P_2(w, e, c)$. Note that there may be several shortest paths, especially since words that are synonymous have almost the same incident semantic edges. Since the candidate shortest paths generally do not differ much from one another (as far as their semantic implications), an arbitrary path is chosen to be P.

Table 3 shows the paths found by the algorithm for some eggcorns.

4.2 Analysis using Dictionary Definitions

As described in §4, the source of many eggcorns is knowledge external to the original word or contexts through some concept or object suggested by the original. In such cases, a semantic network will not suffice to find the reinterpretation path. One possible way of accessing the additional information is to search for w and e in a large corpus, and extract the key words that appear in conjunction with these forms.

However, filtering and extracting the representative information can quickly become a complex problem beyond the scope of this paper. Hence, as a first approximation, we use the dictionary definitions (glosses) that accompany synsets in WordNet. To optimize efficiency and to avoid having noise added by the definitions, the Cornalyzer only resorts to this step if a *sufficiently short path* – that is, a path of length $\leq k$ for some threshold k – is not found when only using word relations. (The results suggest 7 as a good threshold, since most of discovered paths that are longer than 7 tend not to reflect the semantic relationships between the eggcorn and the original form.)

Every gloss from all senses of a lexical item[6] x (for all x in the dictionary) is first tokenized, and punctuation stripped. All tokens are stemmed using the built-in lemmatizer. Only those tokens t that are already present as vertices in G_e are taken into consideration. However, it should be clear that not all tokens t are equally relevant to x. For instance, consider one gloss of the noun "move":

> the act of changing location from one place to another

which gives the tokens *act*, *changing*, *location*, *one*, *place*, *another*. Clearly, the tokens *changing*, *location*, and *place* rank higher than the others in terms of how indicative they are of the meaning of the noun.

[6]A lexical item is a word independent of sense, e.g, all senses of 'bank' constitute a single lexical item.

Table 3: A sample of semantic similarity paths. $x \xrightarrow{R} y$ means "y is an R of x". When relevant, WordNet sense numbers are indicated.

Eggcorn tuple $(word, eggcorn, context)$	Path from word to eggcorn
(mince, mix, 'X words')	mince $\xrightarrow{hypernym}$ change $\xrightarrow{hyponym}$ mix
(few, view, 'name a X')	few $\xrightarrow{deriv}$ fewness $\xrightarrow{hypernym}$ number $\xrightarrow{hypernym}$ amount $\xrightarrow{hypernym}$ magnitude $\xrightarrow{hyponym}$ extent $\xrightarrow{hyponym}$ scope $\xrightarrow{hyponym}$ view
(dissonance, dissidence, cognitive X)	dissonance $\xrightarrow{synonym}$ disagreement (1) $\xrightarrow{homograph}$ disagreement (3) $\xrightarrow{hyponym}$ dissidence
(ado, [to-do, to do], ['much X about nothing', 'without further X'])	ado $\xrightarrow{synonym}$ stir (3) $\xrightarrow{homograph}$ stir (1) $\xrightarrow{hypernym}$ to-do
(jaw, jar, X-dropping)	jaw $\xrightarrow{context}$ dropping $\xrightarrow{inflect}$ drop $\xrightarrow{hypernym}$ displace $\xrightarrow{hyponym}$ jar
(ruckus, raucous, X)	ruckus $\xrightarrow{homograph}$ din $\xrightarrow{deriv}$ cacophonous $\xrightarrow{similar}$ raucous
(segue, segway, X)	segue $\xrightarrow{hypernym}$ passage (1) $\xrightarrow{homograph}$ passage (3) $\xrightarrow{hypernym}$ way $\xrightarrow{supstring}$ segway

One way of reflecting these distinctions in the Cornalyzer is to *weight* these terms appropriately, with something resembling the TF-IDF (Salton and Buckley, 1988) measure used in information retrieval. Let $tf(t, x)$ = the frequency of the token t in the glosses of x, and $idf(t) = \log \frac{N}{df(t)}$ where N = the number of lexical items in the dictionary and $df(t)$ = the number of lexical items in the dictionary whose glosses contain t. Define $W(t, x) = tf(t, x) \cdot idf(t)$.

A new graph G_d is constructed from G_e by adding edges of type *hasdef* from every lexical item x to tokens t in its glosses with the edge-weight $1 + 1/W(t, x)$, and reflexive edges of type *indef* from t to x with the same weight. All existing edges in the original graph G_e are assigned the weight 1.

The semantic path from w to e is found by the process similar to what was described in §4.1.2: first find $P_1(w, e)$ and $P_2(w, e, c)$ as well as $P_3(w, e, c)$ = the shortest path from w to e in G_d, and let $P(w, e, c)$ be the shortest of the three. Since G_d has weighted edges, the shortest path P_3 is computed using Dijkstra's algorithm.

Dictionary-definition-based paths P_2 for some eggcorns are shown in Table 4. The shortest P_2 paths are also shown for comparison. The P_3 paths generally appear to be closer to a human judgment of what the semantic reinterpretation constitutes. In the case of *(bludgeon → bloodgeon)*, for example, P_2 shows no indication of the key connection (bleeding due to being bludgeoned), whereas P_3 captures it perfectly.

Of the 509 eggcorns, paths were found for 238 instances by using only G_s or G_e as the relational graph. Paths for a total of 372 eggcorns were found when using dictionary glosses in the graph G_d.

5 From Generation to Typology

A quick glance at tables 3 and 4 shows that the paths vary in shape and structure: some paths move up and down the hypernym/homonym tree, while others move laterally along synonyms and polysemes; some use no external knowledge, while others make primary use of context information and dictionary glosses. A natural next step, therefore, is to *group the eggcorns* into some number of classes that represent general categories of semantic reanalysis. We can achieve this by clustering eggcorns based on their semantic shortest paths.

5.1 Clustering of Paths

One natural choice for a feature space is the set of all 24 relations (edge-types) used in G_d. An eggcorn (w, e, c) is represented as a vector $[v_1, v_2, \ldots v_{24}]$ where v_i = the number of times that relation R_i (or the reflexive relation of R_i) appears in $P(w, e, c)$.

These vectors are then clustered using k-means

Table 4: Some semantic paths using dictionary glosses. As before, $x \xrightarrow{R} y$ stands for "y is an R of x", and the numbers in parentheses following a lexical item are the WordNet sense numbers corresponding to that word.

Eggcorn tuple	Path from word to eggcorn
(bludgeon, bloodgeon, X)	P_3 (length 6): bludgeon $\xrightarrow{hypernym}$ hit (3) $\xrightarrow{homograph}$ hit (6) $\xrightarrow{hypernym}$ wound $\xrightarrow{indef}$ gore $\xrightarrow{hypernym}$ blood $\xrightarrow{supstring}$ bloodgeon
	P_2 (length 11): bludgeon $\xrightarrow{hypernym}$ club $\xrightarrow{hypernym}$ stick $\xrightarrow{hypernym}$ implement $\xrightarrow{hypernym}$ instrumentality $\xrightarrow{hypernym}$ artefact $\xrightarrow{hyponym}$ structure $\xrightarrow{hyponym}$ area $\xrightarrow{hyponym}$ room $\xrightarrow{hyponym}$ lavatory $\xrightarrow{hyponym}$ loo $\xrightarrow{supstring}$ bloodgeon
(entree, [ontray, on-tray], X)	P_3 (length 4): entree $\xrightarrow{indef}$ meal $\xrightarrow{indef}$ food $\xrightarrow{hasdef}$ tray $\xrightarrow{supstring}$ ontray
	P_2 (length 8): entree $\xrightarrow{hyponym}$ plate (8) $\xrightarrow{homograph}$ plate (4) $\xrightarrow{hypernym}$ flatware $\xrightarrow{hypernym}$ tableware $\xrightarrow{hyponym}$ tea set $\xrightarrow{meronym}$ tea tray $\xrightarrow{hypernym}$ tray $\xrightarrow{supstring}$ on-tray
(praying, preying, X mantis)	P_3 (length 6): praying $\xrightarrow{context}$ mantis $\xrightarrow{indef}$ predacious $\xrightarrow{synonym}$ predatory (3) $\xrightarrow{homograph}$ predatory (2) $\xrightarrow{indef}$ prey $\xrightarrow{inflect}$ preying
	P_2 (length 8): praying $\xrightarrow{context}$ mantis $\xrightarrow{hypernym}$ dictyopterous insect $\xrightarrow{hypernym}$ insect $\xrightarrow{hypernym}$ arthropod $\xrightarrow{hypernym}$ invertebrate $\xrightarrow{hypernym}$ animal $\xrightarrow{hyponym}$ prey $\xrightarrow{inflect}$ preying

and a Euclidean distance metric. We experimented with a few different values of k and found that $k = 5$ produces clusters that are the most semantically coherent.

5.2 Results

The five clusters roughly correspond to the each of the following characteristic paths $P(w, e, c)$:

1. Independent of dictionary glosses and of context, and mostly contain *synonym*, *homograph*, *related*, or *similar to* types of edges.

2. Contain several *hypernym* and *hyponym* edges.

3. Contain several *substring*, *supstring*, and *inflect* or *derivational* edges.

4. Heavily dependent on *context* edges.

5. Heavily dependent on dictionary glosses.

Eggcorns in these clusters can be interpreted to be (1) **Near-synonyms**, (2) **Semantic cousins** – deriving from a common general concept or entity, (3) **Segmentally related** – being linked by morphological operations, (4) **Contextually similar**, or (5) **Linked by implication** – deriving from an implicit concept.

A sample of the cluster membership is shown in Table 5.

6 Discussion

This paper presents a procedure for computationally understanding the semantic reanalyses of words. We identified the two general types of eggcorns, and built the appropriate networks overlying the WordNet graph and dictionary in order to trace the semantic path from a word to its eggcorn.

An obvious drawback to our method stems from the fact that the semantic dictionary is not perfect, or fully reflective of human information. Similarly, dictionary glosses are a limited source of external information. It would hence be worth exploring data-driven methods to augment a source like WordNet, such as building a word graph from co-occurrences in text, or using corpora to derive distributional similarity measures.

The Cornalyzer is only an exploratory first step – there are a wealth of other possible computational problems related to eggcorns. Semantic pathfinding can be extended to defining some measure of eggcorn strength or plausibility. The algorithm can also be used to mine for new eggcorns – a threshold or a set of criteria for an 'eggcornish' path can

Table 5: A look at the clustered eggcorns.

Cluster	Examples
1	(cognitive dissonance → cognitive dissidence), (ado → to-do), (slake thirst → slack thirst), (ruckus → raucous), (sparkle (protests, etc) → spark), (poise to do → pose to do), ...
2	(sow wild oats → sow wild oaks), (name a few → name a view), (whet, wet), (curb hunger → curve hunger), (entree → ontray), (mince words → mix words), ...
3	(utmost → upmost), (valedictorian → valevictorian), (quote unquote → quote on quote), (playwright → playwrite), (no love lost → no love loss), (snub → snob), ...
4	(pied piper → pipe piper), (powerhouse → powerhorse), (jaw-dropping → jar-dropping), (sell (something) down the river → sail (something) down the river), ...
5	(renowned, reknowned), (praying mantis → preying mantis), (expatriate → expatriot), (skim milk → skimp milk), (sopping wet → soaping wet), (pique → peak), ...

be set based on the paths found for known eggcorns, thus helping separate them from false positives (typos and misspellings).

Another possible line of work is finding generalizations in *pronunciation* changes from the original. "The Eggcorn Database" website includes a partial catalogue of phonetic changes like *t-flapping* and *cot/caught merger* – it would be interesting to see if such patterns and categories can be learnt. The basic model of the Cornalyzer can potentially also be extended to applications in other domains of semantic reanalysis like folk etymologies and puns.

Acknowledgments

We would like to thank the anonymous reviewers for their excellent and insightful comments.

References

Alexander Budanitsky and Graeme Hirst. 2001. Semantic distance in wordnet:an experimental, application-oriented evaluation of five measures. In *Proceedings of the ACL Workshop on WordNet and Other Lexical Resources*.

Christiane Fellbaum, editor. 1998. *WordNet: An Electronic Lexical Database*. MIT Press, Cambridge, MA.

Mark Liberman. 2003. Egg corns: folk etymology, malapropism, mondegreen, ??? *http://158.130.17.5/myl/languagelog/archives/000019.html*.

Ruli Manurung, Graeme Ritchie, Helen Pain, Annalu Waller, Dave O'Mara, and Rolf Black. 2008. The construction of a pun generator for language skills development. *Applied Artificial Intelligence*, 22:841–869.

Rani Nelken and Elif Yamangil. 2008. Mining Wikipedia's article revision history for training computational linguistics algorithms. In *Proceedings of the AAAI Workshop on Wikipedia and Artificial Intelligence*.

Gabriella Rundblad and David B Kronenfeld. 1998. Folk-etymology: Haphazard perversion or shrewd analogy? In Julie Coleman and Christian Kay, editors, *Lexicology, Semantics, and Lexicography*. John Benjamins, Manchester.

Gerard Salton and Christopher Buckley. 1988. Term weighting approaches in automatic text retrieval. *Information Processing and Management*, 24(5):513–523.

Phil Scholfield. 1988. Documenting folk etymological change in progress. *English Studies*, 69:341–347.

Oliviero Stock and Carlo Strapparava. 2006. Laughing with hahacronym, a computational humor system. In *Proceedings of the 21st AAAI Conference on Artificial Intelligence*.

Automatically Extracting Word Relationships as Templates for Pun Generation

Bryan Anthony Hong and **Ethel Ong**
College of Computer Studies
De La Salle University
Manila, 1004 Philippines
bashx5@yahoo.com, ethel.ong@delasalle.ph

Abstract

Computational models can be built to capture the syntactic structures and semantic patterns of human punning riddles. This model is then used as rules by a computer to generate its own puns. This paper presents T-PEG, a system that utilizes phonetic and semantic linguistic resources to automatically extract word relationships in puns and store the knowledge in template form. Given a set of training examples, it is able to extract 69.2% usable templates, resulting in computer-generated puns that received an average score of 2.13 as compared to 2.70 for human-generated puns from user feedback.

1 Introduction

Previous works in computational humor have shown that by analyzing the syntax and semantics of how humans combine words to produce puns, computational models can be built to capture the linguistic aspects involved in this creative wordplay. The model is then used in the design of computer systems that can generate puns which are almost at par with those of human-generated puns, as the case of the Joke Analysis and Production Engine or JAPE (Binsted et al, 1997) system.

The computational model used by the JAPE (Binsted, 1996) system is in the form of schemas and templates with rules describing the linguistic structures of human puns. The use of templates in NLP tasks is not new. Information extraction systems (Muslea, 1999) have used templates as rules for extracting relevant information from large, unstructured text. Text generation systems use templates as linguistic patterns with variables (or slots) that can be filled in to generate syntactically correct and coherent text for their human readers.

One common characteristic among these NLP systems was that the templates were constructed manually. This is a tedious and time-consuming task. Because of this, several researches in example-based machine translation systems, such as those in (Cicekli and Güvenir, 2003) and in (Go et al, 2007), have worked on automatically extracting templates from training examples. The learned templates are bilingual pairs of patterns with corresponding words and phrases replaced with variables. Each template is a complete sentence to preserve the syntax and word order in the source text, regardless of the variance in the sentence structures of the source and target languages (Nunez et al, 2008).

The motivation for T-PEG (Template-Based Pun Extractor and Generator) is to build a model of human-generated puns through the automatic identification, extraction and representation of the word relationships in a template, and then using these templates as patterns for the computer to generate its own puns. T-PEG does not maintain its own lexical resources, but instead relies on publicly available lexicons, in order to perform these tasks. The linguistic aspects of puns and the resources utilized by T-PEG are presented in Section 2.

Sections 3 and 4 discuss the algorithms for extracting templates and generating puns, respectively. The tests conducted and the analysis of the results on the learned templates and generated puns follow in Section 5, to show the limitations of T-PEG's approach and the level of humor in the generated puns. The paper concludes with a summary of what T-PEG has been able to accomplish.

Proceedings of the NAACL HLT Workshop on Computational Approaches to Linguistic Creativity, pages 24–31,
Boulder, Colorado, June 2009.

2 Linguistic Resources

Ritchie (2005) defines a pun as "a humorous written or spoken text which relies crucially on phonetic similarity for its humorous effect". Puns can be based on inexact matches between words (Binsted and Ritchie, 2001), where tactics include metathesis (e.g., *throw stones* and *stow thrones*) and substitution of a phonetically similar segment (e.g., *glass* and *grass*).

In T-PEG, punning riddles are considered to be a class of jokes that use wordplay, specifically pronunciation, spelling, and possible semantic similarities and differences between words (Hong and Ong, 2008). Only puns using the question - answer format as shown in example (1) from (Binsted, 1996) are considered. Compound words are also included, underlined in example (2) from (Webb, 1978).

(1) What do you call a beloved mammal?
A dear deer.

(2) What do barbers study? Short-cuts.

The automatic tasks of analyzing human-generated puns in order to build a formal model of the word relationships present in the puns require the use of a number of linguistic resources. These same set of resources are used for later generation. STANDUP (Manurung et al, 2008), for example, uses "a database of word definitions, sounds and syntax to generate simple play-on-words jokes, or puns, on a chosen subject". Aside from using WordNet (2006) as its lexical resource, STANDUP maintains its own lexical database of phonetic similarity ratings for pairs of words and phrases.

Various works have already emphasized that puns can be generated by distorting a word in the source pun into a similar-sounding pun, e.g., (Ritchie, 2005 and Manurung et al, 2008). This notion of phonetic similarity can be extended further by allowing puns containing words that sound similar to be generated, as shown in example (3), which was generated by T-PEG following the structure of (1).

(3) What do you call an overall absence?
A whole hole.

The Unisyn English Pronunciation lexicon (Fitt, 2002) was utilized for this purpose. The dictionary contains about 70,000 entries with phonetic transcriptions and is used by T-PEG to find the pronunciation of individual words and to locate similar sounding words for a given word. Because Unisyn also provides support in checking for spelling regularity, it is also used by T-PEG to check if a given word does exist, particularly when a compound word is split into its constituent syllables and determining if these individual syllables are valid words, such as the constituents "*short*" and "*cuts*" for the compound word "*shortcuts*" in (2).

The wordplay in punning riddles is not based on phonetic similarity alone, but may also involve the semantic links among words that make up the pun. These semantic relationships must also be identified and captured in the template, such that the generated puns are not only syntactically well-formed (due to the nature of templates) but also have consistent semantics with the source human pun, as shown in example (4) from (Binsted, 1996) and T-PEG's counterpart in example (5).

(4) How is a car like an elephant?
They both have trunks.

(5) How is a person like an elephant?
They both have memory.

Two resources are utilized for this purpose. WordNet (2006) is used to find the synonym of a given word, while ConceptNet (Liu and Singh, 2004) is used to determine the semantic relationships of words.

ConceptNet is a large-scale common sense knowledge base with about 1.6 million assertions. It focuses on contextual common sense reasoning, which can be used by a computer to understand concepts and situating these concepts on previous knowledge.

Relationship Types	Examples
IsA	IsA *headache pain* IsA *deer mammal*
PartOf	PartOf *window pane* PartOf *car trunk*
PropertyOf	PropertyOf *pancake flat* PropertyOf *ghost dead*
MadeOf	MadeOf *snowman snow*
CapableOf	CapableOf *sun burn* CapableOf *animal eat*
LocationOf	LocationOf *money bank*
CanDo	CanDo *ball bounce*
ConceptuallyRelatedTo	ConceptuallyRelatedTo *wedding bride* *forest animal*

Table 1. Some Semantic Relationships of ConceptNet (Liu and Singh, 2004)

The concepts can be classified into three general classes – noun phrases, attributes, and activity phrases, and are connected by edges to form an ontology. Binary relationship types defined by the Open Mind Commonsense (OMCS) Project (Liu and Singh, 2004) are used to relate two concepts together, examples of which are shown in Table 1.

3 Extracting Punning Templates

The structural regularities of puns are captured in T-PEG with the use of templates. A template is the combined notion of schemas and templates in (Binsted, 2006), and it contains the relationship between the words (lexemes) in a pun as well as its syntactical structure. The template constrains the set of words that can be used to fill-in the slots during the generation phase; it also preserves the syntactical structure of the source pun, to enable the generated puns to follow the same syntax.

3.1 Templates in T-Peg

A template in T-PEG is composed of multiple parts. The first component is the source punning riddle, where variables replaced the keywords in the pun and also serve as slots that can be filled during the pun generation phase.

Variables can be one of three types. A *regular variable* is a basic keyword in the source pun whose part-of-speech tag is a noun, a verb, or an adjective. Variables in the question-part of the pun are represented with *Xn* while *Yn* represent variables in the answer-part (where *n* denotes the lexical sequence of the word in the sentence starting at index 0).

A *similar-sound variable* represents a word that has the same pronunciation as the regular variable, for example, *deer* and *dear*. A *compound-word variable* contains two regular or similar-sound variables that combine to form a word, for example *sun* and *burn* combine to form the word *sunburn*. A colon (:) is used to connect the variables comprising a compound variable, for example, *X1:X2*.

Word relationships may exist among the variables in a pun. These word relationships comprise the second component of a template and are represented **<var1> <relationship type> <var2>**.

There are four types of binary word relationships captured by T-PEG. *SynonymOf relationships* specify that two variables are synonymous with each other, as derived from WordNet (2006). *Compound-word (or IsAWord) relationships* specify that one variable combined with a second variable should form a word. Unisyn (Fiit, 2002) is used to check that the individual constituents as well as the combined word are valid. *SoundsLike relationships* specify that two variables have the same pronunciation as derived from Unisyn. *Semantic relationships* show the relationships of two variables derived from ConceptNet (Liu and Singh, 2004), and can be any one of the relationship types presented in Table 1.

3.2 Learning Algorithm

Template learning begins from a given corpus of training examples that is preprocessed by the tagger and the stemmer. The tagged puns undergo valid word selection to identify keywords (noun, verb, or adjective) as candidate variables. The candidate variables are then paired with each other to identify any word relationships that may exist between them. The word relationships are determined by the phonetic checker, the synonym checker, and the semantic analyzer. Only those candidate variables with at least one word relationship with another candidate variable will be retained as final variables in the learned template.

Table 2 presents the template for "*Which bird can lift the heaviest weights? The crane.*" (Webb, 1978). Keywords are underlined. All of the extracted word relationships in Table 2 were derived from ConceptNet. Notice that i) some word pairs may have one or more word relationships, for example, "*crane*" and "*lift*"; while ii) some candidate keywords may not have any relationships, i.e, the adjective "*heaviest*", thus it is not replaced with a variable in the resulting template. This second condition will be explored further in Section 5.

Source Pun	Which bird can lift the heaviest weights? The crane.
Template	Which <X1> can <X3> the heaviest <X6>? The <Y1>.
Word Relationships	X1 ConceptuallyRelatedTo X6 X6 ConceptuallyRelatedTo X1 Y1 IsA X1 X6 CapableOfReceivingAction X3 Y1 CapableOf X3 Y1 UsedFor X3

Table 2. Template with *Semantic* Relationships identified through ConceptNet

Table 3 presents another template from the pun "*What do you call a beloved mammal? A dear deer.*" (Binsted, 1996), with the *SynonymOf* relationship derived from WordNet, the *IsA* relationship from ConceptNet, and the *SoundsLike* relationship from Unisyn. Notice the "-0" suffix in variables *Y1* and *Y2*. "*<var>-0*" is used to represent a word that is phonetically similar to *<var>*.

Source Pun	What do you call a beloved mammal? A dear deer.
Template	What do you call a <X5> <X6>? A <Y1> <Y2>.
Word Relationships	X5 **SynonymOf** Y1 X5 **SynonymOf** Y2-0 Y1-0 IsA X6 Y2 IsA X6 Y1 **SoundsLike** Y2 Y1-0 **SoundsLike** Y1 Y2-0 **SoundsLike** Y2

Table 3. Template with *Synonym* Relationships and *Sounds-Like* Relationships

A constituent word in a compound word (identified through the presence of a dash "-") may also contain additional word relationships. Thus, in "*What kind of fruit fixes taps? A plum-ber.*" (Binsted, 1996), T-PEG learns the template shown in Table 4. The compound word relationship extracted is *Y1 IsAWord Y2* (*plum* IsAWord *ber*). *Y1* (*plum*), which is a constituent of the compound word, has a relationship with another word in the pun, *X3* (*fruit*).

Source Pun	What kind of fruit fixes taps? A plum-ber.
Template	What kind of <X3> <X4> taps? A <Y1>:<Y2>.
Word Relationships	Y1 IsA X3 Y1 **IsAWord** Y2 **Y1:Y2** CapableOf X4

Table 4. Template with Compound Word

The last phase of the learning algorithm involves template usability check to determine if the extracted template has any missing link. A template is usable if all of the word relationships form a connected graph. If the graph contains unreachable node/s (that is, it has missing edges), the template cannot be used in the pun generation phase since not all of the variables will be filled with possible words.

Consider a template with four variables named *X3*, *X4*, *Y1* and *Y2*. The word relationships *X3-X4*, *X4-Y1* and *Y1-Y2* form a connected graph as shown in Figure 1(a). However, if only *X3-X4* and *Y1-Y2* relationships are available as shown in Figure 1(b), there is a missing edge such that if variable *X3* has an initial possible word and is the starting point for generation, a corresponding word for variable *X4* can be derived through the *X3-X4* edge, but no words can be derived for variables *Y1* and *Y2*.

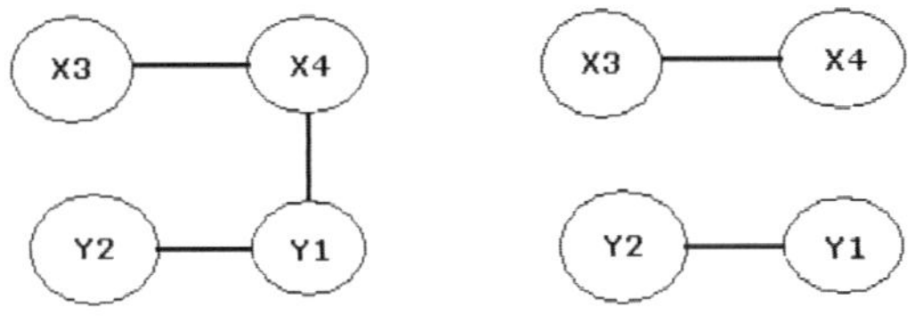

(a) Connected Graph (b) Graph with Missing Edge

Figure 1. Graphs for Word Relationships

This condition is exemplified in Table 5, where two disjoint subgraphs are created as a result of the missing "*house-wall*" and "*wall-wal*" relationships. Further discussion on this is found in Section 5.

Source Pun	What nuts can you use to build a house? Wal-nuts. (Binsted, 1996)
Template	What <X1> can you use to <X6> a <X8>? <Y0>-<Y1>.
Word Relationships	X8 CapableOfReceivingAction X6 X1 SoundsLike Y1 Y0 IsAWord Y1 Y0:Y1 IsA X1
Missing Relations	Y0-0 PartOf X8 Y0-0 SoundsLike Y0

Table 5. Template with Missing Word Relationships where *Y0-0* is the word "*wall*"

4 Generating Puns from Templates

The pun generation phase, having access to the library of learned templates and utilizing the same set of linguistic resources as the template learning algorithm, begins with a keyword input from the user. For each of the usable templates in the library, the keyword is tested on each variable with the same POS tag, except for *SoundsLike* and *IsAWord* relationships where tags are ignored. When a variable has a word, it is used to populate other variables with words that satisfy the word relationships in the template.

T-PEG uses two approaches of populating the variables – forward recursion and backward recursion. *Forward recursion* involves traversing the graph by moving from one node (variable in a template) to the next and following the edges of relationships. Consider the template in Table 6.

Human Joke	How is a window like a headache? They are both panes. (Binsted, 1996)
Template	How is a <X3> like a <X6>? They are both <Y3>.
Word Relationships	Y3-0 SoundsLike Y3 X3 ConceptuallyRelatedTo Y3 Y3 ConceptuallyRelatedTo X3 Y3 PartOf X3 X6 ConceptallyRelatedTo Y3-0 X6 IsA Y3-0 Y3-0 ConceptuallyRelatedTo X6

Table 6. Sample Template for Pun Generation

Given the keyword "*garbage*", one possible sequence of activities to locate words and populate the variables in this template is as follows:

a. "*garbage*" is tried on variable *X6*.
b. *X6* has three word relationships all of which are with *Y3-0*, so it is used to find possible words for *Y3-0*. ConceptNet returns an "*IsA*" relationship with the word "*waste*".
c. *Y3-0* has only one word relationship and this is with *Y3*. Unisyn returns the phonetically similar word "*waist*".
d. *Y3* has two possible relationships with *X3*, and ConceptNet satisfies the "*PartOf*" relationship with the word "*trunk*".

Since two variables may have more than one word relationships connecting them, relationship grouping is also performed. A word relationship group is said to be *satisfied* if at least one of the word relationships in the group is satisfied. Table 7 shows the relationship grouping and the word relationship that was satisfied in each group for the template in Table 6.

Word Relationship	Filled Template
X6 ConceptallyRelatedTo Y3-0 X6 IsA Y3-0 Y3-0 ConceptuallyRelatedTo X6	*garbage* IsA *waste*
Y3-0 SoundsLike Y3	*waste* SoundsLike *waist*
X3 ConceptuallyRelatedTo Y3 Y3 ConceptuallyRelatedTo X3 Y3 PartOf X3	*waist* PartOf *trunk*

Table 7. Relationship Groups and Filled Template

The filled template is passed to the surface realizer, LanguageTool (Naber, 2007), to fix grammatical errors, before displaying the resulting pun "*How is a trunk like a garbage? They are both waists.*" to the user.

The forward recursion approach may lead to a situation in which a variable has been filled with two different sets of words. This usually occurs when the graph contains a cycle, as shown in Figure 2.

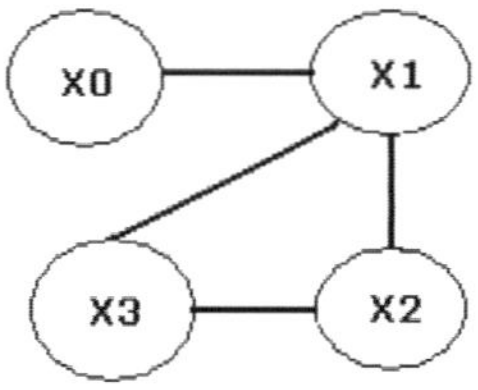

Figure 2. Graph with Cycle

Assume the process of populating the template begins at *X0*. The following edges and resulting set of possible words are retrieved in sequence:

a. *X0-X1* (Words retrieved for X1 → A, B)
b. *X1-X2* (Words retrieved for X2 → D, E, F)
c. *X2-X3* (Words retrieved for X3 → G, H)
d. *X3-X1* (Words retrieved for X1 → B, C)

When the forward recursion algorithm reaches *X3* in step (d), a second set of possible words for *X1* is generated. Since the two sets of words for *X1* do not match, the algorithm gets the intersection of (*A*, *B*) and (*B*, *C*) and assigns this to *X1* (in this case, the word "*B*" is assigned to *X1*). Backward recursion has to be performed starting from step (b) using the new set of words so that other variables with relationships to *X1* will also be checked for possible changes in their values.

5 Test Results

Various tests were conducted to validate the completeness of the word relationships in the learned template, the correctness of the generation algorithm, and the quality of the generated puns.

5.1 Evaluating the Learned Templates

The corpus used in training T-PEG contained 39 punning riddles derived from JAPE (Binsted, 1996) and The Crack-a-Joke Book (Webb, 1978). Since one template is learned from each source pun, the size of the corpus is not a factor in determining the quality of the generated jokes.

Of the 39 resulting templates, only 27 (69.2%) are usable. The unusable templates contain missing word relationships that are caused by two factors. Unisyn contains entries only for valid words and not for syllables. Thus, in (6), the relationship between "*house*" and "*wall*" is missing in the learned template shown in Table 5 because "*wal*" is not found in Unisyn to produce "*wall*". In (7), ConceptNet is unable to determine the relationship between "*infantry*" and "*army*".

(6) What nuts can you use to build a house?
Wal-nuts. (Binsted, 1996)

(7) What part of the army could a baby join?
The infant-ry. (Webb, 1978)

The generation algorithm relies heavily on the presence of correct word relationships. 10 of the 27 usable templates were selected for manual evaluation by a linguist to determine the completeness of the extracted word relationships. A template is said to be *complete* if it is able to capture the essential word relationships in a pun. The evaluation criteria are based on the number of incorrect relationships as identified by the linguist, and includes missing relationship, extra relationship, or incorrect word pairing. A scoring system from 1 to 5 is used, where 5 means there are no incorrect relationship, 4 means there is one incorrect relationship, and so on.

The learning algorithm received an average score of 4.0 out of 5, due to missing word relationships in some of the templates. Again, these were caused by limitations of the resources. For example, in (8), the linguist noted that no relationship between "*heaviest*" and "*weight*" (i.e., PropertyOf *heavy weight*) is included in the learned template presented in Table 2.

(8) What bird can lift the heaviest weights?
The crane. (Webb, 1978)

(9) What kind of fruit fixes taps?
The plum-ber. (Binsted, 1996)

In (9), the linguist identified a missing relationship between "*tap*" and "*plumber*", which is not extracted by the template shown in Table 4.

The linguist also noted that the constituents of a compound word do not always form valid words, such as "*ber*" in *plum-ber* of pun (9), and "*wal*" in *wal-nuts* of pun (6). This type of templates were considered to contain incorrect relationships, and they may cause problems during generation because similar sounding words could not be found for the constituent of the compound word that is not a valid word.

5.2 Evaluating the Generation Algorithm

The generation algorithm was evaluated on two aspects. In the first test, a keyword from each of the source puns was used as input to T-PEG to determine if it can generate back the training corpus. From the 27 usable templates, 20 (74.07%) of the source puns were generated back. Regeneration failed in cases where a word in the source pun has multiple POS tags, as the case in (10), where "*cut*" is tagged as a noun during learning, but verb during generation. In the learning phase, tagging is done at the sentence level, as opposed to a single-word tagging in the generation phase.

(10) What do barbers study? Short-cuts.
(Webb, 1978)

Since a keyword is tried on each variable with the same POS tag in the template, the linguistic resources provided the generation algorithm with a large set of possible words. Consider again the pun in (10), using its template and given the keyword "*farmer*" as an example, the system generated 122 possible puns, some of which are listed in Table 8. Notice that only a couple of these seemed plausible puns, i.e., #3 and #7.

1.	What do *farmers* study?	Egg - plant.
2.	What do *farmers* study?	Power - plant.
3.	What do *farmers* study?	Trans - plant.
4.	What do *farmers* study?	Battle - ground.
5.	What do *farmers* study?	Play - ground.
6.	What do *farmers* study?	Battle - field.
7.	What do *farmers* study?	Gar - field.

Table 8. Excerpt of the Generated Puns Using "*farmer*" as Keyword

In order to find out how this affects the overall performance of the system, the execution times in locating words for the different types of word relationships were measured for the set of 20 regenerated human puns. Table 9 shows the summary for the running time and the number of word relationships extracted for each relationship type.

Another test was also conducted to validate the previous finding. A threshold for the maximum number of possible words to be generated was set to 50, resulting in a shorter running time as depicted in Table 10. A negative outcome of using a threshold value is that only 16 (instead of 20) human puns were regenerated. The other four cases failed because the threshold became restrictive and filtered out the words that should be generated.

Relationship Type	Running Time	# Relationships
Synonym	2 seconds	2
IsAWord	875 seconds	5
Semantic	1,699 seconds	82
SoundsLike	979 seconds	8

Table 9. Running Time of the Generation Algorithm

Relationship Type	Running Time	# Relationships
Synonym	2 seconds	2
IsAWord	321 seconds	4
Semantic	315 seconds	57
SoundsLike	273 seconds	8

Table 10. Running Time of the Generation Algorithm with Threshold = 50 Possible Words

5.3 Evaluating the Generated Puns

Common words, such as *man*, *farmer*, *cow*, *garbage*, and *computer*, were fed to T-PEG so that the chances of these keywords being covered by the resources (specifically ConceptNet) are higher. An exception to this is the use of keywords with possible homonyms (i.e., *whole* and *hole*) to increase the possibility of generating puns with *SoundsLike* relationships.

As previously stated, the linguistic resources provided the generation algorithm with various words that generated a large set of puns. The proponents manually went through this set, identifying which of the output seemed humorous, resulting in the subjective selection of eight puns that were then forwarded for user feedback.

User feedback was gathered from 40 people to compare if the puns of T-PEG are as funny as their source human puns. 15 puns (7 pairs of human-T-PEG puns, with the last pair containing 1 human and 2 T-PEG puns) were rated from a scale of 0 to 5, with 5 being the funniest. This rating system was based on the joke judging process used in (Binsted, 1996), where 0 means it is not a joke, 1 is a pathetic joke, 2 is a "not-so-bad" joke, 3 means average, 4 is quite funny, and 5 is really funny.

T-PEG puns received an average score of 2.13 while the corresponding source puns received an average score of 2.70. Table 11 shows the scores of four pairs of punning riddles that were evaluated, with the input keyword used in generating the T-PEG puns enclosed in parentheses. Pun evaluation is very subjective and depends on the prior knowledge of the reader. Most of the users involved in the survey, for example, did not understand the relationship between *elephant* and *memory*[1], accounting for its low feedback score.

Training Pun	**T-Peg Generated Pun**
What keys are furry? Mon-keys. (Webb, 1978) (2.93)	What verses are endless? Uni-verses. (Keyword: verses) (2.73)
What part of a fish weighs the most? The scales. (Webb, 1978) (3.00)	What part of a man lengthens the most? The shadow. (Keyword: man) (2.43)
What do you call a lizard on the wall? A rep-tile. (Binsted, 1996) (2.33)	What do you call a fire on the floor? A fire-wood. (Keyword: fire) (1.90)
How is a car like an elephant? They both have trunks. (Binsted, 1996) (2.50)	How is a person like an elephant? They both have memory. (Keyword: elephant) (1.50)

Table 11. Sample Puns and User Feedback Scores

Although the generated puns of T-PEG did not receive scores that are as high as the puns in the training corpus, with an average difference rating of 0.57, this work is able to show that the available linguistic resources can be used to train computers to extract word relationships in human puns and to use these learned templates to automatically generate their own puns.

6 Conclusions

Puns have syntactic structures and semantic patterns that can be analyzed and represented in computational models. T-PEG has shown that these computational models or templates can be automatically extracted from training examples of human puns with the use of available linguistic resources. The word relationships extracted are

[1] Elephant characters in children's stories are usually portrayed to have good memories, with the common phrase "An elephant never forgets."

synonyms, is-a-word, sounds-like, and semantic relationships. User feedback further showed that the resulting puns are of a standard comparable to their source puns.

A template is learned for each new joke fed to the T-PEG system. However, the quantity of the learned templates does not necessarily improve the quality of the generated puns. Future work for T-PEG involves exploring template refinement or merging, where a newly learned template may update previously learned templates to improve their quality.

T-PEG is also heavily reliant on the presence of word relationships from linguistic resources. This limitation can be addressed by adding some form of manual intervention to address the missing word relationships caused by limitations of the external resources, thereby increasing the number of usable templates. A different tagger that returns multiple tags may also be explored to consider all possible tags in both the learning and the generation phases.

The manual process employed by the proponents in identifying which of the generated puns are indeed humorous is very time-consuming and subjective. Automatic humor recognition, similar to the works of Mihalcea and Pulman (2007), may be considered for future work.

The template-learning algorithm of T-PEG can be applied in other NLP systems where the extraction of word relationships can be explored further as a means of teaching vocabulary and related concepts to young readers.

References

Kim Binsted. 1996. *Machine Humour: An Implemented Model of Puns*. PhD Thesis, University of Edinburgh, Scotland.

Kim Binsted, Anton Nijholt, Oliviero Stock, and Carlo Strapparava. 2006. Computational Humor. *IEEE Intelligent Systems*, 21(2):59-69.

Kim Binsted and Graeme Ritchie. 1997. Computational Rules for Punning Riddles. *HUMOR, the International Journal of Humor Research*, 10(1):25-76.

Kim Binsted, Helen Pain, and Graeme Ritchie. 1997. Children's Evaluation of Computer-Generated Puns. *Pragmatics and Cognition*, 5(2):309-358.

Iyas Cicekli, and H. Atay Güvenir. 2003. Learning Translation Templates from Bilingual Translation Examples. *Recent Advances in Example-Based Machine Translation*, pp. 255-286, Kluwer Publishers.

Susan Fitt 2002, Unisyn Lexicon Release. Available: http://www.cstr.ed.ac.uk/projects/unisyn/.

Kathleen Go, Manimin Morga, Vince Andrew Nunez, Francis Veto, and Ethel Ong. 2007. Extracting and Using Translation Templates in an Example-Based Machine Translation System. *Journal of Research in Science, Computing, and Engineering*, 4(3):17-29.

Bryan Anthony Hong and Ethel Ong. 2008. Generating Punning Riddles from Examples. *Proceedings of the Second International Symposium on Universal Communication*, 347-352, Osaka, Japan.

Hugo Liu, and Push Singh, 2004. ConceptNet — A Practical Commonsense Reasoning Tool-Kit. *BT Technology Journal*, 22(4):211-226, Springer Netherlands.

Ruli Manurung, Graeme Ritchie, Helen Pain, and Annalu Waller. 2008. Adding Phonetic Similarity Data to a Lexical Database. *Applied Artificial Intelligence*, Kluwer Academic Publishers, Netherlands.

Rada Mihalcea and Stephen Pulman. 2007. Characterizing Humour: An Exploration of Features in Humorous Texts. *Computational Linguistics and Intelligent Text Processing,* Lecture Notes in Computer Science, Vol. 4394, 337-347, Springer Berlin.

Ion Muslea. 1999. Extraction Patterns for Information Extraction Tasks: A Survey. *Proceedings AAAI-99 Workshop on Machine Learning for Information Extraction*, American Association for Artificial Intelligence.

Daniel Naber. 2003. A Rule-Based Style and Grammar Checker.

Vince Andrew Nunez, Bryan Anthony Hong, and Ethel Ong. 2008. Automatically Extracting Templates from Examples for NLP Tasks. *Proceedings of the 22nd Pacific Asia Conference on Language, Information and Computation*, 452-459, Cebu, Philippines.

Graeme Ritchie. 2005. Computational Mechanisms for Pun Generation. *Proceedings of the 10th European Natural Language Generation Workshop*, 125-132. Aberdeen.

Graeme Ritchie, Ruli Manurung, Helen Pain, Annalu Waller, and D. O'Mara. 2006. The STANDUP Interactive Riddle Builder. *IEEE Intelligent Systems* 21(2):67-69.

K. Webb, *The Crack-a-Joke Book*, Puffin Books, London, England, 1978.

WordNet: A Lexical Database for the English Language. Princeton University, New Jersey, 2006.

Gaiku : Generating Haiku with Word Associations Norms

Yael Netzer* and **David Gabay** and **Yoav Goldberg**† and **Michael Elhadad**
Ben Gurion University of the Negev
Department of Computer Science
POB 653 Be'er Sheva, 84105, Israel
{yaeln,gabayd,yoavg,elhadad}@cs.bgu.ac.il

Abstract

creativeness / a pleasing field / of bloom

Word associations are an important element of linguistic creativity. Traditional lexical knowledge bases such as WordNet formalize a limited set of systematic relations among words, such as synonymy, polysemy and hypernymy. Such relations maintain their systematicity when composed into lexical chains. We claim that such relations cannot explain the type of lexical associations common in poetic text. We explore in this paper the usage of Word Association Norms (WANs) as an alternative lexical knowledge source to analyze linguistic computational creativity. We specifically investigate the Haiku poetic genre, which is characterized by heavy reliance on lexical associations. We first compare the density of WAN-based word associations in a corpus of English Haiku poems to that of WordNet-based associations as well as in other non-poetic genres. These experiments confirm our hypothesis that the non-systematic lexical associations captured in WANs play an important role in poetic text. We then present Gaiku, a system to automatically generate Haikus from a seed word and using WAN-associations. Human evaluation indicate that generated Haikus are of lesser quality than human Haikus, but a high proportion of generated Haikus can confuse human readers, and a few of them trigger intriguing reactions.

* Supported by Deutsche Telekom Laboratories at Ben-Gurion University of the Negev.

† Supported by the Lynn and William Frankel Center for Computer Sciences.

1 Introduction

Traditional lexical knowledge bases such as WordNet formalize a limited set of systematic relations that exist between words, such as synonymy, polysemy, hypernymy. When such relations are composed, they maintain their systematicity, and do not create surprising, unexpected word associations.

The human mind is not limited to such systematic relations, and people tend to associate words to each other with a rich set of relations, such as non systematic paradigmatic (*doctor-nurse*) and syntagmatic relations (*mash-potato*) as identified by Saussure (1949). Such associations rely on cultural (*mash-television*), emotional (*math - yuck*) and personal experience (*autumn - Canada*).

In linguistic creativity, such as prose or poetry writing, word associations play an important role and the ability to connect words into new, unexpected relations is one of the key mechanisms that triggers the reader involvement.

We explore in this paper the usage of Word Association Norms (WANs) as an alternative lexical knowledge source to analyze linguistic computational creativity. WANs have been developed in psychological research in the past 40 years. They record typical word associations evoked by people when they are submitted a trigger word. Such associations (*e.g.*, *table* to *chair* or *cloth*) are non-systematic, yet highly stable across people, time (over a period of 30 years) and languages. WANs have been compiled in various languages, and provide an interesting source to analyze word associations in creative writing.

We specifically investigate the Haiku poetic

Proceedings of the NAACL HLT Workshop on Computational Approaches to Linguistic Creativity, pages 32–39,
Boulder, Colorado, June 2009.

genre, which is characterized by heavy reliance on lexical associations. The hypothesis we investigate is that WANs play a role in computational creativity, and better explain the type of word associations observed in creative writing than the systematic relations found in thesauri such as WordNet.

In the rest of the paper, we refine our hypothesis and present observations on a dataset of English Haikus we collected. We find that the density of WAN-based word associations in Haikus is much higher than in other genres, and also much higher than the density of WordNet-based associations. We then present Gaiku, a system we developed to automatically generate Haikus from a seed word using word association norms. Evaluation we performed with a group of 60 human readers indicates that the generated Haikus exhibit interesting creative characteristics and sometimes receive intriguing acclaim.

2 Background and Previous Work

2.1 Computational Creativity

Computational creativity in general and linguistic in particular, is a fascinating task. On the one hand, linguistic creativity goes beyond the general NLP tasks and requires understanding and modelling knowledge which, almost by definition, cannot be formalized (*i.e.*, terms like *beautiful, touching, funny* or *intriguing*). On the other hand, this vagueness itself may enable a less restrictive formalization and allow a variety of quality judgments. Such vague formalizations are naturally more useful when a computational creativity system does not attempt to model the creativity process itself, but instead focuses on 'creative products' such as poetry (see Section 2.3), prose and narrative (Montfort, 2006), cryptic crossword clues (Hardcastle, 2007) and many others. Some research focus on the creative process itself (see (Ritchie, 2006) for a comprehensive review of the field). We discuss in this paper what Boden (1998) calls *P-Creativity* (Psychological Creativity) which is defined relative to the initial state of knowledge, and H-Creativity (Historical Creativity) which is relative to a specific reference culture. Boden claims that, while hard to reproduce, *exploratory creativity* is most successful in computer models of creativity. This is because the other kinds of creativity are *even more elusive* due to *the difficulty of approaching the richness of human associative memory, and the difficulty of identifying our values and of expressing them in computational form.*

We investigate in our work one way of addressing this difficulty: we propose to use associative data as a knowledge source as a first approximation of human associative capabilities. While we do not explain such associations, we attempt to use them in a constructive manner as part of a simple combinational model of creativity in poetry.

2.2 Word Associations and Creativity

Associations and creativity are long known to be strongly connected. Mendick (Mendick, 1969) defines creative thinking as "*the forming of associative elements into new combinations which either meet specified requirements or are in some way useful.*" The *usefulness* criterion distinguishes *original thinking* from *creative thinking*. A creative solution is reached through three main paths: *serendipity* (random stimuli evoke associative elements), *similarity* (stimuli and solution are found similar through an association) and *mediation* (both "problem" and "solution" can be associated to similar elements). In our work, we hypothesize that interesting Haiku poems exhibit creative word associations. We rely on this hypothesis to first generate candidate word associations starting from a seed word and following random walks through WANs, but also to rank candidate Haiku poems by measuring the density of WAN-based associations they exhibit.

2.3 Poetry Generation

Although several automatic and semi-automatic poetry generation systems were developed over the years, most of them did not rise above the level of "party tricks" (Manurung et al., 2000). In his thesis, (Manurung, 2003), defined a poem to be a text that meets three properties: meaningfulness, grammaticality and poeticness. Two of the few systems that attempt to explicitly represent all three properties are reported in (Gervas, 2001) and (Díaz-Agudo et al., 2002). Both systems take as input a prose message provided by the user, and translate it into formal Spanish poetry. The system proposed in (Manurung et al., 2000) is similar in that it focuses on the syntactic and phonetic patterns of the poem, putting less stress on the semantics. The system starts with a simple seed and gradually develops a poem, by making small syntactic and semantic changes at every step.

Specifically in the subfield of Haiku generation, the Haiku generator presented in (Wong and Chun, 2008) produces candidate poems by combining lines taken from blogs. The system then ranks the candidates according to semantic similarity, which is computed using the results returned by a search engine when querying for words in each line. Hitch-Haiku (Tosa et al., 2008), another Haiku generation system, starts from two seed words given by the user. It retrieves two phrases containing these words from a corpus, and then adds a third phrase that connects both input words, using lexical resources.

In our work, we induce a statistical language model of the structure of Haikus from an analysis of a corpus of English Haikus, and explore ways to combine chains of lexical associations into the expected Haiku syntactic structure. The key issues we investigate are the importance of WAN-based associations in the Haiku generation process, and how a chain of words, linked through WAN-based associations, can be composed into a Haiku-like structure.

2.4 Haiku

Haiku is a form of poetry originated in Japan in the sixteenth century. The genre was adopted in Western languages in the 20th Century. The original form of a poem is of three lines of five, seven and five syllables (although this constraint is loosened in non-Japanese versions of Haiku (Gilbert and Yoneoka, 2000)). Haiku, by its nature, aims to reflect or evoke emotion using an extremely economical linguistic form; most Haiku use present tense and use no judgmental words; in addition, functional or syntactic words may be dropped. Traditional Haiku involve reference to nature and seasons, but modern and western Haiku are not restricted to this theme[1].

We adopt the less "constraining" definition of the author Jack Kerouac (2004) for a Haiku "I propose that the "Western Haiku" simply say a lot in three short lines in any Western language. Above all, a Haiku must be very simple and free of all poetic trickery and make a little picture and yet be as airy and graceful as a Vivaldi Pastorella." (pp. *x-xi*). In addition, we are guided by the saying " *The best haiku should leave the reader wondering* " (Quoted in (Blasko and Merski, 1998))

2.5 Word Association Norms

The interest in word associations is common to many fields. Idiosyncrasy of associations was used as a diagnostic tool at the beginning of the 20th century, but nowadays the majority of approaches deal less with particular associations and more with general patterns in order to study the structure of the mental lexicon and of semantic memory (Rubinsten et al., 2005).

Word Association Norms (WAN) are a collection of cue words and the set of free associations that were given as responses to the cue, accompanied with quantitative and statistical measures. Subjects are given a word and asked to respond immediately with the first word that comes to their mind. The largest WAN we know for English is the University of South Florida Free Association Norms (Nelson et al., 1998).

Word Association Norms and Thesauri in NLP Sinopalnikova and Smrz (2004) have shown that when building and extending semantic networks, WANs have advantages over corpus-based methods. They found that WANs cover semantic relations that are difficult to acquire from a corpus: 42% of the non-idiosyncratic cue-target pairs in an English WAN never co-appeared in a 10 words window in a large balanced text corpus. From the point of view of computational creativity, this is encouraging, since it suggests that association-based content generation can lead to texts that are both sensible and novel. (Duch and Pilichowski, 2007)'s work, from a neuro-cognitive perspective, generates neologisms based, among other data, on word association. (Duch and Pilichowski, 2007) sums "creativity requires prior knowledge, imagination and filtering of the results."

3 WordNet vs. Associations

Word association norms add an insight on language that is not found in WordNet or are hard to acquire from corpora, and therefore can be used as an additional tool in NLP applications and computational

[1] *Senryu* poetry, similar in form to Haiku, is the Japanese genre of poems that relate to human and relationships, and may be humorous. Hereafter, we use Haiku for both the original definition and the Senryu as well.

creativity.

We choose the Haiku generation task using word associations, since this genre of poetry encapsulates meaning in a special way. Haiku tend to use words which are connected through associative or phonological connections (very often ambiguous).

We hypothesize that word-associations are good catalyzers for creativity, and use them as a building block in the creative process of Haiku generation. We first test this hypothesis by analyzing a corpus of existing Haiku poems.

3.1 Analyzing existing text

Can the creativity of text as reflected in word associations be quantified? Are Haiku poems indeed more associative than newswire text or prose? If this is the case, we expect Haiku to have more associative relations, which cannot be easily recovered by WordNet than other type of text. We view the WAN as an undirected graph in which the nodes are stemmed words, and two nodes are connected *iff* one of them is a cue for the other. We take the *associative distance* between two words to be the number of edges in the shortest path between the words in the associations-graph. Interestingly, almost any word pair in the association graph is connected with a path of at most 3 edges. Thus, we take two words to be associatively related if their associative distance is 1 or 2. Similarly, we define the *WordNet distance* between two stemmed words to be the number of edges in the shortest path between any synset of one word to any synset of the other word[2]. Two words are WordNet-related if their WordNet distance is less than 4 (this is consistent with works on lexical-cohesion, (Morris and Hirst, 1991)).

We take the *associativity* of a piece of text to be the number of associated word pairs in the text, normalized by the number of word pairs in the text of which both words are in the WAN.[3] We take the *WordNet-relations level* of a piece of text to be the number of WordNet-related word pairs in the text.

[2]This is the inverse of the path-similarity measure of (Pedersen et al., 2004).

[3]This normalization is performed to account for the limited lexical coverage of the WAN. We don't want words that appear in a text, but are not covered by the WAN, to affect the associativity level of the text.

SOURCE	AVG. ASSOC RELATIONS (<3)	AVG. WORDNET RELATIONS (<4)
News	0.26	2.02
Prose	0.22	1.4
Haiku	0.32	1.38

Table 1: Associative and WordNet relations in various text genres

We measure the average associativity and WordNet levels of 200 of the Haiku in our Haiku Corpus (Section 4.1), as well as of random 12-word sequences from Project Gutenberg and from the NANC newswire corpus.

The results are presented in Table 1.

Perhaps surprisingly, the numbers for the Gutenberg texts are lower on all measures. This is attributed to the fact that Gutenberg texts have many more pronouns and non-content words than the Haiku and newswire text. Haiku text appears to be more associative than newswire text. Moreover, newswire documents have many more WordNet-relations than the Haiku poems – whenever words are related in Haiku, this relatedness tends to be captured via the association network rather than via the WordNet relations. The same trend is apparent also when considering the Gutenberg numbers: they have about 15% less associations than newswire text, but about 30% less WordNet-relations. This supports the claim that associative information which is not readily available in WordNet is a good indicator of creative content.

3.2 Generating creative content

We now investigate how word-associations can help in the process of generating Haikus. We define a 5 stage generative process: **theme selection** in which the general theme of the Haiku is decided, **syntactic planning**, which sets the Haiku form and syntactic constraints, **content selection / semantic planning** which combines syntactic and aesthetic constraints with the theme selected in the previous stages to form good building blocks, **filtered over-generation** of many Haiku based on these selected building blocks, and finally **re-ranking** of the generated Haiku based on external criteria.

The details of the generation algorithm are presented in Section 4.2. Here we focus on the creative aspect of this process – theme selection. Our main claim is that WANs are a good source for interesting themes. Specifically, interesting themes can be obtained by performing a short *random walk* on the association graph induced by the WAN network.

Table 2 presents the results of several random walks of 3 steps starting from the seed words "Dog", "Winter", "Nature" and "Obsession". For comparison, we also present the results of random walks over WordNet glosses for the same seeds.

We observe that the association network is better for our needs than WordNet. Random walks in WordNet are more likely to stay too close to the seed word, limiting the poetic options, or to get too far and produce almost random connections.

4 Algorithm for generating Haiku

4.1 Dataset

We used the Word Association Norms (WAN) of the University of South Florida [4] (Nelson et al., 1998) for discovering associations of words. The dataset (Appendix A, there) includes 5,019 cue words and 10,469 additional target that were collected with more than 6,000 participants since 1973.

We have compiled a Haiku Corpus, which includes approximately 3,577 Haiku in English of various sources (amateurish sites, children's writings, translations of classic Japanese Haiku of Bashu and others, and 'official' sites of Haiku Associations (*e.g., Haiku Path - Haiku Society of America*).

For the content selection part of the algorithms, we experimented with two data sources: a corpus of 1TB web-based N-grams supplied by Google, and the complete text of Project Gutenberg. The Gutenberg data has the advantage of being easier to POS-tag and contains less restricted-content, while the Google Web data is somewhat more diverse.

4.2 Algorithm Details

Our Haiku generation algorithm includes 5 stages: theme selection, syntactic planning, content selection, filtered over generation, and ranking.

The **Theme Selection** stage is in charge of dictating the overall theme of our Haiku. We start with a user-supplied seed word (*e.g.* `WINTER`). We then consult the Association database in order to enrich the seed word with various associations. Ideally, we would like these associations to be close enough to the seed word to be understandable, yet far enough away from it as to be interesting. After some experimenting, we came up with the following heuristic, which we found to provide adequate results. We start with the seed word, and conduct a short random walk on the associations graph. Each random step is comprised of choosing a random direction (either "Cue" or "Target") using a uniform distribution, and then a random neighbor according to its relative frequency. We conduct several (8) such walks, each with 3 steps, and keep all the resulting words. This gives us mostly close, probable associations, as well as some less probable, further away from the seed.

The **syntactic planning** stage determines the form of the generated Haiku, setting syntactic and aesthetic constraints for the generative process. This is done in a data-driven way by considering common line patterns from our Haiku corpus. In a training stage, we POS-tagged each of the Haiku, and then extracted a pattern from each of the Haiku lines. A line-pattern is a sequence of POS-tags, in which the most common words are lexicalized to include the word-form in addition to the POS-tag. An example for such a line pattern might be `DT_the JJ NN`. We kept the top-40 frequent patterns for each of the Haiku lines, overall 120 patterns. When generating a new Haiku, we choose a random pattern for the first line, then choose the second line pattern conditioned on the first, and the third line pattern conditioned on the second. The line patterns are chosen with a probability proportional to their relative frequencies in the training corpus. For the second and third lines we use the conditional probabilities of a pattern appearing after the previous line pattern. The result of this stage is a 3-line Haiku skeleton, dictating the number of words on each line, their POS-tags, and the placement of specific function words.

In the **Content Selection** stage, we look for possible Haiku lines, based on our selected theme and syntactic structure. We go over our candidate lines[5], and extract lines which match the syntactic patterns and contain a stemmed appearance of one of the stemmed theme words. In our current implementation, we require the first line to contain the seed word, and the second and third line to contain any of

[4]http://w3.usf.edu/FreeAssociation/

[5]These are POS-tagged n-grams extracted from a large text corpora: the Google T1 dataset or Project Gutenberg

SEED	WAN	WORDNET
Dog	puppy adorable cute	heel villain villainess
Dog	cat curious george	hound scoundrel villainess
Winter	summer heat microwave	wintertime solstice equinox
Winter	chill cold alergy	midwinter wintertime season
Nature	animals instinct animals	world body crotch
Nature	natural environment surrounding	complexion archaism octoroon
Obsession	cologne perfume smell	fixation preoccupation thought
Obsession	compulsion feeling symptom	compulsion onomatomania compulsion

Table 2: Some random walks on the WordNet and WAN induced graphs

the theme words. Other variations, such as choosing a different word set for each line, are of course possible.

The **over generation** stage involves creating many possible Haiku candidates by randomly matching lines collected in the content selection stage. We filter away Haiku candidates which have an undesired properties, such as repeating the same content-word in two different lines.

All of the generated Haiku obey the syntactic and semantic constraints, but not all of them are interesting. Thus, we **rank** the Haiku in order to weed out the better ones. The top-ranking Haiku is the output of our system. Our current heuristic prefers highly associative Haikus. This is done by counting the number of 1st and 2nd degree associations in each Haiku, while giving more weight to 2nd degree associations in order to encourage "surprises". While all the candidate Haiku were generated based on a common theme of *intended* associative connections, the content selection and adherence to syntactic constraints introduce additional content words and with them some new, *unintended* associative connections. Our re-ranking approach tries to maximize the number of such connections.[6]

5 Evaluation

The ultimate goal of a poetry generation system is to produce poems that will be considered good if written by a human poet. It is difficult to evaluate to what extent a poetry generation system can meet this goal (Ritchie, 2001; Manurung et al., 2000). Difficulties arise from two major sources: first, since a creative work should be novel, it cannot be directly evaluated by comparison to some gold standard. Second, it is hard for people to objectively evaluate the quality of poetry. Even determining whether a text is a poem or not is not an easy task, as readers expect poetry to require creative reading, and tolerate, to some extent, ungrammatical structures or cryptic meaning.

5.1 "Turing Test" Experiment

To evaluate the quality of Gaiku, we asked a group of volunteers to read a set of Haiku, indicate how much they liked each one (on a scale of 1-5), and classify each Haiku as written by a human or by a computer.

We compiled two sets of Haiku. The first set (AUTO) contained 25 Haiku. 10 Haiku chosen at random from our Haiku corpus, and 15 computer generated ones. The computer generated Haiku were created by identifying the main word in the first line of each human-written Haiku, and passing it as a seed word to the Haiku generation algorithm (in case a first line in human-written Haiku contained two main words, two Haiku were generated). We included the top-ranking Haiku returning from a single run of the system for each seed word. The only human judgement in compiling this set was in the identification of the main words of the human Haiku.

The second set (SEL) was compiled of 9 haiku poems that won awards[7], and 17 computer Haiku that were selected by us, after several runs of the automatic process. (Again, each poem in the automatic poems set shared at least one word with some poem in the human Haiku set).

The subjects were not given any information about the number of computer-generated poems in the sets.

[6]While this heuristic works well, it leaves a lot to be desired. It considers only the quantity of the associations, and not their quality. Indeed, when looking at the Haiku candidates produced in the generation stage, one can find many interesting pieces, where some of the lower ranking ones are far better than the top ranking.

[7]Gerald Brady Memorial Award Collection http://www.hsa-haiku.org/bradyawards/brady.htm 2006-2007

The AUTO questionnaire was answered by 40 subjects and the SEL one by 22. (Altogether, 52 different people took part in the experiment, as some subjects answered both versions). The subjects were all adults (age 18 to 74), some were native English speakers and others were fully fluent in English. Except a few, they did not have academic background in literature.

5.2 Results and Discussion

Results are presented in Table 3 and Figure 1.

Overall, subjects were correct in 66.7% of their judgements in AUTO and 61.4% in SEL. The average grade that a poem - human or machine-made - received correlates with the percentage of subjects who classified it as human. The average grade and rate of acceptance as written by human were significantly higher for the Haiku written by people. However, some computer Haiku rivaled the average human poem in both measures. This is true even for AUTO, in which both the generation and the selection processes were completely automatic. The best computer Haiku of SEL scored better than most human Haiku in both measures.

The best computer poem in SEL was:

early dew / the water contains / teaspoons of honey

which got an average grade of 3.09 and was classified as human by 77.2% of the subjects.

At the other extreme, the computer poem (SEL):

space journey / musical instruments mythology / of similar drugs

was classified as human by only 9% of the subjects, and got an average grade of 2.04.

The best Haiku in the AUTO set was:

cherry tree / poisonous flowers lie / blooming

which was classified as human by 72.2% of the subjects and got an average grade of 2.75.

The second human-like computer generated Haiku in each set were:

spring bloom / showing / the sun's pyre

(AUTO, 63.8% human) and:

blind snakes / on the wet grass / tombstoned terror

(SEL, 77.2% human).

There were, expectedly, lots of disagreements. Poetry reading and evaluation is subjective and by

		Human Poems	Gaiku
AUTO	avg. % classified as Human	72.5%	37.2%
	avg. grade	2.86	2.11
SEL	avg. % classified as Human	71.7%	44.1%
	avg. grade	2.84	2.32

Table 3: Turing-test experiment results

itself (in particular for Haiku) a creative task. In addition, people have very different ideas in mind as to a computer's ability to do things. (One subject said, for example, that the computer generated

holy cow / a carton of milk / seeking a church

is *too stupid* to be written by a computer; however, content is very strongly connected and does not seem random). On the other end, subjects often remarked that some of the human-authored Haiku contained metaphors which were *too obvious* to be written by a human.

Every subject was wrong at least 3 times (at least once in every direction); every poem was wrongly-classified at least once. Some really bad auto-poems got a good grade here and there, while even the most popular human poems got a low grade sometimes.

6 Discussion and Future Work

Word association norms were shown to be a useful tool for a computational creativity task, aiding in the creation of an automatic Haiku-generation software, which is able to produce "human-like" Haiku. However, associations can be used for many other tasks.

In the last decade, *lexical chains* are often used in various NLP tasks such as text summarization or text categorization; WordNet is the main resource for detecting the cohesive relationships between words and their relevance to a given chain (Morris and Hirst, 1991). We believe that using word association norms can enrich the information found in WordNet and enable the detection of more relevant words.

Another possible application is for assisting word-finding problem of children with specific language impairments (SLI). A useful tactic practiced as an assistance to retrieve a forgotten word is by saying all words that come to mind. The NLP task, therefore, is for a set of a given associations, reconstruct the targeted word.

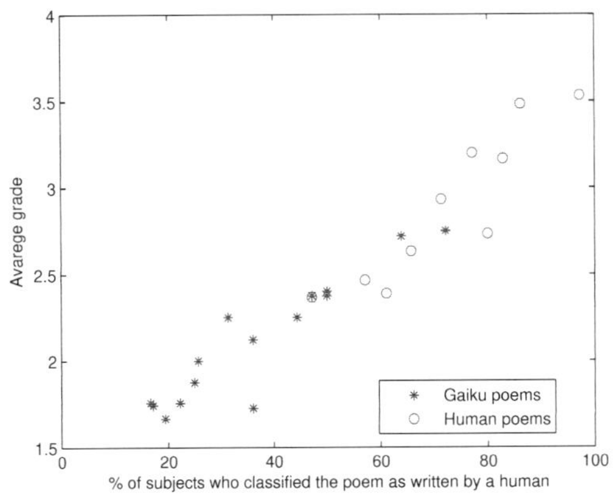

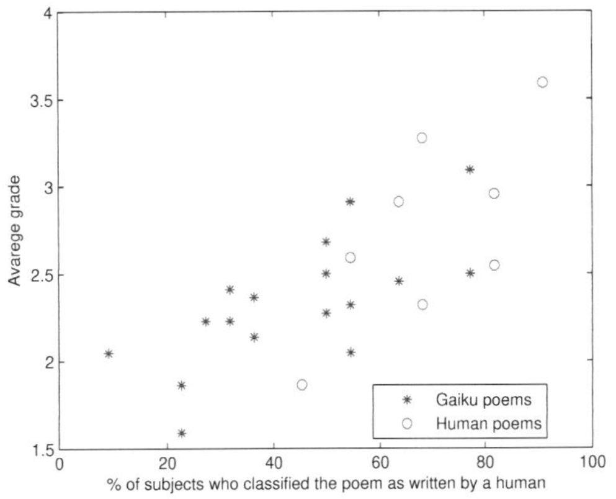

Figure 1: Average grades and percentages of subjects who classified poems as written by humans, for AUTO (left) and SEL. Circles represent Haiku written by people, and stars represent machine-made Haiku

References

D.G. Blasko and D.W. Merski. 1998. Haiku poetry and metaphorical thought: An invention to interdisciplinary study. *Creativity Research Journal*, 11.

M.A. Boden. 1998. Creativity and artificial intelligence. *Artificial Intelligence*, 103(1–2).

F. de Saussure, C. Bally, A. Riedlinger, and A. Sechehaye. 1949. *Cours de linguistique generale*. Payot, Paris.

B. Díaz-Agudo, P. Gervás, and P. A. González-Calero. 2002. Poetry generation in COLIBRI. In *Proc. of EC-CBR*.

W. Duch and M. Pilichowski. 2007. Experiments with computational creativity. *Neural Information Processing, Letters and Reviews*, 11(3).

P. Gervas. 2001. An expert system for the composition of formal Spanish poetry. *Journal of Knowledge-Based Systems*, 14.

R. Gilbert and J. Yoneoka. 2000. From 5-7-5 to 8-8-8: An investigation of Japanese Haiku metrics and implications for English Haiku. *Language Issues: Journal of the Foreign Language Education Center*.

D. Hardcastle. 2007. Cryptic crossword clues: Generating text with a hidden meaning BBKCS-07-04. Technical report, Birkbeck College, London.

J. Kerouac. 2004. *Book of Haikus*. Enitharmon Press.

H.M. Manurung, G. Ritchie, and H. Thompson. 2000. Towards a computational model of poetry generation. In *Proc. of the AISB'00*.

H.M. Manurung. 2003. *An evolutionary algorithm approach to poetry generation*. Ph.D. thesis, University of Edinburgh.

S.A. Mendick. 1969. The associative basis of the creative process. *Psychological Review*.

N. Montfort. 2006. Natural language generation and narrative variation in interactive fiction. In *Proc. of Computational Aesthetics Workshop at AAAI 2006*, Boston.

J. Morris and G. Hirst. 1991. Lexical cohesion computed by thesaural relations as an indicator of the structure of text. *Computational Linguistics*, 17.

D.L. Nelson, C.L. Mcevoy, and T.A. Schreiber. 1998. The University of South Florida Word Association, Rhyme, and Word Fragment Norms. http://www.usf.edu/FreeAssociation/.

T. Pedersen, S. Patwardhan, and J. Michelizzi. 2004. Wordnet::similarity - measuring the relatedness of concepts. In *HLT-NAACL 2004: Demonstrations*.

G. Ritchie. 2001. Assessing creativity. In *Proc. of AISB'01 Symposium*.

G. Ritchie. 2006. The transformational creativity hypothesis. *New Generation Computing*, 24.

O. Rubinsten, D. Anaki, A. Henik, S. Drori, and Y. Faran. 2005. Free association norms in the Hebrew language. *Word Norms in Hebrew*. (In Hebrew).

A. Sinopalnikova and P. Smrz. 2004. Word association thesaurus as a resource for extending semantic networks. In *Communications in Computing*.

N. Tosa, H. Obara, and M. Minoh. 2008. Hitch haiku: An interactive supporting system for composing haiku poem. In *Proc. of the 7th International Conference on Entertainment Computing*.

M. Tsan Wong and A. Hon Wai Chun. 2008. Automatic Haiku generation using vsm. In *Proc. of ACACOS'08*, April.

Automatic Generation of Tamil Lyrics for Melodies

Ananth Ramakrishnan A
AU-KBC Research Centre
MIT Campus, Anna University
Chennai, India
ananthrk@au-kbc.org

Sankar Kuppan
AU-KBC Research Centre
MIT Campus, Anna University
Chennai, India
sankar@au-kbc.org

Sobha Lalitha Devi
AU-KBC Research Centre
MIT Campus, Anna University
Chennai, India
sobha@au-kbc.org

Abstract

This paper presents our on-going work to automatically generate lyrics for a given melody, for phonetic languages such as Tamil. We approach the task of identifying the required syllable pattern for the lyric as a sequence labeling problem and hence use the popular CRF++ toolkit for learning. A corpus comprising of 10 melodies was used to train the system to understand the syllable patterns. The trained model is then used to guess the syllabic pattern for a new melody to produce an optimal sequence of syllables. This sequence is presented to the Sentence Generation module which uses the Dijkstra's shortest path algorithm to come up with a meaningful phrase matching the syllabic pattern.

1 Introduction

In an attempt to define poetry (Manurung, 2004), provides three properties for a natural language artifact to be considered a poetic work, viz., Meaningfulness (M), Grammaticality (G) and Poeticness (P). A complete poetry generation system must generate texts that adhere to all the three properties. In this work, our attempt would be to generate meaningful lyrics that match the melody and the poetic aspects of the lyric will be tackled in future works.

According to on-line resources such as *How to write lyrics* (Demeter, 2001), the generated lyric must have Rhythm, Rhyme and Repetition.

One of the recent attempts for automatically generating lyrics for a given melody is the Tra-la-Lyrics system (Oliveira et al., 2007). This system uses the *ABC* notation (Gonzato, 2003) for representing melody and the corresponding suite of tools for analyzing the melodies. The key aspect of the system is its attempt to detect the strong beats present in the given melody and associating words with stressed syllables in the corresponding positions. It also evaluates three lyric generation strategies (Oliveira et al., 2007) – random words+rhymes, sentence templates+rhymes and grammar+rhymes. Of these strategies, the sentence templates+rhymes approach attempts for syntactical coherence and the grammar+rhymes approach uses a grammar to derive Portuguese sentence templates. From the demo runs presented, we see that the system can generate grammatical sentences (when using an appropriate strategy). However, there is no attempt to bring Meaningfulness in the lyrics.

2 Lyric Generation for Tamil

Tamil, our target language for generating lyrics, is a phonetic language. There is a one-to-one relation between the grapheme and phoneme. We make use of this property in coming up with a generic representation for all words in the language. This representation, based on the phonemic syllables, consists

Proceedings of the NAACL HLT Workshop on Computational Approaches to Linguistic Creativity, pages 40–46,
Boulder, Colorado, June 2009. ©2009 Association for Computational Linguistics

of the following three labels: *Kuril* (short vowel, represented by K), *Nedil* (long vowel, represented by N) and *Mei* (consonants, represented by M). For example, the word *thA-ma-rai* (*lotus*) will be represented as N-K-N (long vowel followed by short vowel followed by another long vowel). This representation scheme, herein after referred as *KNM* representation, is used throughout our system - training, melody analysis and as input to the sentence generation module.

3 Approach

Our approach to generating lyrics for the given melody is a two-step process (Figure 1). The first step is to analyze the input melody and output a series of syllable patterns in *KNM* representation scheme along with tentative word and sentence boundary. The subsequent step involves filling the syllable pattern with words from the corpus that match the given syllable pattern and any rhyme requirements. We approach the first aspect as a Sequence Labeling problem and use the popular CRF++ toolkit (Kudo, 2005) to label the input melody in *ABC* notation (Gonzato, 2003) with appropriate syllable categories (*Kuril*, *Nedil* and *Mei*). This system is trained with sample film songs and their corresponding lyrics (in *KNM* scheme) as input. The trained model is then used to label the given input melody. The syllable pattern, thus generated for the input melody, is provided to a Sentence Generation Module that finds suitable lyrics satisfying the following constraints: a.) Words should match the syllable pattern b.)The sequence of words should have a meaning. We achieve this by using the popular Dijkstra's Shortest Path Algorithm (Cormen et al., 1990) against a pre-built corpus of Unigram and Bigram of Words.

4 Melody Analysis

The goal of the Melody Analysis is to analyze the input melody and suggest a possible *KNM* representation scheme that will match the melody. Since our representation of melody is based on the *ABC* Notation (Gonzato, 2003), which is textual, we approach this problem as labeling the *ABC* notation using the *KNM* representation scheme.

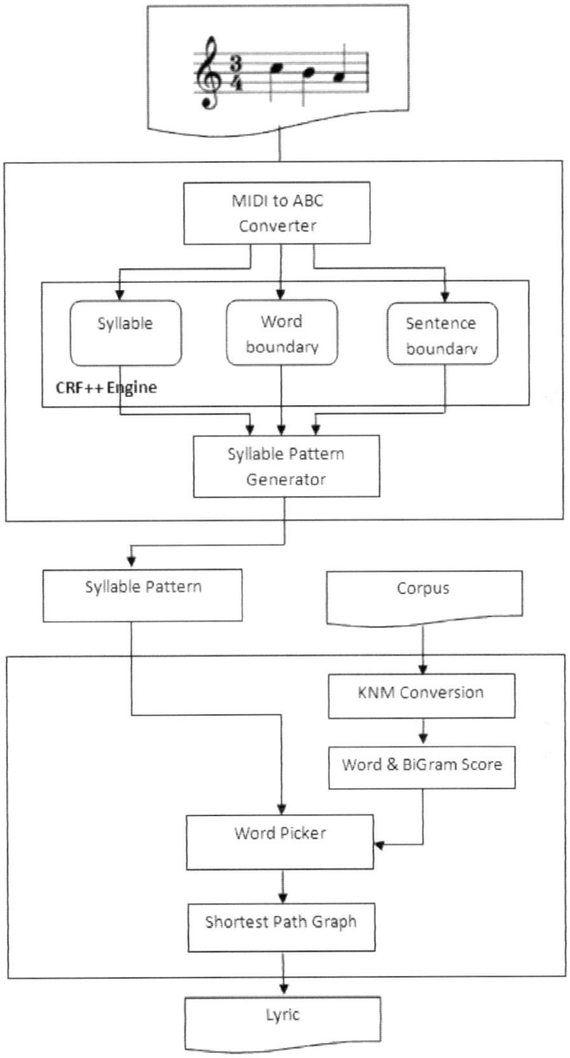

Figure 1. System Approach

4.1 Characteristics of Melody

Every melody follows a *Meter*, which provides the basic design principles in music. Some of the most frequently used meters we encountered in the film songs that we used are 2/4, 3/4, 4/4, 6/8, 9/8 and 12/8 – that indicate the number of Notes played in the given interval. Each Note is represented by the character set A, B, C, D, E, F and G – which are called as main notes and A#, C#, D#, F# and G# - which are called Sharp Notes. Thus, for any given Meter in the melody, we can find the sequence of Notes with the corresponding duration for which the Note is played in that meter.

For the purpose of generating lyrics, we need to fit one syllable for each of the notes in the melody.

4.2 Conditional Random Fields

Conditional Random Fields(*CRF*) (Lafferty et al., 2001) is a Machine Learning technique that has performed well for sequence labeling problems such as POS tagging, Chunking and Named Entity Recognition. It overcomes the difficulties faced in other techniques like Hidden Markov Models(*HMM*) and Maximum Entropy Markov Model(*MEMM*).

(Lafferty et al., 2001) define Conditional Random Fields as follows: "Let **G** = (**V**, **E**) be a graph such that $\mathbf{Y} = (\mathbf{Y}_v)_{v \in V}$, so that **Y** is indexed by the vertices of **G**. Then (**X**,**Y**) is a conditional random field in case, when conditioned on **X**, the random variables $\mathbf{Y}_v$ obey the Markov property with respect to the graph: $p(\mathbf{Y}_v|\mathbf{X},\mathbf{Y}_w,w\neq v) = p(\mathbf{Y}_v|\mathbf{X},\mathbf{Y}_w,w\sim v)$, where w~v means that w and v are neighbors in **G**". Here **X** denotes a sentence and **Y** denotes the label sequence. The label sequence y which maximizes the likelihood probability $p_\Theta(\mathbf{y}|\mathbf{x})$ will be considered as the correct sequence, while testing for new sentence x with CRF model . The likelihood probability $p_\Theta(\mathbf{y}|\mathbf{x})$ is expressed as follows.

$$p_\theta(\mathbf{y} \mid \mathbf{x}) \propto \exp\left(\sum_{e\in E,k} \lambda_k f_k(e,\mathbf{y}|_e,\mathbf{x}) + \sum_{v\in V,k} \mu_k g_k(v,\mathbf{y}|_v,\mathbf{x})\right)$$

where λ_k and μ_k are parameters from *CRF* model $\boldsymbol{\theta}$ and f_k and g_k are the binary feature functions that we need to give for training the *CRF* model. This is where we integrate the specific features of the problem into the machine learning models like *CRF*.

4.3 Feature Templates

There are three models that need to be learnt, viz, labeling notes with *KNM* scheme, identifying word boundaries and identifying line boundaries. We present below the features used to learn each of the above.

4.3.1 Learning *KNM* labels

In addition to the labels K, N and M, there are also other non-syllable features that need to be identified in the melody. Thus, the complete list of labels include, K, N, KM, NM, TIE, OPEN, CLOSE, PRE and BAR.

K – short vowel
N – long vowel
KM – short vowel followed by consonant
NM – long vowel followed by consonants
TIE – presence of a Tie in the meter
OPEN – opening of a tie
CLOSE – closing of a tie
PRE – Note that follows a tie
BAR – End of meter.

The following are the list of features considered:

- Current Note
- Previous Note + Current Note + Next Note
- Previous-to-previous Note + Previous Note + Current Note + Next Note + Next-to-next Note
- Current Note/Duration
- Previous Note/Duration + Current Note/Duration + Next Note/Duration
- Previous-to-previous Note/Duration + Previous Note/Duration + Current Note/Duration + Next Note/Duration + Next-to-next Note/Duration.

4.3.2 Word Boundary

Another important aspect in analyzing the melody is to spot potential word boundaries. While in many cases, the presence of bars could indicate potential word boundaries, there are also cases where a given word can span a bar (especially due to the presence of Ties). Hence, we need to explicitly train our system to identify potential word boundaries. The features used to identify the boundaries of words are mostly the same as for learning the *KNM* labels, but with the addition of considering two more previous notes along with their durations.

4.3.3 Sentence Boundary

As with Word Boundary ,we cannot assume sentence boundaries based on the musical notation and hence we also train our system to identify potential sentence boundaries. Sentence boundary identification happens after the word boundaries are identified and hence this additional feature is used along with the above-mentioned features for sentence boundary training.

5 Sentence Generation

The goal of the Sentence Generation module is to generate a meaningful phrase that matches the input pattern given in *KNM* scheme. For example, given an input pattern such as *'KMKM NKM NKN'*, it should generate a phrase consisting of three words each of them matching their respective pattern.

5.1 Corpus selection and pre-processing

Since we are interested in generating lyrics for melody, the corpus we chose consisted mainly of poems and short stories. The only pre-processing involved was to remove any special characters (such as "( ), $ % &, etc.) from the text. From this corpus, we index all Unigram and Bigram of Words. Each word is marked with its *KNM* syllable pattern and their frequency of occurrence in the corpus. The Bigram list contains only the frequency of occurrence.

5.2 Graph Construction

Given an input pattern (say *'KMKM NKM NKN'*), we construct a directed graph with the list of words satisfying each pattern, as represented by Figure 2.

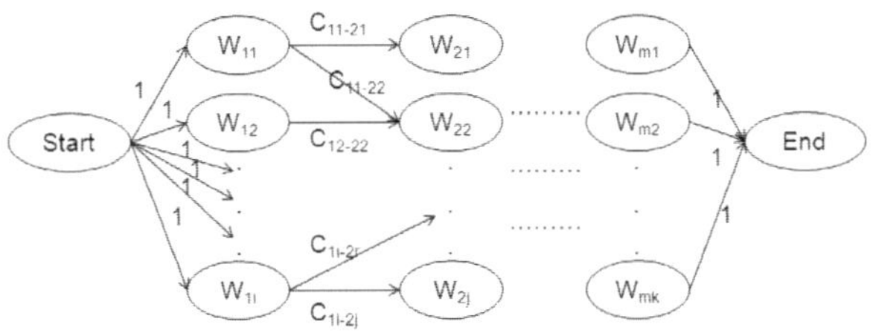

Figure 2. Graph Construction

The edge from word W_{ij} (of, say pattern *KMKM*) to W_{rs} (of, say pattern *NKM*) is weighted based on the frequency values collected from the corpus and is calculated as follows:

$$P(W_{rs} / W_{ij}) = \frac{\#\,(W_{ij} \text{ followed by } W_{rs})}{\#\,(W_{ij})} \qquad \textit{(Eqn. 1)}$$

Since the Shortest Path Algorithm picks the path with the least cost, we need to weight the edges in such a way that a higher probability sequence gets the least cost (C). Thus, we measure $Cost(W_{rs}/W_{ij})$ as:

$$Cost(W_{rs}/W_{ij}) = 1 - P(W_{rs}/W_{ij}) \qquad \textit{(from Eqn. 1)} \quad \textit{(Eqn. 2)}$$

By default, the cost from the START node to the first list of words and the cost from the last list of words to END node is fixed as 1.

5.3 Preferential selection of paths

One of the shortcomings of using the Shortest Path Algorithm is that, for the given input pattern and the given Corpus, the algorithm will always generate the same phrase (with the least cost). In addition to this problem, when the melody demands, we need to generate rhyming words. Lastly, we need to handle the case where the corpus may not have a phrase that matches the complete pattern. We tackle all the above issues by biasing the Shortest Path Algorithm by changing the cost of the edges.

5.3.1 Bias initial word

In order to generate different phrases for the same pattern (say *KMKM NKM NKN*), we pick a random word that matches the initial pattern (*KMKM*) and fix the cost of the edge from START to the random word to 0. As the default cost from START to all leading words is 1, this biases the algorithm to find a pattern that starts with the random word. However, if there exists a phrase, whose "overall cost" is still less than the one starting with the random phrase, the algorithm will output the same phrase. In order to avoid this, we provide multiple random words and pick the one that truly generates a unique phrase.

5.3.2 Rhyming Words

When there is a need to generate phrases that rhyme with any previously generated phrases, especially in line endings, we use the same biasing technique to prefer certain words over others. The motivation to concentrate on line endings is based on our assumption that the notes in melody would be similar for the rhyming words and thus our representation scheme involving Mei(M) (consonants) would handle the stressed syllables. The path finding algorithm, can take as input a word and a position, with which the new phrase should rhyme in the given position. In this case, we generate all the words that rhyme with the given word by using the *Maximum substring matching technique*. That is, the word with the maximum substring common to the input word, in word endings, is considered as a rhyming word. For example, given an input word '*kOyil*' (*temple*), the rhyming words would be '*vAyil*' (*gate*) and '*veyil*' (*sun*). As can be seen, both the words have the suffix '*yil*' common with the input word. Thus, as earlier, the cost of the edges in the paths leading to such rhyming words will be set to 0, thus biasing the algorithm to pick these paths. One another way would be have only those nodes corresponding to the rhyming words (discarding other non-rhyming words). However, in the case where no rhyming words are present in the corpus, this approach can lead to a graph with an incomplete path. Hence we use the approach of biasing the graph paths that can pick the rhyming words, if present and provide a non-rhyming word, if none was available.

5.3.3 Edit-Distance Matching

There can also be cases when there is no phrase that exactly matches the given input pattern sequence, though the corpus might contain individual words matching each pattern in the sequence. In this case, we relax the matches using the *Edit-Distance* metric. Thus, for the given pattern *NKN*, we also list words that match *NKK*, *KKN*, etc. Since the input patterns are deemed to fit the given melody, an Edit-Distance Matching can turn up words that need not match the given melody and hence should be used only when there are no phrases matching the input pattern. Another approach, though practically not possible, is to have a "*big enough corpus*" that contains at least one phrase matching each pattern.

6 Experiments

We conducted the experiments as two separate steps, one for the *CRF* engine and another for the Sentence Generation module.

For the *CRF* engine, we collected and used Tamil film songs' tune and lyrics, as they were easily available from the web. The tunes were converted to the *ABC* notation and their lyrics were converted to the *KNM* representation scheme. The notes from the tune and the syllables in the corresponding lyric (in their respective representation schemes) were manually mapped with each other. An example training file for the *CRF* engine for learning the *KNM* representation scheme is presented below:

Note	Duration	Label
B	½	K
C	½	N
B	½	K
A	½	KM
G	½	K
-	0	tie
[	0	open
A	½	pre
G	½	K
]	0	close
B	4	K

Table 1. *KNM* scheme learning – training file

Similarly, for the word boundary identification, the same input is used but with the labels corresponding to word boundaries such as W-B (word beginning), W-I (word intermediate), etc. (Table 2):

Note	Duration	Label
B	½	W-B
C	½	W-I
B	½	W-I
A	½	W-I
G	½	W-B
-	0	Tie
[	0	open
A	½	pre
G	½	W-I
]	0	close
B	4	W-I

Table 2. Word boundary learning – training file

For sentence boundary identification, the output from the word boundary identification is used and hence it is run after the word boundary identification is complete. Thus, the input to the CRF engine in this case would be like the one in (Table 3), with labels corresponding to sentence boundary such as S-B (sentence beginning) and S-I (sentence intermediate):

Note	Duration	Word Boundary	Sentence Boundary
B	½	W-B	S-B
c	½	W-I	S-I
B	½	W-I	S-I
A	½	W-I	S-I
G	½	W-B	S-I
-	0	Tie	S-I
[	0	Open	S-I
A	½	Pre	S-I
G	½	W-I	S-I
]	0	close	S-I
B	4	W-I	S-B

Table 3. Sentence boundary learning – training file

For the Sentence Generation module, we used short stories, poems and Tamil lyrics across various themes such as love, appreciation of nature, patriotism, etc. From this, all the special characters were removed and the list of Unigram and Bigram Words were collected along with their frequencies.

Based on the limited experiments performed on the trained CRF model, we observe that the feature set presented for Syllable identification seem to perform reasonably and identifies the syllables with 70% accuracy for manually tagged melodies. However, we could not objectively evaluate the Word and Sentence Boundary identification process as the resulting boundaries can also be considered as valid boundaries. In general, the word and sentence boundaries are the choice of the lyricist and hence the results can be considered as another valid way to generate lyric. Also, we feel that the number of training samples (10 melodies) supplied for training the CRF engine is very less for it to reasonably learn the nuances that are present in real-word lyrics.

Some of the syllable patterns identified from the tune and the corresponding sentences generated are given below:

Pattern: '*KK KK KKK*
NKKM KMKK'

Output: ஒரு சிறு வயது
ஞாபகம் வந்தது

Translation: *In small age*
I recollected

As the syllable patterns get longer, we had to resort to using Edit Distance in order to find matching sentences. One such output is presented below:

Pattern: '*KMKMKM KMKM NKN*
NKMKM NMKKM NKN'

Output: தமிழில் இங்கு காணலாம்
என்று முறைப்புடன் சொல்லி

Translation: *We can see here in Tamil*
Proclaiming aloud

7 Limitations and Future Work

From the initial set of experiments, we see that it is possible to generate a syllable pattern that closely matches the input tune. Currently, we do not consider the identification of strong beats in the melody and are expecting the presence of Mei (M) to take care of stressed syllables. We also expect the same strategy to work for other South Indian languages as well. The current Lyric Generation algorithm is simplistic, in that it can generate short meaningful phrases, but generating longer phrases require adding constraints (such as closest matching patterns) that defeats the purpose of matching with the tune. Also, the current method generates phrases that are independent of the previous phrases. This leads to lyrics that are meaningful in parts, but meaningless on the whole.

Future work can involve introducing "*semantic similarity*" across phrases in a lyric, thereby generating lyrics that provide a coherent meaning. Also, experiments can be conducted with different domain corpus to generate lyrics for a given situation (such as Love, Death, Travel, etc.) Other sentence generation strategies, such as an *Evolutionary Algorithm* (as suggested in (Manurung, 2004)) can also be attempted. Once a coherent meaningful lyric is generated, further improvements can be towards incorporating poetic aspects in the lyric.

References

Demeter. 2001. *How to write Lyrics* http://everything2.com/index.pl?node=How to write lyrics.

Guido Gonzato. 2003. *The ABCPlus Project* http://abcplus.sourceforge.net.

Hanna M. Wallach. 2004. *Conditional Random Fields: An Introduction*. Technical Report MS-CIS-04-21. Department of Computer and Information Science, University of Pennsylvania.

Hisar Maruli Manurung. 2004. *An evolutionary approach to poetry generation*. Ph.D. Thesis, University of Edinburg.

Hugo R. Goncalo Oliveira, F. Amilcar Cardoso, and F. Camara Perreira. 2007. *Tra-La Lyrics: An approach to generate text based on rhythm*. Proceedings of the Fourth International Joint Workshop on Computational Creativity, IJWCC'07, London:47-54.

Hugo R. Goncalo Oliveira, F. Amilcar Cardoso, and F. Camara Perreira. 2007. *Exploring difference strategies for the automatic generation of song lyrics with Tra-La Lyrics*. Proceedings of the Portuguese Conference on Artificial Intelligence (EPIA 2007), Guimarães, Portugal:57-68

John Lafferty, Andrew McCallum, and Fernando Pereira. 2001. *Conditional Random Fields: Probabilistic Models for Segmenting and Labeling Sequence data*. Proceedings of the Eighteenth International Conference on Machine Learning (ICML 2001), Williams College, Willamstown, MA, USA:282-289

Taku Kudo. 2005. *CRF++: Yet Another CRF toolkit*. http://crfpp.sourceforge.net.

Thomas H. Cormen., Charles E. Leiserson., Ronald L. Rivest. 1990. *Introduction to Algorithms*. Prentice-Hall: 527-531.

Quantifying Constructional Productivity with Unseen Slot Members

Amir Zeldes
Institut für deutsche Sprache und Linguistik
Humboldt-Universität zu Berlin
Unter den Linden 6, 10099 Berlin, Germany
amir.zeldes@rz.hu-berlin.de

Abstract

This paper is concerned with the possibility of quantifying and comparing the productivity of similar yet distinct syntactic constructions, predicting the likelihood of encountering unseen lexemes in their unfilled slots. Two examples are explored: variants of comparative correlative constructions (CCs, e.g. *the faster the better*), which are potentially very productive but in practice lexically restricted; and ambiguously attached prepositional phrases with the preposition *with*, which can host both large and restricted inventories of arguments under different conditions. It will be shown that different slots in different constructions are not equally likely to be occupied productively by unseen lexemes, and suggested that in some cases this can help disambiguate the underlying syntactic and semantic structure.

1 Introduction

Some syntactic constructions[1] are more productive than others. Innovative coinages like the CC: *The bubblier the Mac-ier* (i.e. the more bubbly a program looks, the more it feels at home on a Macintosh computer) are possible, but arguably more surprising and marked than: *I have a bubblier operating system with a Mac-ier look* in their respective construction, despite the same novel lexemes. The aim of this paper is to measure differences in the productivity of slots in such partially-filled constructions and also to find out if this productivity can be used to disambiguate constructions.

As one of the defining properties of language, productivity has received much attention in debates about the nature of derivational processes, the structure of the mental lexicon and the interpretation of key terms such as compositionality, grammaticality judgments or well-formedness. However in computational linguistics it is probably fair to say that it can be regarded most of all as a problem. Familiar items present in training data can be listed in lexical resources, the probabilities of their different realizations can be estimated from corpus frequency distributions etc. Thus using lexical information (statistically extracted or handcrafted resources) is the most successful strategy in resolving syntactic ambiguities such as PP-attachment (Hindle and Rooth, 1993; Ratnaparkhi, 1998; Stetina and Nagao, 1997; Pantel and Lin, 2000; Kawahara and Kurohashi, 2005), basing decisions on previous cases with identical lexemes or additional information about those lexemes. Yet because of productivity, even very large training data will never cover examples for all inputs being analyzed.

In morphological theory (and corresponding computational linguistic practice), the situation has been somewhat different: a much larger part of the word formations encountered in data can be listed in a lexicon, with neologisms being the exception, whereas in syntax most sentences are novel, with recurring combinations being the exception.[2] The focus in morphology has therefore often been on which word formation processes are productive and to what extent, with the computational counterpart being whether or not corresponding rules should be built into a morphological analyzer. Syntacticians, conversely, may ask which apparently regular constructions are actually lexicalized or have at least partly non-compositional properties (e.g. collocations, see Choueka, 1988, Evert, 2005,

[1] I use the term 'construction' in a construction grammar sense following Goldberg (1995, 2006) to mean mentally stored hierarchically organized form-meaning pairs with empty, partially-filled or fully specified lexical material. In this sense, both comparative adjectives and the pattern *The [COMP] the [COMP]* are constructions, and the productivity of such patterns is the quantity being examined here.

[2] Compounding represents an exception to this generalization, standing, at least for some languages, between syntax and word formation and often generating an unusually large amount of items unlisted in lexica (cf. Bauer, 2001:36-7).

Proceedings of the NAACL HLT Workshop on Computational Approaches to Linguistic Creativity, pages 47–54,
Boulder, Colorado, June 2009.

2009; multiword expressions, Sag et al., 2002; lexical bundles, Salem, 1987, Altenberg and Eeg-Olofsson, 1990, Biber et al., 1999, 2004).

In morphology, the realization that productivity is a matter of degree, rather than a binary trait of word formation processes (see e.g. Bauer, 2001:125-162), has lead to the exploration of quantitative measures to assess and compare different aspects of the fertility of various patterns (esp. the work of Baayen, 2001, 2009). Yet syntactic applications of these measures have only very recently been proposed, dealing with one slot of a pattern much like the stem operated on by a morphological process (cf. Barðdal, 2006; Kiss, 2007).

In this paper I will examine the application of measures based on Baayen's work on morphology to different variants of syntactic constructions with more or less variable slots. The goal will be to show that different constructions have inherently different productivity rates, i.e. they are more or less liable to produce new members in their free slots. If this view is accepted, it may have consequences both theoretically (novelty in certain positions will be more surprising or marked) and practically, e.g. for parsing ambiguous structures with novel arguments, since one parse may imply a construction more apt to novelty than another.

The remainder of this article is structured as follows: the next section introduces concepts underlying morphological productivity and related corpus-based measures following Baayen (2009). The following two sections adapt and apply these measures to different types of CCs (such as *the faster the better*) and NP/VP-attached PPs, respectively, using the BNC[3] as a database. The final section discusses the results of these studies and their implications for the study of syntactic productivity.

2 Morphological Productivity Measures

Productivity has probably received more attention as a topic in morphology than in syntax, if for no other reason than that novel words are comparatively rare and draw attention, whereas novel phrases or sentences are ubiquitous. The exact definition of a novel word or 'neologism' is however less than straightforward. For the present purpose we may use Bauer's (2001:97-98) working definition as a starting point:

> *[Productivity] is a feature of morphological processes which allow for new coinages, [...] coining must be repetitive in the speech community [...] Various factors appear to aid productivity: type frequency of appropriate bases, phonological and semantic transparency, naturalness, etc., but these are aids to productivity, not productivity itself.*

For Bauer, productivity is defined for a morphological process, which is ideally frequently and consistently found and coins ideally transparent novel forms. The word 'coining' in this context implies that speakers use the process to construct the transparent novel forms in question, which in turn means the process has a regular output. Yet novelty, transparency and regularity are difficult to judge intuitively, and the definitions of "new" vs. "existing" words cannot be judged reliably for any one speaker, nor with any adequacy for a speaker community (cf. Bauer, 2001:34-35).

This problem has led researchers to turn to corpus data as a sort of 'objective' model of language experience, in which the output of a process can be searched for, categorized and tagged for evaluation. Baayen (e.g. 2001, 2009) proposes three corpus-based measures for the productivity of word formation processes. The first measure, which he terms *extent of use*, is written V(C,N) and is simply the proportion of types produced by a process C in a corpus of size N, e.g. the count of different nouns in *-ness* out of all the types in N. According to this measure, *-ness* would have a much higher *realized productivity* than the *-th* in *warmth* since it is found in many more words. However, this measure indiscriminately deals with all existing material – all words that have already been generated – and hence it cannot assess how likely it is that novel words will be created using a certain process.

Baayen's other two measures address different aspects of this problem and rely on the use of *hapax legomena*, words appearing only once in a corpus. The intuitive idea behind looking at such words is that productively created items are one-off unique occurrences, and therefore they must form a subset of the hapax legomena in a corpus. Baayen uses V(1,C,N), the number of types from category C occurring once in a corpus of N words and V(1,N), the number of all types occurring once in a corpus of N words. The second measure, termed *hapax-conditioned degree of productivity* is said to measure *expanding productivity*, the rate at

[3] The British National Corpus (http://www.natcorp.ox.ac.uk/), with over 100 million tokens of British English.

which a process is currently creating neologisms. It is computed as V(1,C,N)/V(1,N), the proportion of hapax legomena from the examined category C within the hapax legomena from all categories in the corpus. Intuitively, if the amount of hapax legomena could be replaced by 'true' neologisms only, this would be the relative contribution of a process to productivity in the corpus, which could then be compared between different processes[4].

The third measure, *category-conditioned degree of productivity* measures the *potential productivity* of a process, meaning how likely it is to produce new members, or how saturated a process is. This measure is the proportion of hapax legomena from category C divided by N(C), the total token count from this category: V(1,C,N)/N(C). It intuitively represents the probability of the next item from category C, found in further corpus data of the same type, to be a hapax legomenon.

Baayen's measures (hence p1, p2 and p3 respectively) are appealing since they are rigorously defined, easily extractable from a corpus (provided the process can be identified reliably in the data) and offer an essential reduction of the corpus wide behavior of a process to a number between 1 and 0, that is, an item producing no hapax legomena would score 0 on p2 and p3, and an item with 100% hapax legomena would score 1 on p3, even if it is overall rather insignificant for productivity in the corpus as a whole (as reflected in a low score for p2). The measure p3 is the most important one in the present context, since it allows us to reason conversely that, given that an item is novel and could belong to one of two processes, it is more likely to have come from whichever process is more productive, i.e. has a higher p3 score.

Indeed the assumptions made in these measures do not necessarily fit syntactic productivity at a first glance: that the process in question has a clearly defined form (e.g. a suffix such as *-ness*) that it accommodates one variable slot (the stem, e.g. *good-* in *goodness*), and that each different stem forms a distinct type. Applying these measures to syntactic constructions requires conceptual and mathematical adaptation, which will be discussed in the next section using the example of comparative correlative constructions.

3 Measuring Productivity in CCs

Comparative correlatives are a complex yet typologically well attested form of codependent clauses expressing a corresponding monotonous positive or negative change in degree between two properties (see den Dikken, 2005 for a cross-linguistic overview). For example, in *the faster we go, the sooner we'll get there*, speed is monotonously correlated with time of arrival. A main reason for syntactic interest in this type of sentence is a proposed 'mismatch' (see McCawley, 1988, Culicover and Jackendoff, 1999) between its syntax, which appears to include two identically constructed paratactic clauses, and its semantics, which imply possible hypotaxis of the first clause as a sort of 'conditional' (*if and in so much as we go fast...*).

Two other noteworthy features of this construction in use (the following examples are from the BNC) are the frequent lack of a verb (*the larger the leaf the better quality the tea*) and even of a subject noun (*the sooner the better*) [5] and a tendency for the (at least partial) lexicalization of certain items. The verbless variant often houses these, e.g. *the more the merrier*, but also with verbs, e.g. *the bigger they come the harder they fall.* A context-free grammar might describe a simplified variant of such clauses in the following terms:

S_{cc} > *the* COMP (NP (VP))
S > S_{cc} S_{cc}

where S_{cc} is one of the comparative correlative clauses, COMP represents either English comparative allomorph (in *-er* like *bigger* or analytic with *more* or *less* in *more/less important*), and NP and VP are optional subjects and corresponding predicates for each clause.[6]

However like many CFG rules, these rules may be too general, since it is clearly the case that not

[4] This statement must be restricted somewhat: in items showing multiple processes, e.g. *bullishness*, the processes associated with the suffixes *-ish* and *-ness* are not statistically independent, creating a difficulty in using such cases for the comparison of these two processes (see Baayen, 2009). In syntax the extent of this problem is unclear, since even occurrences of NPs and VPs are not independent of each other.

[5] The latter form has been analyzed as a case of ellipsis of the copula *be* (Culicover and Jackendoff, 1999:554; similarly for German: Zifonun et al., 1997:2338). It is my position that this is not the case, as the bare construction has distinct semantic properties as well as different productive behavior, see below.

[6] These rules should be understood as agnostic with respect to the parataxis/hypotaxis question mentioned above. The parentheses mean NP may appear without VP but not vice versa.

all comparatives, nouns and verbs fit in this construction, if only because of semantic limitations, i.e. they must be plausibly capable of forming a pair of monotonously correlated properties. Corpus data shows that comparatives in CC clauses select quite different lexemes than comparatives at large, that the first and second slots (hence cc1 and cc2) have different preferences, and that the presence or absence of a VP and possibly a subject NP also interact with these choices. Table 1 shows comparatives in the BNC sorted by frequency in general, along with their frequencies in cc1 and cc2. Some frequent comparatives do not or hardly appear in CCs given their frequency[7] while others prefer a certain slot exclusively (e.g. *more likely* in cc2) or substantially (e.g. *higher* in cc1). Columns Ø1 and Ø2 show bare comparatives (no subject or verb) in cc1 or 2 and the next two columns show subsets of bare cc1 or 2 given that the other clause is also bare. The last columns show CCs with only NPs and no verb, either in one clause or both. In bare CCs we find that *better* selects cc2 exclusively, in fact making up some 88% of cc2s in this construction (*the* COMP *the better*) in the BNC.

word	comp	cc1	cc2	Ø1	Ø2	Ø1 (Ø2)	(Ø1) Ø2	n1	n2	n1 (n2)	(n1) n2
further	21371										
better	20727	15	143		89		51	9	22	5	15
higher	15434	97	39	4	2	3		84	23	44	21
greater	13883	82	171	1	1			75	92	35	80
lower	10983	20	27		2			18	12	7	12
older	8714	24	1	1		1		3		1	
…											
longer	3820	45	15	3	1	3		11	3	9	3
bigger	3469	43	13	4	1	3		30	8	15	8
more likely	3449		28						2		1
…											
more wholistic	1										
zanier	1	1						1			

Table 1. Comparative frequencies independently and in cc1/cc2, with or without nominal subjects/verbs in one or both clauses.

[7] Occurrences of items which cannot serve attributively, such as *more* with no adjective and *sooner*, have been excluded, since they are not comparable to the other items. Most occurrences of the most frequent item, *further*, should arguably be excluded too, since it is mostly used as a lexicalized adverb and not a canonical comparative. However comparative usage is also well-attested, e.g.: *he was going much further than that.*

A look at the list of lexemes typical to cc1 vs. cc2 shows that cc1 tends to express a dependent variable with spatiotemporal semantics (*higher, older, longer*), whereas cc2 typically shows an independent evaluative (*better, more likely*), though many common lexemes appear in both.[8]

Although the results imply varying degrees of preference and lexicalization in different constructions, they do not yet tell us whether or not, or better how likely, we can expect to see new lexemes in each slot. This can be assessed using Baayen's measures, by treating each construction as a morphological process and the comparative slot as the lexical base forming the type (see Kiss, 2007 for a similar procedure).[9] The results in Table 2 show that all constructions are productive to some extent, though clearly some yield fewer new types.

	toks	types	hpx	p1	p2	p3
comp	266703	5988	2616	0.00772	0.00651	0.0098
cc1	802	208	140	0.00026	0.00034	0.1745
cc2	802	181	126	0.00023	0.00031	0.1571
bare1	58	45	37	5.80E-05	9.22E-05	0.6379
bare2	58	7	5	9.03E-06	1.24E-05	0.0862

Table 2. Productivity scores for comparatives, cc-clauses in general and specifically for bare CCs

p1 and p2 show that CCs are responsible for very little of the productive potential of comparatives in the corpus. This is not only a function of the relative rarity of CCs: if we look at their rate of vocabulary growth (Figure 1), general comparatives gather new types more rapidly than CCs even for the same sample size[10]. Using a Finite Zipf Mandelbrot Model (FZM, Evert, 2004), we can extrapolate from the observed data to predict the gap will grow with sample size.

[8] I thank Livio Gaeta and an anonymous reviewer for commenting on this point.

[9] In fact, one could also address the productivity of the construction as a whole by regarding each argument tuple as a type, e.g. <*more ergonomic*, *better*> could be a hapax legomenon despite *better* appearing quite often. Since each slot multiplies the chances a construction has to be unique, the nth root of the value of the measure would have to be taken in order to maintain comparability, thus the square root of p_k for 2 slots, the cube root for 3 slots and so on. Another option, if one is interested in the chance that any particular slot will be unique, is to take the average of p_k for all slots. However for the present purpose the individual score of each slot is more relevant.

[10] The comparative curve is taken from 2000 occurrences evenly distributed across the sections of the BNC, to correspond topically to the CCs, which cover the whole corpus.

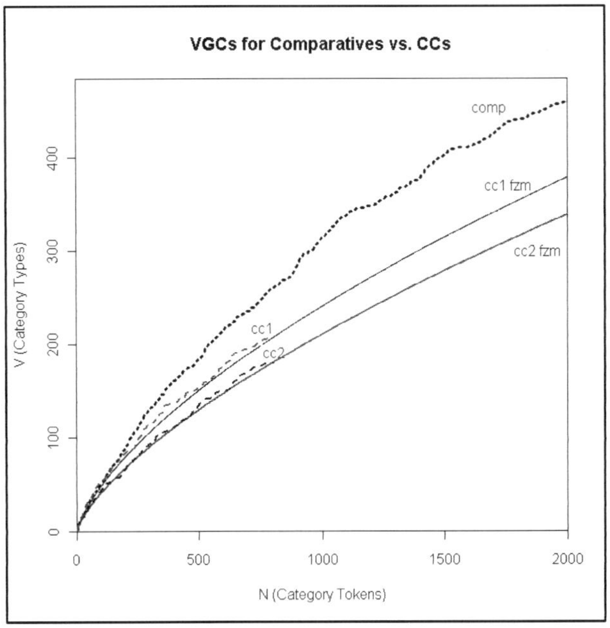

Figure 1. Vocabulary growth curves and FZM extrapolations for comparatives in cc1, cc2 and at large in the BNC.

However, p3 shows the surprising result that CCs have more potential productivity than comparatives in general, with the bare cc1 slot leading, both general CC slots somewhat behind, and the bare cc2 last. This means our data does not begin to approach covering this category – the next CC is much likelier to be novel, given the data we've seen so far.

With this established, the question arises whether a CFG rule like the one above should take account of the likelihood of each slot to contain novel vs. familiar members. For instance, if a PCFG parser correctly identifies a novel comparative and the input matches the rule, should it be more skeptical of an unseen bare cc1 than an unseen bare cc2 (keeping in mind that the latter have so far been *better* in 88% of cases)? To illustrate this, we may consider the output of a PCFG parser (in this case the Stanford Parser, Klein and Manning, 2003) for an ambiguous example.

Since CCs are rather rare, PCFGs will tend to prefer most other parses of a sentence, if these are available. Where no other reading is available we may get the expected two clause structure, as in the example in Figure 2.[11]

[11] The X nodes conform to the Penn Treebank II Bracketing Guidelines for CCs (Bies et al., 1995:178).

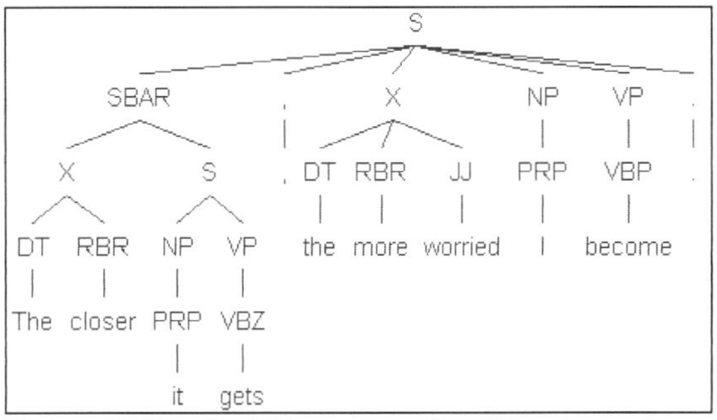

Figure 2. Stanford Parser tree for: *The closer it gets, the more worried I become.*

The Stanford Parser fares quite well in cases like these, since the pronoun (*it*, *I*) can hardly be modified by the comparative (*[$_{NP}$ *the closer it*] or *[$_{NP}$ *the more worried I*]), and similarly for NPs with articles (*[$_{NP}$ *the closer the time*]). Yet article-less NPs and bare CCs cause problems, as in the tree in Figure 3.

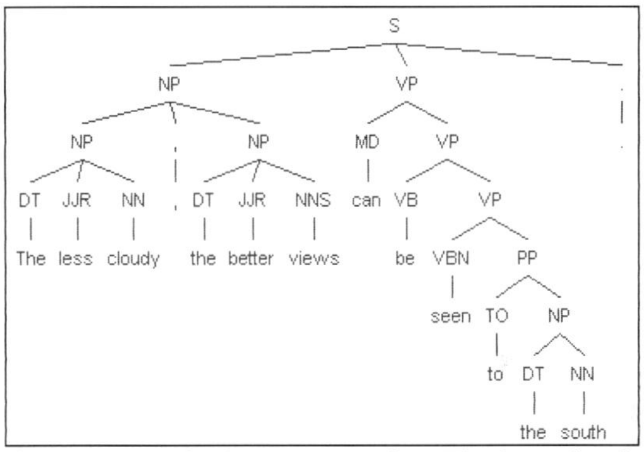

Figure 3. Stanford Parser tree for: *The less cloudy, the better views can be seen to the south.*

Here *The less cloudy* and *the better views* form one NP, separate from the VP complex. Such a reading is not entirely impossible: the sentence could mean 'less cloudy, better views' appositively. However despite the overall greater frequency of appositions and the fact that *less cloudy* has probably not been observed in cc1 in training data, the pattern of a novel form for cc1 and *better* in cc2 is actually consistent with a novel CC. With these ideas in mind, the next section examines the potential of productivity to disambiguate a much more prevalent phenomenon, namely PP attachment.

4 PP Attachment and Productivity

The problem of attaching prepositional phrases as sister nodes of VP or as adjuncts to its object nouns is a classic case of syntactic ambiguity that causes trouble for parsers (see Hindle and Rooth, 1993; Manning and Schütze, 1999:278-287; Atterer and Schütze, 2007), e.g. the difference between *I ate a fish with a fork* and *I ate a fish with bones*[12], i.e. denoting the instrument or an attribute of the fish. There are also two further common readings of the preposition *with* in this context, namely attached either high or low in the VP in a comitative sense: *I ate a fish with Mary* and *I ate a fish with potatoes* respectively, though most approaches do not distinguish these, rather aiming at getting the attachment site right.

Already in early work on PP attachment (Hindle and Rooth, 1993) it was realized that the lexical identity of the verb, its object, the preposition and in later approaches also the prepositional object noun (Ratnaparkhi et al., 1994) are useful for predicting the attachment site, casting the task as a classification of tuples <*v*, *n1*, *p*, *n2*> into the classes V (VP attachment) and N (NP attachment). Classifiers are commonly either supervised, with disambiguated training data, or more recently unsupervised (Ratnaparkhi, 1998) using data from unambiguous cases where no *n1* or *v* appears. Other approaches supplement this information with hand-built or automatically acquired lexical resources and collocation databases to determine the relationship between the lexemes, or, for lexemes unattested in the tuples, for semantically similar ones (Stetina and Nagao, 1997; Pantel and Lin, 2000).

Although the state of the art in lexically based systems actually approaches human performance, they lose their power when confronted with unfamiliar items. For example, what is the likeliest attachment for the following BNC example: *I can always eat dim-sum with my dybbuk*? It is safe to assume that the (originally Hebrew) loan-word *dybbuk* '(demonic) possession' does not appear in most training datasets, though *dim-sum* is attested more than once as an object of *eat* in the BNC. Crucially, the triple (*eat*, *dim-sum*, *with*) alone cannot reliably resolve the attachment site (consider *soy-sauce* vs. *chopsticks* as n2). It is thus worth examining how likely a novel item is in the relevant slot of each reading's construction. The rest of this section therefore examines productivity scores for the slots in *eat NP with NP* and their correlation with different readings as an example.

Since these cases cannot be identified automatically in an unparsed text with any reliability, and since there is not enough hand-parsed data containing these constructions, a conservative proximity assumption was made (cf. Ratnaparkhi, 1998) and all occurrences of *eat* and related forms within ten words of *with* and with no intervening punctuation in the BNC were evaluated and tagged manually for this study. This also allowed for head-noun and anaphor resolution to identify the referent of a slot in the case of pronominal realization; thus all slot types in the data including pronouns are evaluated in terms of a single head noun.

Results show that out of 131 hits, the largest group of PPs (59 tokens) were object noun modifiers, almost all comitatives[13], justifying the prevalent heuristic to prefer low attachment. However verbal instrumentals and high comitatives (25 and 23 respectively) come at a very close second. The remaining 24 cases were adverbial modifications (e.g. *with enthusiasm*). Looking at hapax legomena in the respective slots we can calculate the measures in Table 3.

	n1 slot		n2 slot		total
	hapax	p3	hapax	p3	tokens
n	39	0.661	45	0.7627	59
v adv	15	0.625	21	0.875	24
v com	8	0.3478	20	0.8696	23
v inst	15	0.6	4	0.16	25

Table 3. p3 for the first and second head noun in nominal and three types of verbal PP attachment for *eat* n *with* n in the BNC.

The scores show that the verbal instrumental reading is the least likely to exhibit a novel head at the n2 slot, which is semantically plausible – the repertoire of eating instruments is rather conventionalized and slow to expand. The comitative reading is very likely to innovate in n2, but much less so in n1, fitting e.g. the "dim-sum with dybbuk"-scenario. This fits the fact that one may eat together with many distinct persons etc., but when

[12] Though in some cases the distinction is not so tenable, e.g. *we have not signed a settlement agreement with them* (Manning and Schütze, 1999:286), where *with them* can arguably be attached low or high. Incidentally, the 'fish' examples are actually attested in the BNC in a linguistic context.

[13] Only 4 hits were truely non-comitative noun modifiers, e.g. <*eat*, *anything*, *with*, *preservatives*>, where a comitative reading is clearly not intended. Since the group was so small, all noun modifiers have been treated here together.

these are specified, the exact nature of the meal or food is often left unspecified[14]. The adverbial reading is likely to innovate in both slots, since many ways or circumstances of eating can be specified and these hardly restrict the choice of object for *eat*. Interestingly, the choice of object maintains a very stable productivity in all but the high comitative construction. n2 innovation in nominal modifiers is actually lower than for adverbials and comitatives, meaning low attachment may not be the preferred choice for unknown nouns.

While these results imply what some reasonable expectations may be to find a novel member of each slot in each reading, they do not take the identity of the lexemes into account. In order to combine the general information about the slot with knowledge of a known slot member, we may simultaneously attempt to score the productivity of the construction's components, namely the noun or verb in question, for PP modifiers. This raises the problem of what exactly should be counted. One may argue that high-attached comitatives and adverbials should be counted separately, since they are almost always optional regardless of the verb (one can equally well eat or do anything else with someone in some way), unlike instrumentals which may be more closely linked to the verb. On the other hand, the exact constructional sense of such PPs is colored by the verb, e.g. eating a meal with someone has a rather particular meaning (as opposed to coincidentally performing the act of eating alongside another eater). If the decision is only between high and low attachment, then grouping all variants together may be sensible in any case.

Depending on the argument and verb, it is possible to make fine distinctions, provided enough cases are found. For *dim-sum*, for example, no cases of NP modifying *with* (novel or otherwise) are found, making the (correct) high comitative reading likely. By contrast, for the head noun *fish*, which is a common object of *eat*, 37 hits with *with*-PPs are found in the BNC, forming 32 prepositional object noun types of which 28 are hapax legomena in this slot. All high readings of *with*-PPs with *eat* (including intransitive *eat*) form 92 tokens, 68 noun types and 44 hapax legomena. Thus *fish + PP* scores p3=0.756 while *eat + PP* scores 0.478, corresponding to less productivity. This means novel prepositional objects are substantially less probable for the high attachment given that the direct object is *fish*.

5 Conclusion

The above results show that similar yet distinct constructions, which vary slightly in either constituent structure (high vs. low attachment), semantics (comitative or instrumental PPs), number of arguments (more and less bare CCs) or position (cc1 vs. cc2), show very different lexical behavior, exhibiting more or less variety in different slots and differing proportions of hapax legomena. The inference which should become apparent from the sharp contrasts in slot scores (especially in p3) given the size of the data, is that these differences are not coincidental but are indicative of inherently different productivity rates for each slot in each construction. These properties need not be attributed to system internal, linguistic reasons alone, but may also very well reflect world knowledge and pragmatic considerations.[15] However, from a construction grammar point of view, the entrenchment of these constructions in speakers and therefore in data is inextricably connected with interaction in the world, thus making syntactic productivity a plausible and relevant quantity both theoretically and potentially for NLP practice.

It remains to be seen whether or not productivity scores can help automatically disambiguate structures with unseen arguments (e.g. PP attachment with unencountered n2), or even distinguish semantic classes such as comitatives, instrumentals etc. for novel nouns, for which a classification into helpful semantic categories (animate, human and so forth) is not available. A large-scale evaluation of this question will depend on how easily and reliably productivity scores can be extracted automatically from data for the relevant constructions.

References

Bengt Altenberg and Mats Eeg-Olofsson. 1990. Phraseology in Spoken English. In: Jan Aarts and Willem Meijs, editors, *Theory and Practice in Corpus Linguistics*. Rodopi, Amsterdam: 1-26.

[14] In fact the non-food specific nouns *breakfast*, *lunch*, *dinner*, *dish* and *meal* cover 16 of the high comitative n1 tokens, almost 70%.

[15] In this context it is worth mentioning that similar ongoing examinations of German CCs reveal different lexical preferences, implying that some of this behavior is language dependent and to some extent language internally lexicalized.

Michaela Atterer and Hinrich Schütze. 2007. Prepositional Phrase Attachment without Oracles. *Computational Linguistics*, 33(4): 469-476.

R. Harald Baayen. 2001. *Word Frequency Distributions*. (Text, Speech and Language Technologies 18.) Kluwer Academic Publishers, Dordrecht / Boston / London.

R. Harald Baayen. 2009. Corpus Linguistics in Morphology: Morphological Productivity. In: Anke Lüdeling and Merja Kytö, editors, *Corpus Linguistics. An International Handbook, vol. 2*. Mouton de Gruyter, Berlin: 899-919.

Jóhanna Barðdal. 2006. Predicting the Productivity of Argument Structure Constructions. In: *The 32nd Annual Meeting of the Berkeley Linguistics Society*. Berkeley Linguistics Society, Berkeley. Available at: http://ling.uib.no/barddal/BLS-32.barddal.pdf.

Laurie Bauer. 2001. *Morphological Productivity*. (Cambridge Studies in Linguistics 95.) Cambridge University Press, Cambridge, UK.

Ann Bies, Mark Ferguson, Karen Katz and Robert MacIntyre. 1995. *Bracketing Guidelines for Treebank II Style Penn Treebank Project*. Technical report, University of Pennsylvania.

Douglas Biber, Susan Conrad and Viviana Cortes. 2004. If you look at...: Lexical Bundles in University Teaching and Textbooks. *Applied Linguistics*, 25(3): 371-405.

Douglas Biber, Stig Johansson, Geoffrey Leech, Susan Conrad and Edward Finegan. 1999. *The Longman Grammar of Spoken and Written English*. Longman, London.

Yaacov Choueka. 1988. Looking for Needles in a Haystack. In: *Proceedings of RIAO '88*. Cambridge, MA, 609-623.

Peter W. Culicover and Ray Jackendoff. 1999. The View from the Periphery: The English Comparative Correlative. *Linguistic Inquiry* 30(4): 543-571.

Marcel den Dikken. 2005. Comparative Correlatives Comparatively. *Linguistic Inquiry*, 36(4): 497-532.

Stefan Evert. 2004. A simple LNRE model for random character sequences. In: *Proceedings of JADT 2004*: 411-422.

Stefan Evert. 2005. *The Statistics of Word Cooccurrences: Word Pairs and Collocations*. PhD dissertation, University of Stuttgart.

Stefan Evert. 2009. Corpora and Collocations. In: Anke Lüdeling and Merja Kytö, editors, *Corpus Linguistics. An International Handbook, vol. 2*. Mouton de Gruyter, Berlin: 1212-1248.

Adele E. Goldberg. 1995. *Constructions: A Construction Grammar Approach to Argument Structure*. University of Chicago Press, Chicago and London.

Adele E. Goldberg. 2006. *Constructions at Work: The Nature of Generalization in Language*. Oxford University Press, Oxford, UK.

Donald Hindle and Mats Rooth. 1993. Structural Ambiguity and Lexical Relations. *Computational Linguistics*, 19(1): 103-130.

Daisuke Kawahara and Sadao Kurohashi. 2005. PP-Attachment Disambiguation Boosted by a Gigantic Volume of Unambiguous Examples. In: *Proceedings of the 2nd International Joint Conference on Natural Language Processing (IJCNLP-05)*: 188-198.

Tibor Kiss. 2007. Produktivität und Idiomatizität von Präposition-Substantiv-Sequenzen. *Zeitschrift für Sprachwissenschaft*, 26(2): 317-345.

Dan Klein and Christopher D. Manning. 2003. Accurate Unlexicalized Parsing. In: *Proceedings of the 41st Meeting of the Association for Computational Linguistics*: 423-430.

Christopher D. Manning and Hinrich Schütze. 1999. *Foundations of Statistical Natural Language Processing*. MIT Press, Cambridge, MA.

James D. McCawley. 1988. The Comparative Conditional in English, German and Chinese. In: *Proceedings of the Fourteenth Annual Meeting of the Merkeley Linguistics Society*. Berkeley Linguistics Society, Berkeley: 176-187.

Patrick Pantel and Dekang Lin. 2000. An Unsupervised Approach to Prepositional Phrase Attachment using Contextually Similar Words. In: *Proceedings of the 38th Annual Meeting of the Association for Computational Linguistics*: 101-108.

Adwait Ratnaparkhi. 1998. Statistical Models for Unsupervised Prepositional Phrase Attachment. In: *Proceedings of COLING-ACL98, Montreal Canada*: 1079-1085

Adwait Ratnaparkhi, Jeff Reynar and Salim Roukos. 1994. A Maximum Entropy Model for Prepositional Phrase Attachment. In: *Proceedings of the ARPA Human Language Technology Workshop*. Plainsboro, NJ: 250-255.

Ivan Sag, Timothy Baldwin, Francis Bond, Ann Copestake and Dan Flickinger. 2002. Multiword Expressions: A Pain in the Neck for NLP. In: *Proceedings of the Third International Conference on Intelligent Text Processing and Computational Linguistics (CICLING 2002)*. Mexico City, Mexico: 1-15.

André Salem. 1987. *Pratique des segments répétés*. Institut National de la Langue Française, Paris.

Jiri Stetina and Makoto Nagao. 1997. Corpus Based PP Attachment Ambiguity Resolution with a Semantic Dictionary. In: Jou Zhao and Kenneth Church, editors, *Proceedings of the Fifth Workshop on Very Large Corpora*. Beijing and Hong Kong: 66-80.

Gisela Zifonun, Ludger Hoffmann and Bruno Strecker, editors. 1997. *Grammatik der deutschen Sprache, Bd. 3*. (Schriften des Instituts für deutsche Sprache 7.) De Gruyter, Berlin / New York.

Curveship: An Interactive Fiction System for Interactive Narrating

Nick Montfort
Program in Writing and Humanistic Studies
Massachusetts Institute of Technology
Cambridge, MA 02139, USA
nickm@nickm.com

Abstract

Interactive fiction (often called "IF") is a venerable thread of creative computing that includes *Adventure, Zork,* and the computer game *The Hitchhiker's Guide to the Galaxy* as well as innovative recent work. These programs are usually known as "games," appropriately, but they can also be rich forms of text-based computer simulation, dialog systems, and examples of computational literary art. Theorists of narrative have long distinguished between the level of underlying content or story (which can usefully be seen as corresponding to the simulated world in interactive fiction) and that of expression or discourse (corresponding to the textual exchange between computer and user). While IF development systems have offered a great deal of power and flexibility to author/programmers by providing a computational model of the fictional world, previous systems have not systematically distinguished between the telling and what is told. Developers were not able to control the content and expression levels independently so that they could, for instance, have a program relate events out of chronological order or have it relate events from the perspective of different characters. Curveship is an interactive fiction system which draws on narrative theory and computational linguistics to allow the transformation of the narrating in these ways. This talk will briefly describe interactive fiction, narrative variation, and how Curveship provides new capabilities for interactive fiction authors.

1 Curveship and Its Contexts

This paper addresses those interested in aesthetic and computational, work with language, whether or not they are familiar with interactive fiction or narrative theory. I describe the twofold motivation behind Curveship, explaining why I find interactive fiction compelling and why I find narrative variation a worthwhile capability for a literary computer system. I then sketch the way that Curveship works, pointing to aspects of the system that will, I hope, interest interactive fiction authors and also have relevance beyond interactive fiction.

Several histories of interactive fiction are available, including book-length (Montfort 2003) and briefer ones (Nelson 2001, Montfort 2007a). This paper focuses on how interactive fiction works, and on explaining its conventions, rather than on detailing the history of the first interactive fiction, *Adventure* (written in 1976 by Will Crowther and Don Woods), the "mainframe" games that followed, interactive fiction in the commercial marketplace (including the many notable contributions of Infocom), and the surge in development by individual, non-commercial interactive fiction authors. This paper also doesn't provide any information about how to download or run interactive fiction, and very little about how to play it, although several FAQs and other resources are available online with that information (IFWiki 2009, Aiken 2008, Cadre n.d.).

After offering some of the motivation for this work, this paper provides a high-level introduction to Curveship and its capabilities. The details on narrative variation and on how it has been implemented computationally are available in the

Proceedings of the NAACL HLT Workshop on Computational Approaches to Linguistic Creativity, pages 55–62,
Boulder, Colorado, June 2009.

author's dissertation (Montfort 2007b). While the interface to the system has been streamlined and other changes are being made to facilitate the use of Curveship by interactive fiction authors, the approach to narrative variation that is described there remains current.

2 The Interactive Fiction Tradition

Since the release of the first work of interactive fiction in 1976, those working in the form have developed conventions and traditions and have undertaken many different sorts of exploration and innovation.

A snippet of a transcript from this author's *Book and Volume* (2005) gives a basic idea of what interaction is like:

> **Your Apartment Building's Lobby**
> Clean, if not homey. The doorman waits in a Plexiglas cube that looks curiously bulletproof.
>
> >leave
> Onward, into the intentional city. nWare crafted it well -- built from the ground up with security and scalability in mind, it's fully pedestrianized but hums, almost full-size, like a city center.
>
> The night sky is completely cloudless. The dry warmth of the air hints at the desert that surrounds nTopia.
>
> **Abalone & Fifth**
> Your apartment building is on the southwest corner. Opposite it is a windowless, blocky building. On the southeast corner Pharmicopia sprawls. Otto's Automat is to the northwest.
>
> A window pops up in the lower right corner of your nLap. In it, the uncanny red stapler wiggles its hinged head to the accompaniment of a cheery robot voice:
>
> *I see you're outside! Hey, the nice thing about this city is that it uses the grid system, so you can just go NORTH, EAST, SOUTH, or WEST, and you'll pretty much always end up somewhere else!*
>
> The window winks away.
>
> >go to the automat
>
> **Otto's Automat**
> Someone, perhaps nWare's monarchically wealthy founder, shellf, really got into *Dark City*. There couldn't be any other excuse for this combination vending machine and cafeteria, even though it may strain to look modern and appetizing. Pixelated smiley faces in an urgent red decorate everything, even the edges of the food-dispensing wall.
>
> The opportunity to avoid social contact during food selection is appealing.
>
> >buy some food
> Food does seem like a good idea. You select something palatable from the food-dispensing wall and begin to consume it, face flickering with mammalian happiness.
>
> A guy you met during new employee reorientation -- Knut, you think his name is -- furtively joins you as you're dining. He looks even more feverish and high-strung than he did a few days ago.
>
> "Hi. Hi again. Gotta tell. Tell you something."

Here, the player character — the one controlled by the player via textual commands — begins in the lobby of his apartment building. The player then types a command for that character to "leave," which he does, ending up outside at an intersection. Because the player character happens to be carrying his laptop computer, which is turned on, an annoying animated agent appears and dispenses some advice. The next command, "go to the automat," directs the character to enter a different building. ("Go northwest," "walk northwest," "northwest," or simply "nw" would have all done the same thing.) Finally, the character is commanded to "buy some food," which the character does — something that is only possible because the character has his electronic cash device, isn't sated, and is in place where food is sold. Although these are not dramatically interesting actions, they, in this game and in others, can be part of figuring out the nature of an unusual world.

Of course, not every input works as smoothly as these did in this context. Actions often work if they are warranted by the situation in some way; so "buy some food" is appropriate in an automat while "donate my organs to science" isn't. A character can be commanded to walk in a particular direction, or to enter a building that is nearby, but not, usually, to "go to Tangiers." And there is usually no need for fine-grained positioning or describing the manner in which an action is done, so instead of issuing the command "hop spryly over to the coffee table" to prepare for setting down one's mug, it's fine to just go directly to typing "put my mug on the coffee table."

Moving a character around using compass directions is a very notable convention originating with *Adventure,* although there were other ways to get around in that game. However it's done, traversing a virtual space is very important to interactive fiction.

There are four important characteristics of interactive fiction that make it interesting from a research standpoint as well as from the standpoint of poetics. A work of interactive fiction is:

- A limited domain that serves as a simulated "microworld." It has a complete model of the things that can be manipulated in the simulation and can be usefully talked about.

- A dialog system. Natural language is provided as output, and the system accepts commands that, although simple and short, are instances of English text.

- A computer game, providing enjoyment and fun. Although not the preeminent form of computer entertainment today, as it was around 1980, interactive fiction is something that many people find enjoyable and interact with for its own sake.

- A form of aesthetic expression and literary art. As with any form or medium, only a few use a significant amount of this potential. But the computational, literary nature of interactive fiction gives it the capability to do aesthetic work that could not otherwise be done.

Since many people don't realize that interactive fiction extends beyond the cave setting and fantasy genre, it's worth mentioning a few examples of work from the last few years, work that gives an idea of the range of interactive fiction today — all of which is available for free download and easily found online:

Anchorhead, by Michael Gentry, 1998: An expansive interactive fiction with deep secrets and action that runs over several days, inspired in tone and style by H. P. Lovecraft.

Bad Machine, by Dan Shovitz, 1998: Manifesting itself as confusing a mix of status reports, error messages, this interactive fiction takes place in a strange robot-run factory.

Narcolepsy, by Adam Cadre, 2003: A seemingly contemporary, ordinary interactive fiction that branches hilariously into strange genre scenarios.

Slouching toward Bedlam, by Star C. Foster and Daniel Ravipinto, 2003: A steampunk science fiction piece set in an asylum and involving technological and kabbalistic themes.

Savoir-Faire, by Emily Short, 2002: The return to a childhood home provides opportunities to remember the past and requires that the player figure out an intricate system of sympathetic magic.

Spider and Web, by Andrew Plotkin, 1998: A science-fiction spy thriller that has the player reenact past events to the satisfaction of an interrogator.

Interactive fiction as it exists now is a type of virtual reality, a simulation of not only a space and the characters and things in that space but also of physical and metaphysical laws that obtain in a world. Furthermore, it's a virtual reality that works well, one in which conventions have evolved about the level of abstraction and the types of commands that will work. An effective way of interacting has been negotiated.

Although more could be done to better simulate a world and to better understand language in interactive fiction, the Curveship project has a different goal. Curveship is being developed to add to interactive fiction's well-established capability for simulation a new capability for narration, one that will allow the telling to be parametrically varied.

3 Narrative Variation

For more than three decades, interactive fiction programs have simulated fictional worlds. By allowing control over settings, characters, and the incidents that happen, they have provided very useful facilities. However, literary works are not powerful and compelling merely because of what happens in them. They also rely on these events being told in an interesting way, on the different types of narrating that can be done. The interactive fiction system I am describing, Curveship, uses natural language generation to allow the narrating to be varied parametrically. To understand why this is a significant capability, it is worth turning to non-digital novels, stories, and narrative poems to see how they accomplish their effects.

We may consider different novels, stories, and poems to be "great" — powerful, affecting, transforming, deeply pleasing to read — but whichever ones we prefer, it is unlikely that we appreciate them simply because of what happens in them. The way these events are narrated is also important. A paraphrase or summary is generally not considered to be as interesting as is a great work of literature, even an ancient one. A timeline of events would hardly compare to *The Odyssey*, in which Odysseus tells some of the events himself, in which he weeps as he hears a bard, who does not know Odysseus's identity, relating the events of the Trojan War and his own exploits to him. This is not to say that there can be no interesting retellings of *The Odyssey,* only that any telling will be interesting or not based on how the narrating is done.

The study of narrating, of how the same underlying events can be told in different ways, has been undertaken systematically in the field of narrative theory or *narratology*, in which the distinction between story/content and discourse, between that

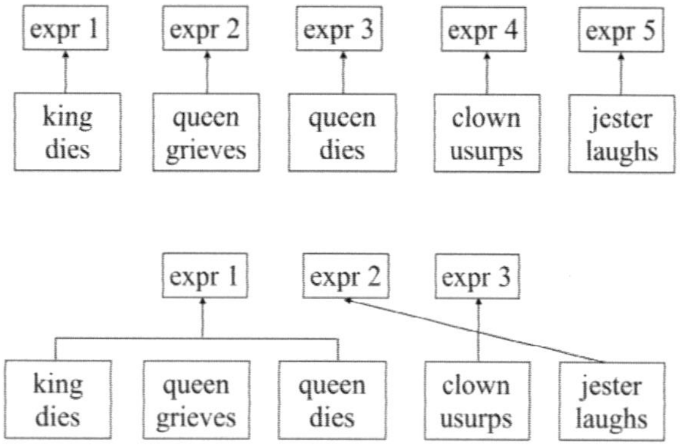

Figure 1. The same underlying events can be represented in a straightforward chronological way (above) or with different frequency, speed, and order (below).

which is *narrated* the *narrative* itself, has been central. Specifically, the model that Gérard Genette presents in *Figures III,* translated into English as *Narrative Discourse* (Genette 1980) and later revised in *Narrative Discourse Revisited* (Genette 1988), has provided the basis for narrative variation in Curveship.

A variant of a simple story given as an example by E. M. Foster is represented in figure 1. There are five underlying events: The death of the king, the grieving of the queen, the death of the queen, the usurping of the throne by a clown, and the laughing of the jester. These can be told one after another in their chronological order, as the top part of the diagram shows. But it is also possible to narrate the same underlying contest by saying "The king and queen died. The jester laughed — after the clown usurped the throne." This telling represented in the bottom part of the diagram, and corresponds to changes in three of Genette's categories: *frequency* (whether there is one telling per event, one for several events, or several for one event), *speed* (how rapidly or slowly events are related), and *order* (the sequence in which events are represented as compared to their chronological order in the story world). In this case, the king and queen's death are both narrated with a single statement, a change in frequency; the queen's grief is skipped over as rapidly as is possible and thus omitted entirely, a change in speed; and the clown's usurping of the throne is mentioned last, after the jester's laughter, which it apparently occasioned — a change in order.

Genette describes several other categories of variation, two of which are important for this paper. The *time of narrating* describes the temporal relationship between the narrating and the events of the story. For instance, in "I was driving down the road and it started raining frogs" the narrating is happening after the events, but a different (and still perfectly plausible) telling of this story, "So I'm driving down the road and all of the sudden it starts raining frogs," the narrating and the events take place at the same time, giving a more immediate feel to the narrative. We could gloss this different as one of "past tense" and "present tense," but this simple reference to grammar breaks down as a story gets more complex. If the narrator-character were to continue by noting "I had just had the wiper blades replaced" in the first case and "I just had the wiper blades replaced," the story would no

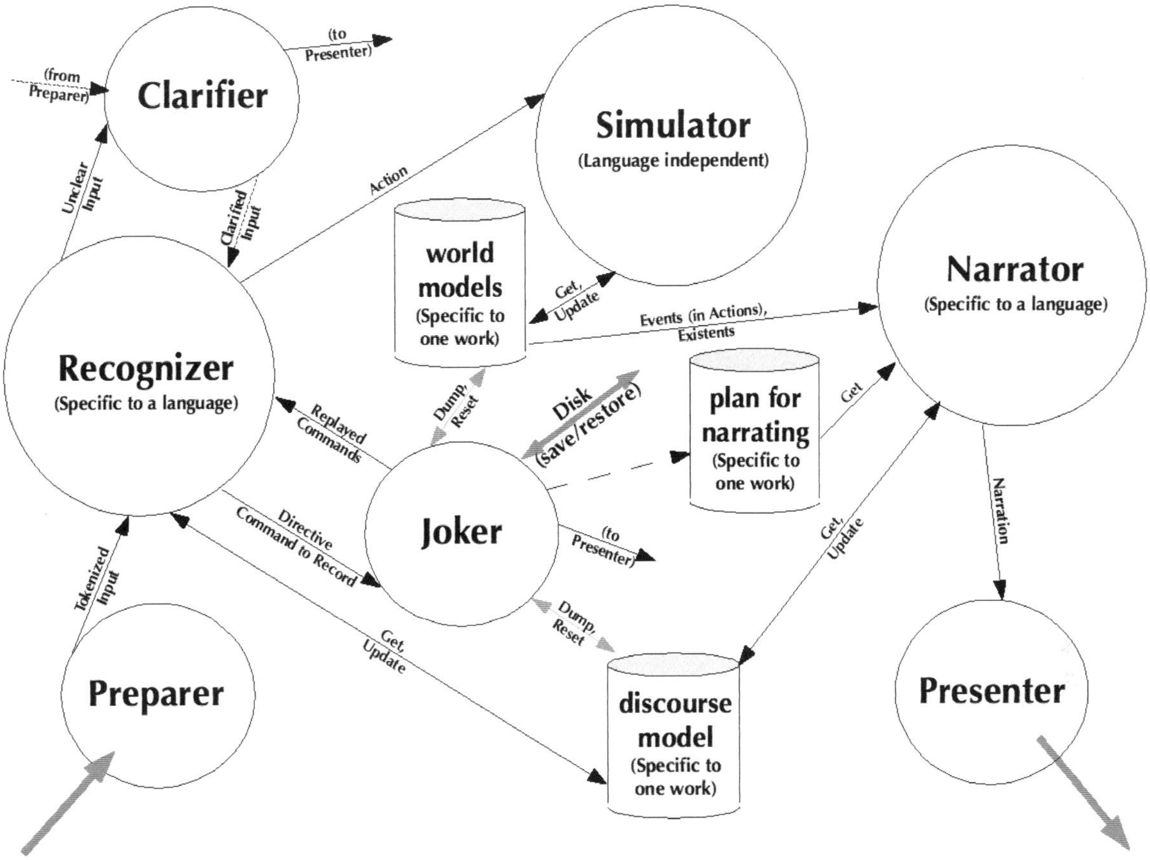

Figure 2. The architecture of Curveship. Each module is responsible for one more or less complex function; for instance, the Joker allows for *save, restore, restart,* and similar manipulation of the game state. The Simulator determines what events transpire in the IF world, while the Narrator deals with how to represent those events.

longer be entirely in the simple present or simple past. The important difference here, although it is reflected in the grammar, is actually a narrative one.

Focalization, briefly, describes the way that the information available to the narrator is regulated. If the narrative follows a character and tells us only what that character knows, it is focalized by that character. Whether the character is referred to in the main level of the narrative as "I," in the third person (as in a typical Hemingway story), or even as "you" (the standard case in interactive fiction) is a separate matter. Specifically, that has to do with who the narrator and naratee are and if there are characters within the story who have this role.

4 The Architecture of Curveship

State-of-the-art IF systems (including TADS 3 and Inform 7) have innovated in many ways, but they are similar in offering two main modules, the "parser," which deals with recognizing intended actions based on typed user input, and the rest of the program, which handles both the simulation of the IF world and the narrating of events and description of existents in that world.

Curveship has a parser as well (the Recognizer) but, as shown in figure 2, it is further separated into modules that deal with different functions the interactive fiction system and program have to carry out. Significantly, it has separate Simulator and Narrator modules. The Simulator is potentially independent of the human language of a particular interactive fiction, although Curveship has only been implemented in English as yet. It updates the world models to reflect the new state of the underlying simulated world and the new theories that characters have about this world. Then, the Narrator module, which is quite specific to a particular human language, builds a narrative reply using a world model and a plan for narrating. The Simulator is the only module that updates the world models. Similarly, the discourse model is written only by the Recognizer (which updates this model to reflect the user's contributions to the discourse) and the Narrator (which produces the system's contributions to the discourse and updates the model to reflect these).

Curveship's somewhat unusual name is meant to call attention to how the system models the essential qualities of variation — the curve of a story through its telling — just as friendship and authorship represent the essence of being a friend and author.[1] The word "curveship" was coined by Hart Crane (1899-1932) in the last line of his poem "To Brooklyn Bridge," in which he addresses the bridge: "And of the curveship lend a myth to God."

5 Order and Time of Narrating

The order of events as narrated does not have to correspond to the order of events in a fictional, simulated, or historical world. Genette represents the order of events in the narrating as a sequqnce, of the form "3451267," but he also notes that events can be reordered in many different ways, for different purposes and to different effects. For instance, in "3451267," the earliest two events, "12," may have been narrated as what is commonly called flashback (which Genette calls an analepsis). But perhaps not: perhaps "345," "12," and "67" all fell into different categories, and the narration was done according to these categories — using syllepsis, in Genette's system. Or, perhaps the events have been jumbled at random to confuse the reader about their temporal relationship; this is called achrony. Cue words and tense will be used differently in these three cases, so "3451267" is not an adequate representation when text is to be generated, rather than just analyzed.

Instead of representing the order of events in the narrative as a sequence, Curveship uses an ordered tree representation called a reply structure. It describes not only the sequence of events but also which level each event is at and what its relationship is to the level above. To determine the tense, the system uses a theory that relates how three

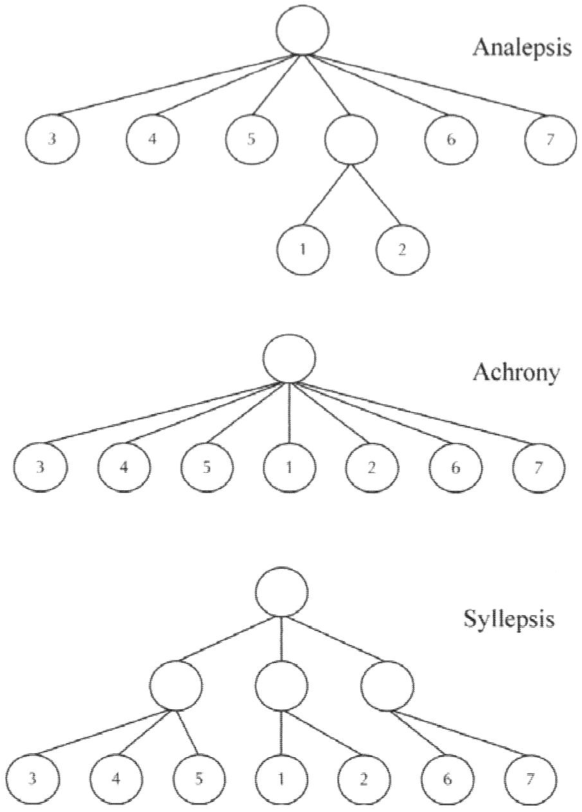

Figure 3. The reply structures corresponding to three different orderings, all of which would look the same if a simple sequence were used as a representation.

points in time — speech time (S), reference time (R), and event time (E) — correspond to a particular grammatical tense (Reichenbach 1947). Event time is supplied by the simulator; the other two times are determined based on the plan for narrating and the reply structure as text generation are done. The reply structure representation allows for different orderings to be composed, so, for instance, within a flashforward, the events can be jumbled achronously, and within each sylleptic category the narration can be done in a different temporal way.

6 Focalization

Curveship implements a system for changing focalization based on Marie Laure-Ryan's concept of a Fictional Actual World which the reader recenters upon (Ryan 2001). In the formulation of this concept for interactive fiction, it is useful to consider an Interactive Fiction Actual World that

[1] This may seem like an obscure name, but at least it's better than the name the system previously had, during the main phase of my research work: "nn." People often couldn't even identify this as a word, whether it was spoken or written.

represents what is actual, or real, to the characters in the game. Each character, then — each potential focalizer — has his or her own world model, a theory of this world which may be mistaken and almost certainly is partial. The Narrator, then, never even sees the underlying simulation, but instead relates events based on the focalizer's current theory of the world.

Because the Narrator may tell about things that happened before the current state of the world, each focalizer maintains not only a current theory of the world but also a history of how the world appeared in the past.

7 Text Generation in Curveship

The Narrator, which does text generation in Curveship, is organized into a standard three-stage pipeline. First comes the highest-level operation of content selection and ordering, which is done by the Reply Planner (essentially a document planner, but here part of a discourse is being planned). Then, the Microplanner determines the grammatical specifics of the output based on the plan for narrating. Finally, the Realizer accepts the paragraph proposals from the Microplanner and produces a string.

The problem of authoring for generation is a difficult one. Interactive fiction authors would like to be able to write as they do now, simply associating strings with objects and events. This representation is not suitable for the generation task, however. Something more general is needed to allow narrative variation to be automatically produced.

Advanced research and commercial text generation system use highly abstract representations of sentences (different ones for each system) to allow text to be flexibly transformed, aggregated, and changed in tense, aspect, and person. While the power of this approach is unquestionable, taking this direction is also unsuitable, because it would require a tremendous investment on the part of authors, who would spend perhaps a hundred times the time and effort to create the same textual output that they could jot off in the typical interactive fiction system. It is unlikely that anyone would undertake this voluntarily, and, if people did, it would almost certainly disrupt the authorship process.

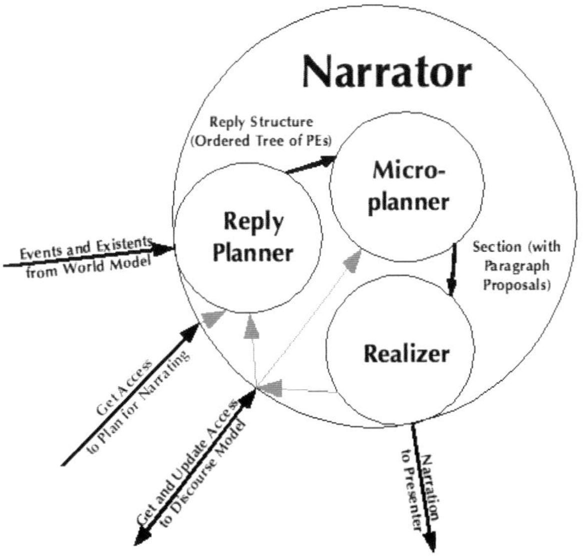

Figure 4. The Narrator module uses a standard three-stage pipeline for text generation.

As a compromise, Curvseship uses a string-with-slots representation that offers significant flexibility in generation without the extreme complexity of most sentence representations. It allows authors to "cheat" and indicate that something should be treated as an entity in the discourse even if there is no model of it in the simulation. For instance, the text at the beginning of *Adventure* can be generated from the following strings:

```
'S_FC V_stand_PROG at the_end of
 a_road before
 a_small_brick_building'
'a_small_stream V_flow_S out of
 the_building and down a_gully'
```

The first slot, S_FC, indicates that the focalizing character is to be named there (pronominalized if appropriate) and will be the subject of the sentence. The next, V_stand_PROG, says that the verb "stand" is to appear in the progressive. It is not necessary to specify the number; without such a specification, the verb will agree in number with the subject. The rest of the first string looks ordinary, except that noun phrases have been connected with underscores. This indicates that they should be treated as entities in the discourse even though they are not simulated: The system will, for instance, output "a road" the first time around and, since the road is then given in the discourse, it will output "the road" afterwards. Finally, in the second string, there is the slot V_flow_S. The subject of the sentence is not indicated, but it is not necessary, since the "_S" indicates that the verb "flow" should be output in the singular.

Depending on the plan for narrating and the state of the discourse, this can produce:

> You are standing at the end of a road before a small brick building. A small stream flows out of the building and down a gully.

As well as:

> You were standing at the end of the road before the small brick building. The small stream flowed out of the building and down the gully.

Along with more exotic strings that result from unusual narrative settings and the use of text filters.

References

Aiken, Jim. "Getting Started with Interactive Fiction," 2008. http://www.musicwords.net/if/if_getting_started.htm

Cadre, Adam. "Interactive Fiction — Getting Started." http://adamcadre.ac/content/if.txt

Genette, Gérard. *Narrative Discourse: An Essay in Method.* Trans. J. E. Lewin. Ithaca, NY: Cornell University Press. 1980.

Genette, Gérard. *Narrative Discourse Revisited.* Trans. J. E. Lewin. Ithaca, NY: Cornell University Press. 1988.

IFWiki. "Interactive Fiction FAQ," 2009. http://ifwiki.org/index.php/FAQ

Montfort, Nick. *Twisty Little Passages: An Approach to Interactive Fiction*. The MIT Press, 2003.

Montfort, Nick. "Generating Narrative Variation in Interactive Fiction." Dissertation, University of Pennsylvania, 2007a.

Montfort, Nick. "Riddle Machines: The History and Nature of Interactive Fiction." In A Companion to Digital Literary Studies, pp. 267–282. Editors, Ray Siemens and Susan Schreibman. Basil Blackwell, 2007b.

Nelson, Graham. "A short history of interactive fiction." *The Inform Designer's Manual* section 46, 4th edition, 2001. http://www.inform-fiction.org/manual/html/s46.html

Reichenbach, Hans. *Elements of Symbolic Logic.* New York: Macmillan. 1947.

Ryan, Marie-Laure. *Narrative as Virtual Reality.* Baltimore: Johns Hopkins University Press. 2001.

Planning Author and Character Goals for Story Generation

Candice Jean Solis, Joan Tiffany Siy, Emerald Tabirao, and **Ethel Ong**
College of Computer Studies
De La Salle University
Manila, Philippines
candice_solis13@yahoo.com, emeraldtabirao_dlsu@yahoo.com.ph,
joan.tiffany.siy@gmail.com, ethel.ong@delasalle.ph

Abstract

The design and content of the planning library of a story generation system dictates the content quality of the story it produces. This paper presents the story planner component of Picture Books, a system that generates stories for children aged 4 to 6 years based on a set of picture elements selected by the user. The planning library separates the design for the story patterns from the design of the semantic ontology that supplies the story's domain knowledge. An evaluation of the system shows that the coherency and completeness of the plot is attributed to the story pattern design structure while the appropriateness of the content is attributed to the semantic ontology.

1 Introduction

Several researchers have developed story generators capable of generating stories that closely resemble human-made stories. Some of these include TALE-SPIN (Meehan, 1977) that generates stories through problem solving, MINSTREL (Turner, 1992) that uses an episodic memory scheme for storing past problem-solving cases, and MAKEBELIEVE (Liu and Singh, 2002) that constructs stories with the use of logical reasoning.

Callaway and Lester (2002) observed that most story generators (SG), such as TALE-SPIN and MAKEBELIEVE, concentrated on the generation of plots and the characters, with less emphasis on linguistic phenomena, resulting in stories that have good narrative quality but lacking in linguistic structures. Their STORYBOOK system addresses this by applying full-scale linguistic approaches to the narrative prose generation architecture of AUTHOR (Callaway, 2000).

Loenneker (2005) made a similar observation regarding SG whose implicit goal is to generate a coherent narrative in a given genre with less emphasis on discourse structure, and skipping document structuring and microplanning (Reiter and Dale, 2000) stages.

In this paper, we present our story generator, Picture Books, which generates stories for children aged four to six. Picture Books derives the story elements from a given input set of picture elements (backgrounds, characters, and objects). The genre (fables) and story goal (moral lessons) are applied as separate parts of the system's planning library, which contains story planning goals to convert abstract story specifications to coherent stories suitable for the target age group.

The rest of this paper is subdivided as follows. Section 2 presents some background information on the specifications of a children's story as well as the semantic ontology used by the planners of Picture Books. Section 3 discusses the design of the plan library and the planning process involved in story generation, followed by the evaluation results on the content and grammar of the stories generated by the system in Section 4. The paper ends with a summary of future work that can be done to improve the generated stories.

2 Storytelling and Picture Books

The motivation behind Picture Books is twofold. First is the realization that stories are combinations of various genres to produce a differing effect. The genres can be considered as templates that dictate the plot of the story. It is therefore possible to create a story by indicating the story elements (i.e., characters, events, and settings), the genres, and the goal of the story to automatically produce a narrative text. The second motivation is that stories serve as rich sources of information that help develop a child's knowledge. However, young children recognize images of objects easily compared to words (Fields et al, 2003), accounting for the popularity of picture-based story books that allow readers to relate stories by using not only words, but pictures depicting the story.

Proceedings of the NAACL HLT Workshop on Computational Approaches to Linguistic Creativity, pages 63–70,
Boulder, Colorado, June 2009.

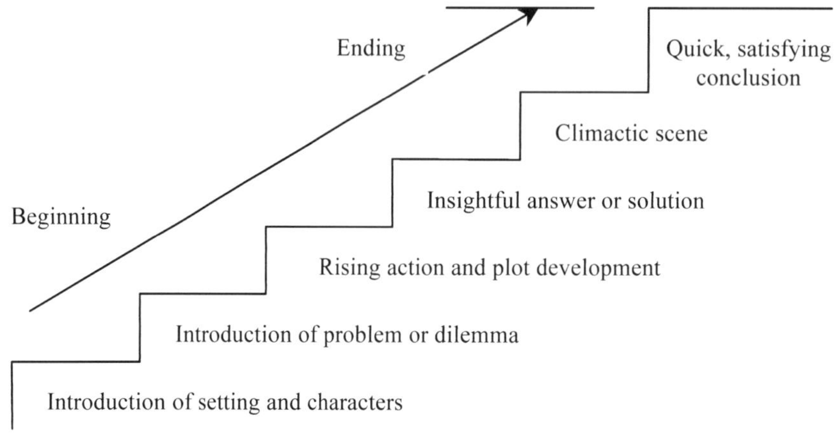

Figure 0. Common and Classic Story Pattern Form (Machado, 2003)

2.1 Story Specifications

Interviews with child educators revealed that most of the published storybooks for children focus on themes to teach them lessons about proper behavior. These themes revolve around everyday activities like eating on time and brushing your teeth with lessons on being careful, being honest, and the value of sharing. Themes also dictate the objects that can be used in the story, for example, in the *eating healthy foods* theme, possible positive objects supporting good behavior are apples and bananas, while cakes and candies are considered negative objects in cases of misbehavior (i.e., unhealthy foods).

Another common characteristic of children's stories is the use of the fable form, wherein the story characters are portrayed by animals that can capture the imagination and attention of the target readers. The animals have simple traits that children can relate with, such as loyalty for dogs, playfulness for cats, kindness for rabbits, and bravery for tigers. They are also given names, such as *Ellen the elephant*, *Rizzy the rabbit*, and *Leo the lion*, to give the impression that the characters are friends that the children are getting to know better through reading the story.

In the linguistic aspect, stories for four year olds have simple sentence structures and contain line redundancy. This is lessened as the child grows older. The words used in the stories are not only simple and easy to understand, but also vary depending on the child's age in order to introduce new words to his vocabulary. Lessons and rules are emphasized by positive praises while improper behaviors are emphasized by revealing their consequences.

Another aspect to consider in storytelling is the story's title. Story titles are short and often contain the story's theme as a hint to what the story is about. The main character's name should also be included in the title, such as "*Leo the Lion Learns to Eat on Time*".

In general, Machado (2003) showed that stories follow a common and classic story pattern depicted in Figure 0, which flows from negative to positive and has the following outline:

i. The main character wants something.
ii. The main character is informed of the rules and/or restrictions.
iii. The main character disobeys the rule.
iv. The main character is either caught or experiences natural consequences of disobedience (e.g. a tooth ache from eating too much candy).
v. The main character learns a lesson.

2.2 Semantic Ontology

The knowledge resource dictates the amount of information that an SG system can output, thus highlighting its importance. Picture Books uses an ontology to have a flexible knowledge resource that provides relevant concepts familiar to the target age group as well as applicable to the story being planned. Its design was adapted from ConceptNet (Liu and Singh, 2004a), a semantic resource with structure closely resembling that of WordNet (2006).

The nodes used by ConceptNet are of three general classes representing noun phrases, attributes, and activity phrases. A *semantic relationship* connects two concepts while a *semantic category* classifies them. The semantic relationships are binary relation types defined by Open Mind Commonsense project (Liu and Singh, 2004b). Table 1 lists some of these relationships defined in Picture Books following the form *<relationship>(<concept1>, <concept2>)*.

Semantic Category	Semantic Relationships
Things	***IsA***(headache, pain) - corresponds loosely to hypernym in WordNet ***PropertyOf***(apple, healthy) ***PartOf***(window, pane) – corresponds loosely to holonym in WordNet ***MadeOf***(toy car, clay)
Events	***FirstSubeventOf***(tell bedtime story, sleep) ***EventForGoalEvent***(go to grocery store, buy food) ***EventForGoalState***(clean up, be neat) ***EventRequiresObject***(play, toy)
Actions	***EffectOf***(become dirty, itchy) ***EffectOfIsState***(make friends, friendship) ***CapableOf***(toy car, play)

Table 1. ConceptNet semantic relationships (Liu and Singh, 2004b) with sample concepts of Picture Books

3 Planning the Story

Picture Books has three major components – a *picture editor*, a *story planner*, and a *sentence planner*. The *Picture Editor* is provided for users to specify the background or setting of the story (kitchen), and to select and "stick" into the background the set of characters (little sheep and mama sheep) and objects (cake, bread). An example picture is shown in Figure 2.

The first child character placed in the picture will be the protagonist of the story, while the first adult sticker placed in the picture will be the parent of the protagonist. If there is no adult character, the protagonist's biological parent will be chosen as the adult character needed in the story. The first object sticker placed in the picture will assume the **%object%** variable used in planning the story - especially in ontology accesses. The rest are discarded.

All elements in the picture, namely the background, the characters and the objects (including sequence of placement), and the name and age of the user, are stored in an *input content representation* (ICR) and passed on to the *story planner*.

The *Story Planner* takes in the abstract ICR then performs three planning steps – i) *theme planning* to select an appropriate theme for the story, ii) *plot planning* to instantiate the story plots depicting the theme, and iii) *presentation planning* to handle the planning of the story's title, introduction and appropriate ending. A *Story Organizer* arranges these resulting story events as it is supposed to be presented to the user in an abstract story tree.

The *Sentence Planner* then converts the abstract story tree representation to sentence specifications by performing *referring expression generation*, *lexicalization*, and *phrase specification mapping*. The *Surface Realizer* uses the *simplenlg* realiser (Venour and Reiter, 2008) to convert the sentence specifications to actual sentences that comprise the story.

Figure 2. Sample Picture with Stickers

3.1 Plan Library

The plan library contains the set of instructions and information on creating the plot of a story, and has three parts: (1) the *story elements* containing information regarding the characters, objects and settings of a story; (2) a set of *story patterns* to direct the story goal towards attainment of the moral lesson; and (3) a *semantic ontology* containing concepts applicable to the target domain, in this case, fables.

Picture Books uses a set of predefined characters, objects and backgrounds, as inputs. These story elements are used to determine the actors, the setting and the theme of a story. Information on characters, such as the parents, is useful for identifying other characters in the story. The background serves as the main setting of the story, and combined with the selected objects, is used to determine the theme. Given a *bedroom* background, the set of available themes include *being brave*, *being neat*, *being careful*, *being honest*, and *sleeping early*. Objects that are available for this background include an *alarm clock*, *a lamp, a pillow*, and *toys*.

The story pattern is used to direct the goal of the story and is composed of the theme, story plot, author goal and character goal. Each component is designed to subsume the next (i.e., theme subsumes story plot, and story plot subsumes author goal) to support different granularity of story details and to lessen the redundancy as common story details are subsumed by a higher-level component.

A **theme** dictates the plot of a story and is composed of four story plots (see Figure 3) namely, the *problem*, *rising action*, *solution* and *climax* which, according to Machado (2003), are the four fundamental stages of the main plot of any story. In the theme *take_bath*, these four plots would contain the following:

Problem:	Defy by not doing the rule
Rising Action:	Experience consequence
Solution:	Do the lesson
Climax:	Learn the benefit

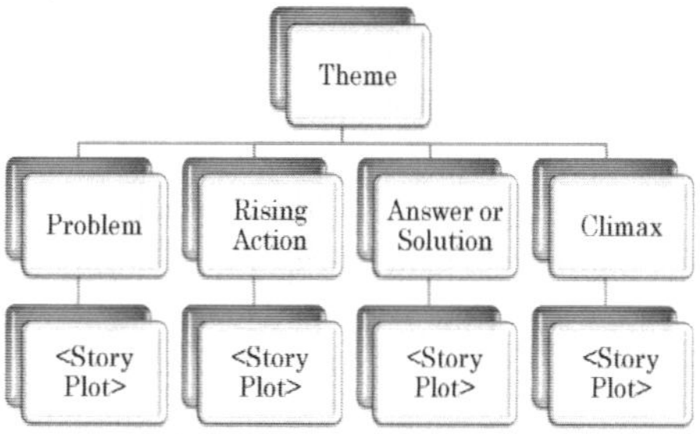

Figure 3. Theme Structure

The theme is executed through the **story plot**. A story plot represents the major events in the theme and contains at least two author goals (shown in Figure 4) that represent the scenes comprising the event.

Figure 4. Story Plot Structure

Figure 5. Author Goal Structure

An **author goal** (**Figure** 5) is composed of a *goal* of the scene and the corresponding *consequence* of the goal to ensure consistency in the scene. Each goal and consequence component of an author goal is in turn filled up by at least one character goal.A **character goal** (Figure 6) represents the unit of action a character or two characters do in order to depict the goal/consequence of the scene. This design of the character goal is based from the action operators of Uijlings (2006) and can be directly converted to simple declarative sentences.

A character goal has five fields – the *action*, the *agens* or doer of the action, the *patiens* or receiver of the action, the *target*, and the *instrument*. One character goal generates one sentence in the story with the *agens* as the subject, the *action* as the verb, the *patiens* as the character or object that undergoes the action verb, the *target* as the location or object of the action verb, and the *instrument* as the object used to perform the verb. This design allows all fields to be empty except for *action* and *agens*.

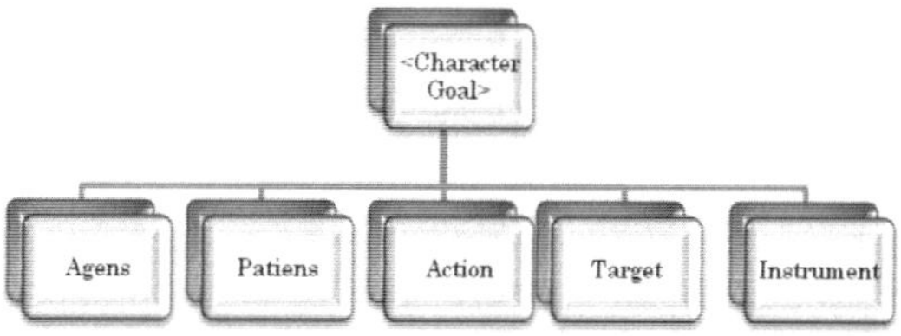

Figure 6. Character Goal Data Structure

The character goal is generic so that it only contains default values for *action*, *agens* and *patiens*. During instantiation of a character goal for a particular scene, attribute values are passed to the character goal at the author goal level. For example, given the generic character goal *adult tells main character* (CGL01) has the following default attributes:

action:	tell
agens:	adult
patiens:	main character

When a scene requires the adult to inform the main character of the lesson, the *target* attribute would then be assigned with the lesson value to denote that the adult is talking to the main character about the lesson. The invocation of the character goal in the author goal level would be:

CGL01(*target*:lesson)

This customizes the character goal to "*adult tells the lesson to the main character*" to fit the scene.

Parameters for character goal attributes include not only the story variables (i.e. object, lesson, background), but invocations to inner character goals and ontology accesses as well. An *inner character goal* is a character goal assigned as an attribute of an outer character goal.

It represents a clause in a sentence and is usually assigned as a value of the *target* attribute in the outer character goal, for example:

CGL03(*target*:CGL05(*target*:lesson))

Picture Books would interpret the inner character goal "*main character is not doing the lesson* (CGL05)" first before appending it to the outer character goal "*secondary character told the adult character* (CGL03)", resulting in the following sentence specification:

secondary character tells an adult that the main character is not doing the lesson

The *instrument* attribute in a character goal may have the following value which would trigger an ontology search for a concept:

onto<semantic_category>(%object%)

The *<semantic category>* constrains the search coverage to concepts that are directly connected to the given input concept *(%object%)*. For example, *ontoSpatial(play)* triggers a search for all concepts connected to *play* within the *spatial* semantic category (e.g., "*locationOf*" and "*oftenNear*" semantic relationships).

Character goals can also be created dynamically during runtime and are used to increase the length and the variation of the generated story. Dynamic character goals necessitate the search for relationship paths in the ontology. Two input concepts, the source and destination concepts, and the semantic category that constrains the search coverage, are needed when searching for relationship paths.

Consider the following attribute value of a character goal:

ontoEvent(break object, punishment)

This denotes that a search for a series of semantic relationships within the *Event* semantic category must be performed to relate *break object* to *punishment*. The resulting path is shown in Figure 7.

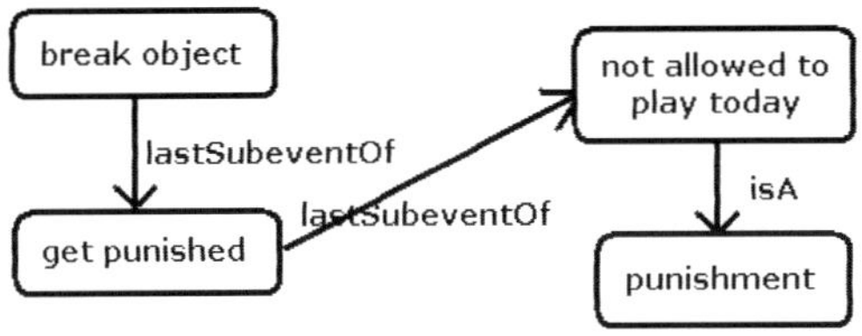

Figure 7. Sample Ontology Path Search Result

Each relationship in the resulting path, excluding *isA* (hypernym) and *conceptuallyRelatedTo* relationships, is mapped to a dynamic character goal. For example, in the first *lastSubeventOf* relationship in Figure 7, the second concept ("*get punished*") is assigned to the *action* attribute of the dynamic character goal, resulting in the abstract output sentence specifications "*Main character gets punished*" and "*Main character is not allowed to play today*".

3.2 Planning Process

The *Theme Planner* selects a theme by matching the input objects against the applicable objects of the candidate themes for a specified background. When the theme with the highest score has been determined, the *Plot Planner* instantiates the story plots of the chosen theme, beginning with the *problem*, followed by the *rising action,* then the *solution* and finally the *climax*. Given the theme *eat_on_time* with the following corresponding story plots:

eat_on_time(defy_break_rule, experience_consequence, inform_lesson, realize _benefit) [1]

the first (*problem*) story plot, *defy_break_rule*, suggests that the main character will disobey an adult character's rule/instruction. Executing this plot entails executing the author goals within it.

defy_break_rule(inform_character_rule, ignore _rule)

Then the first author goal, *inform_character _rule,* suggesting that the adult character informs the main character of the rule first, is executed:

inform_character_rule(adult_talk_character, character_not_want)

Finally, the character goals in the author goal, *adult_talk_character* and *character_not_want*, are executed. Notice that it is only in the character goal level that instantiation of characters and objects are made.

adult_talk_character("tell", "Mommy Audrey", "Simon", "eat on time", null) [2]
character_not_want("not want", "Simon", null, "eat on time", null)

These phrase specifications of character goals will be forwarded later to the surface realizer for translation to simple sentences to generate the text "*Mommy Audrey told Simon to eat on time.*" and "*Simon did not want to eat on time.*", respectively.

---

[1] Theme format:
Theme(problem, rising action, solution, climax)
[2] Character Goal format:
CG(action, agens, patiens, target, instrument)

The planning process continues by backtracking to the first story plot and iterating until it exhausts all the theme's story plots. A depth-first tree traversal algorithm is employed to recursively traverse the theme tree. An excerpt from the theme *eat_on_time,* starting from the story plot *defy_break_rule*, and its tree traversal, is shown in Figure 8.

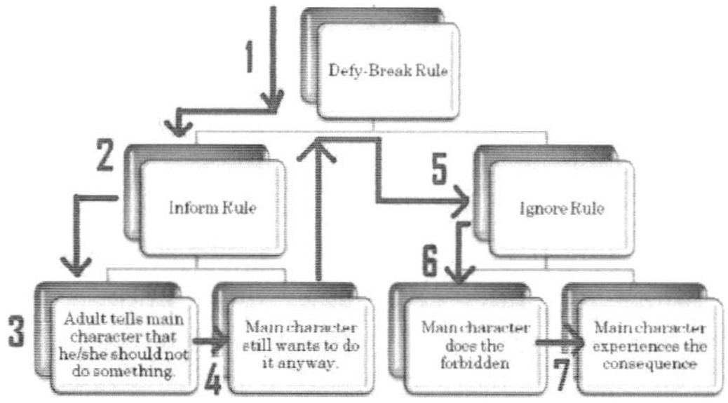

Figure 8. Tree Traversal for the Problem "*Defy Break Rule*" of the "*Eat_On_Time*" Theme

3.3 Planning for Linguistic Variation

Sentences generated by Picture Books vary in length and word complexity according to the user's age. The variation in length is handled by *specificity character goals* (SCG) that are appended as supporting details to their respective character goals. SCGs are designed so that their existence will give more detail to the preceding character goal while ensuring consistency, and that their non-existence will still make the story complete. SCG is not executed when the user is four years old, one SCG is executed when the user is five years old, and all of SCGs are executed when the user is six years old.

Age	Story Excerpt
Four	Ellen was scared. She was ***sad***. Teacher Sara saw that Ellen was crying. Teacher Sara told Ellen to be brave.
Five	Ellen was scared. She was ***lonely***. Teacher Sara saw that Ellen was crying. <u>Teacher Sara asked Ellen if everything was okay.</u> She told her to be brave.
Six	Ellen was scared. She was ***upset***. Teacher Sara saw that she was crying. <u>Teacher Sara asked Ellen if everything was okay. Ellen told teacher Sara that she was scared</u>. Teacher Sara told Ellen to be brave.

Table 2. Excerpts of Stories with Linguistic Variation

Word complexity is addressed by storing different synonymous lexical items in the lexicon. The appropriateness of the lexical items to the target age group was verified by child educators. Table 2 contains excerpts from Picture Books' stories for various ages, with ***boldfaced italics*** showing lexical variation, while <u>underlined sentences</u> are the executed SCGs. Additional sentences and lexical items can be generated by encoding more SCGs into the plan library and the ontology, respectively.

4 Results and Analysis

The knowledge base of Picture Books currently contains 9 backgrounds, 11 themes, 40 characters, 37 objects, 77 author goals, and 61 character goals. The lexicon has been populated with 419 words appropriate for the target age group, while the ontology has 240 concepts and 369 semantic relationships. 15 exemplary stories generated by the system, consisting of five themes that vary per age (4, 5, and 6), were selected. Two child educators and a linguist manually validated the appropriateness of the content and the linguistic correctness of the 15 stories, respectively.

Each story was rated per criterion from 1 to 4, with 4 being the highest. A rate of 4 means that the criterion is completely present in the story, 3 means that the criterion is present but incomplete, 2 means the criterion is partially present, and 1 means the criterion is not present.

4.1 Evaluating the Story Content

The evaluation on the story patterns' role in ensuring that the story goal is met is shown in Table 3, while the evaluation of the semantic ontology's role in supplying domain knowledge to the story is shown in Table 4.

The evaluators gave the stories high ratings in terms of *plot completeness*, validating that the stories have all the essential story elements (problem, rising action, the solution and the climax to the problem) as well as the introduction of the time and setting of the story. This was attributed to the plan library structure consisting of themes, plots, author goals, and character goals. Because of this coherency in the plot, the *understandability* criterion received a high average score of 3.47.

Criteria	Average
Story is understandable	3.47
The settings of the story were described	3.86
The characters in the story were described	3.67
Objects are present in the story	4.00
General Average	**3.75**

Table 3. Evaluation on the Story Patterns

Criteria	Average
Sentences are coherent	2.67
The story has transition	3.47
The actions of the characters make sense	3.93
Story is appropriate to target age	3.80
Objects in the story were described	2.80
General Average	**3.33**

Table 4. Evaluation of the Semantic Ontology

Evaluations on the effectiveness of the semantic ontology, on the other hand, produced varying scores. The coherency of the sentences received a low average score of 2.67, because as seen in the excerpt below, a sentence (such as the underlined text) depicting that *Ellen the elephant* did something to show she is trying to be brave was missing in the generated story.

She wanted to be brave. Ellen was brave. She wanted to play with others. She bravely introduced herself. Ellen made friends.

Since the ontology did not contain any other information of what to do in order to be brave, the story content planner did not place any detail describing the action of the main character depicting her attempt to be brave. This can be remedied by adding more semantic relationships (that can be converted to sentences) between concepts.

The excerpt from the generated story "*Rizzy the Rabbit Learns to be Honest*" below also affected the coherency criterion when the second character, *Denise the dog*, suddenly appeared in the middle of the story when she could have been introduced with the first character, *Rizzy the rabbit*, at the start of the story.

The evening was warm. Rizzy the rabbit was in the dining room. She played near a lamp. Rizzy broke the lamp. She was scared. Mommy Francine saw that the lamp was broken. Rizzy told Mommy Francine that Denise broke the lamp.

The criterion regarding story transition pertains to the ease of transition of events that can be attributed to the path of relationships retrieved from the semantic ontology, which more often than not, introduce event transitions including character actions.

The criterion on appropriateness of the story content to the target age received a high average score of 3.80 mainly because the semantic ontology has been populated with concepts specifically for the target age group.

While the presence of objects in the stories received a high score of 4.00 (see Table 3), the description of objects received a low score of 2.80 (see Table 4), because although objects are present in the stories, as in "*She played near a lamp.*", they were not described, i.e., "*breakable lamp*". This was remedied by adding object descriptions in the ontology. However, the selection of which description to be used was currently not dictated by the story theme, nor was the description subsequently used to direct the sequences of events in the rest of the story.

4.2 Evaluating the Linguistic Aspect

Table 5 summarizes the evaluation on the grammatical aspect of the generated stories. Since mostly simple sentences are generated, they are grammatically correct and coherent.

CRITERIA	AVG
Sentences are grammatically correct	3.20
Sentences are coherent	3.60
Pronouns are used correctly	3.45
Articles are used correctly	3.20
The story has transition	3.00
General Average	**3.29**

Table 5. Evaluation on Grammar Correctness

Most of the generated stories contain correct usage of pronouns, except for sentences such as "*Teacher Sara told Ellen that Ellen should be brave*", where the second reference to "*Ellen*" should be replaced with the pronoun "*she*". The evaluators, however, noted the lack of possessive pronouns in the text below (the underlined words are the identified missing pronouns).

Porky wanted to play. He played with his toys. His toys were scattered.

There are also occurrences of missing articles, as shown in the excerpt below (the underlined words are the missing articles).

He played near a glass of water. Simon broke the glass of water. He was scared. Daddy Gary saw that the glass of water was broken.

The generated stories received an average score of 3.0 for the transition criterion due to missing transitional devices, as shown in the excerpt below (the underlined words are the missing transitional devices).

He apologized to her. Mommy Patricia then helped Porky to clean up. Soon he found the lost toys.

5 Conclusion and Recommendations

The design of Picture Books' plan library, combined with planning operators in the form of story plots and character goals, demonstrated that grammatically correct and coherent stories for children aged 4 to 6 can be generated from a given set of predefined pictures, provided that the appropriate domain knowledge is present. The semantic ontology whose design was adapted from ConceptNet provided the domain knowledge that supplies factual information to the story. The theme structure and its components model the way humans perform storytelling and also ensured that the generated stories will contain the four basic elements of *problem, rising action, solution,* and *climax*. The separation of the plan library which dictates the story patterns from the semantic ontology gives flexibility to Picture Books such that it could easily be adapted to generate other story domain.

Currently, Picture Books generates stories with simple declarative sentences. A future improvement of the system is to extend the design of the character goal to generate stories with dialogues. Although common animals that young children can relate with have been used as the main characters of the story, their traits, such as loyalty, bravery, and kindness, have not been considered in determining the flow of the story. A similar claim can be made for describing the objects used in the story, such that a story promoting the value of "*being thrifty*" can use the "*expensive lamp*" as an object, while the value of "*being careful*" can use the "*breakable lamp*" instead. These are aspects of storytelling that can be investigated in a future work.

From a linguistic perspective, the current implementation of Picture Books can generate pronouns and articles, as well as a transitional device at the last sentence in the story. However, possessive pronouns, the consistent use of articles, and the generation of appropriate transitional devices in several parts of the story should be further explored. The design of the character goals can be extended by adding an attribute indicating a connection or the passage of time between sentences. Rhetorical Structure Theory (Mann and Thompson, 1988) can also be applied to author goals and character goals for an effective discourse structure that would provide a smoother story flow.

References

Charles B. Callaway, and James C. Lester. 2002. Narrative Prose Generation. *Artificial Intelligence*, 139(2): 213-252.

Charles B. Callaway. 2000. *Narrative Prose Generation*. PhD thesis, North Carolina State University, Raleigh, NC.

Robert Dale, and Ehud Reiter. 2000. *Building Natural Language Generation Systems*. Cambridge: Cambridge University Press.

Marjorie Fields, Lois Groth, and Katherine Spangler. 2003. *Let's Begin Reading Right: A Developmental Approach to Emergent Literacy, 5/E*. Prentice Hall.

Hugo Liu, and Push Singh. 2004a. Commonsense Reasoning in and over Natural Language. In *Proceedings of the 8th International Conference on Knowledge-Based Intelligent Information and Engineering Systems*, 293-306, Wellington, New Zealand. Springer Berlin.

Hugo Liu, and Push Singh, 2004b. ConceptNet — A Practical Commonsense Reasoning Tool-Kit. *BT Technology Journal*, 22(4): 211-226. Springer Netherlands.

Hugo Liu, and Push Singh. 2002. Makebelieve: Using Commonsense Knowledge to Generate Stories. In *Proceedings of the Eighteenth National Conference on Artificial Intelligence*, 957-958, Edmonton, Alberta, Canada. AAAI Press.

Birte Loenneker. 2005. Narratological Knowledge for Natural Language Generation. In *Proceedings of the Tenth European Workshop on Natural Language Generation*, 91-100, Aberdeen, Scotland.

Jeanne Machado. 2003. Storytelling. In *Early Childhood Experiences in Language Arts: Emerging Literacy*, 304-319. Clifton Park, N.Y. Thomson/Delmar Learning.

William C. Mann, Sandra A. Thompson. 1988. Rhetorical Structure Theory: Toward a Functional Theory of Text Organization. *Text*, 8(3), 243-281.

James Meehan. 1977. TALE-SPIN, An Interactive Program that Writes Stories. *Proceedings of the 5th International Joint Conference on Artificial Intelligence*, 91-98. Cambridge, M.A.

Scott R. Turner. 1992. *Minstrel: A Computer Model of Creativity and Storytelling*. Los Angeles, California: University of California.

Jasper Uijlings. 2006. Designing a Virtual Environment for Story Generation. MSc Thesis, University of Amsterdam, Amsterdam.

Chris Venour, Ehud Reiter. 2008. A Tutorial for Simplenlg (version 3.7) http://www.csd.abdn.ac.uk/~ereiter/simplenlg/

WordNet: A Lexical Database for the English Language. Princeton University, New Jersey, 2006.

An Unsupervised Model for Text Message Normalization

Paul Cook
Department of Computer Science
University of Toronto
Toronto, Canada
pcook@cs.toronto.edu

Suzanne Stevenson
Department of Computer Science
University of Toronto
Toronto, Canada
suzanne@cs.toronto.edu

Abstract

Cell phone text messaging users express themselves briefly and colloquially using a variety of creative forms. We analyze a sample of creative, non-standard text message word forms to determine frequent word formation processes in texting language. Drawing on these observations, we construct an unsupervised noisy-channel model for text message normalization. On a test set of 303 text message forms that differ from their standard form, our model achieves 59% accuracy, which is on par with the best supervised results reported on this dataset.

1 Text Messaging

Cell phone text messages—or SMS—contain many shortened and non-standard forms due to a variety of factors, particularly the desire for rapid text entry (Grinter and Eldridge, 2001; Thurlow, 2003).[1] Furthermore, text messages are written in an informal register; non-standard forms are used to reflect this, and even for personal style (Thurlow, 2003). These factors result in tremendous linguistic creativity, and hence many novel lexical items, in the language of text messaging, or *texting language*.

Normalization of non-standard forms—converting non-standard forms to their standard forms—is a challenge that must be tackled before other types of natural language processing can take place (Sproat et al., 2001). In the case of text messages, text-to-speech synthesis may be particularly useful for the visually impaired; automatic translation has also been considered (e.g., Aw et al., 2006). For texting language, given the abundance of creative forms, and the wide-ranging possibilities for creating new forms, normalization is a particularly important problem, and has indeed received some attention in computational linguistics (e.g., Aw et al., 2006; Choudhury et al., 2007; Kobus et al., 2008).

In this paper we propose an unsupervised noisy channel method for texting language normalization, that gives performance on par with that of a supervised system. We pursue unsupervised approaches to this problem, as large collections of text messages, and their corresponding standard forms, are not readily available.[2] Furthermore, other forms of computer-mediated communication, such as Internet messaging, exhibit creative phenomena similar to text messaging, although at a lower frequency (Ling and Baron, 2007). Moreover, technological changes, such as new input devices, are likely to have an impact on the language of such media (Thurlow, 2003).[3] An unsupervised approach, drawing on linguistic properties of creative word formations, has the potential to be adapted for normalization of text in other similar genres—such as Internet discussion forums—without the cost of developing a large training corpus. Moreover, normalization may be particularly important for such genres, given the

[1]The number of characters in a text message may also be limited to 160 characters, although this is not always the case.

[2]One notable exception is Fairon and Paumier (2006), although this resource is in French. The resource used in our study, Choudhury et al. (2007), is quite small in comparison.

[3]The rise of other technology, such as word prediction, could reduce the use of abbreviations, although it's not clear such technology is widely used (Grinter and Eldridge, 2001).

Proceedings of the NAACL HLT Workshop on Computational Approaches to Linguistic Creativity, pages 71–78,
Boulder, Colorado, June 2009.

Formation type	Freq.	Example
Stylistic variation	152	*betta* (*better*)
Subseq. abbrev.	111	*dng* (*doing*)
Prefix clipping	24	*hol* (*holiday*)
Syll. letter/digit	19	*neway* (*anyway*)
G-clipping	14	*talkin* (*talking*)
Phonetic abbrev.	12	*cuz* (*because*)
H-clipping	10	*ello* (*hello*)
Spelling error	5	*darliog* (*darling*)
Suffix clipping	4	*morrow* (*tomorrow*)
Punctuation	3	*b/day* (*birthday*)
Unclear	34	*mobs* (*mobile*)
Error	12	*gal* (**girl*)
Total	400	

Table 1: Frequency of texting forms in the development set by formation type.

need for applications such as translation and question answering.

We observe that many creative texting forms are the result of a small number of specific word formation processes. Rather than using a generic error model to capture all of them, we propose a mixture model in which each word formation process is modeled explicitly according to linguistic observations specific to that formation.

2 Analysis of Texting Forms

To better understand the creative processes present in texting language, we categorize the word formation process of each texting form in our development data, which consists of 400 texting forms paired with their standard forms.[4] Several iterations of categorization were done in order to determine sensible categories, and ensure categories were used consistently. Since this data is only to be used to guide the construction of our system, and not for formal evaluation, only one judge (a native English speaking author of this paper) categorized the expressions. The findings are presented in Table 1.

Stylistic variations, by far the most frequent category, exhibit non-standard spelling, such as representing sounds phonetically. Subsequence abbreviations, also very frequent, are composed of a subsequence of the graphemes in a standard form, often omitting vowels. These two formation types account for approximately 66% of our development data; the remaining formation types are much less frequent. Prefix clippings and suffix clippings consist of a prefix or suffix, respectively, of a standard form, and in some cases a diminutive ending; we also consider clippings which omit just a *g* or *h* from a standard form as they are rather frequent.[5] A single letter or digit can be used to represent a syllable; we refer to these as syllabic (syll.) letter/digit. Phonetic abbreviations are variants of clippings and subsequence abbreviations where some sounds in the standard form are represented phonetically. Several texting forms appear to be spelling errors; we took the layout of letters on cell phone keypads into account when making this judgement. The items that did not fit within the above texting form categories were marked as unclear. Finally, for some expressions the given standard form did not appear to be appropriate. For example, *girl* is not the standard form for the texting form *gal*; rather, *gal* is an English word that is a colloquial form of *girl*. Such cases were marked as errors.

No texting forms in our development data correspond to multiple standard form words, e.g., *wanna* for *want to*.[6] Since such forms are not present in our development data, we assume that a texting form always corresponds to a single standard form word.

It is important to note that some text forms have properties of multiple categories, e.g., *bak* (*back*) could be considered a stylistic variation or a subsequence abbreviation. In such cases, we simply attempt to assign the most appropriate category.

The design of our model for text message normalization, presented below, uses properties of the observed formation processes.

3 An Unsupervised Noisy Channel Model for Text Message Normalization

Let S be a sentence consisting of *standard forms* $s_1 s_2 ... s_n$; in this study the standard forms are reg-

[4] Most texting forms have a unique standard form; however, some have multiple standard forms, e.g., *will* and *well* can both be shortened to *wl*. In such cases we choose the category of the most frequent standard form; in the case of frequency ties we choose arbitrarily among the categories of the standard forms.

[5] Thurlow (2003) also observes an abundance of g-clippings.

[6] A small number of similar forms, however, appear with a single standard form word, and are therefore marked as errors.

ular English words. Let T be a sequence of *texting forms* $t_1 t_2 ... t_n$, which are the texting language realization of the standard forms, and may differ from the standard forms. Given a sequence of texting forms T, the challenge is then to determine the corresponding standard forms S.

Following Choudhury et al. (2007)—and various approaches to spelling error correction, such as, e.g., Mays et al. (1991)—we model text message normalization using a noisy channel. We want to find $\text{argmax}_S P(S|T)$. We apply Bayes rule and ignore the constant term $P(T)$, giving $\text{argmax}_S P(T|S)P(S)$. Making the independence assumption that each t_i depends only on s_i, and not on the context in which it occurs, as in Choudhury et al., we express $P(T|S)$ as a product of probabilities: $\text{argmax}_S \left(\prod_i P(t_i|s_i)\right) P(S)$.

We note in Section 2 that many texting forms are created through a small number of specific word formation processes. Rather than model each of these processes at once using a generic model for $P(t_i|s_i)$, as in Choudhury et al., we instead create several such models, each corresponding to one of the observed common word formation processes. We therefore rewrite $P(t_i|s_i)$ as $\sum_{wf} P(t_i|s_i, wf)P(wf)$ where wf is a word formation process, e.g., subsequence abbreviation. Since, like Choudhury et al., we focus on the word model, we simplify our model as below.

$$\text{argmax}_{s_i} \sum_{wf} P(t_i|s_i, wf)P(wf)P(s_i)$$

We next explain the components of the model, $P(t_i|s_i, wf)$, $P(wf)$, and $P(s_i)$, referred to as the word model, word formation prior, and language model, respectively.

3.1 Word Models

We now consider which of the word formation processes discussed in Section 2 should be captured with a word model $P(t_i|s_i, wf)$. We model stylistic variations and subsequence abbreviations simply due to their frequency. We also choose to model prefix clippings since this word formation process is common outside of text messaging (Kreidler, 1979; Algeo, 1991) and fairly frequent in our data. Although g-clippings and h-clippings are moderately frequent, we do not model them, as these very specific word formations are also (non-prototypical) subsequence abbreviations. We do not model syllabic letters and digits, or punctuation, explicitly; instead, we simply substitute digits with a graphemic representation (e.g., *4* is replaced by *for*), and remove punctuation, before applying the model. The other less frequent formations—phonetic abbreviations, spelling errors, and suffix clippings—are not modeled; we hypothesize that the similarity of these formation processes to those we do model will allow the system to perform reasonably well on them.

graphemes	w	i	th	ou	t
phonemes	w	ɪ	θ	au	t

Table 2: Grapheme–phoneme alignment for *without*.

3.1.1 Stylistic Variations

We propose a probabilistic version of edit-distance—referred to here as edit-probability—inspired by Brill and Moore (2000) to model $P(t_i|s_i, \text{stylistic variation})$. To compute edit-probability, we consider the probability of each edit operation—substitution, insertion, and deletion—instead of its cost, as in edit-distance. We then simply multiply the probabilities of edits as opposed to summing their costs.

In this version of edit-probability, we allow two-character edits. Ideally, we would compute the edit-probability of two strings as the sum of the edit-probability of each partitioning of those strings into one or two character segments. However, following Brill and Moore, we approximate this by the probability of the partition with maximum probability. This allows us to compute edit-probability using a simple adaptation of edit-distance, in which we consider edit operations spanning two characters at each cell in the chart maintained by the algorithm.

We then estimate two probabilities: $P(g_t|g_s, pos)$ is the probability of texting form grapheme g_t given standard form grapheme g_s at position pos, where pos is the beginning, middle, or end of the word; $P(h_t|p_s, h_s, pos)$ is the probability of texting form graphemes h_t given the standard form phonemes p_s and graphemes h_s at position pos. h_t, p_s, and h_s can be a single grapheme or phoneme, or a bigram.

We compute edit-probability between the graphemes of s_i and t_i. When filling each cell in the chart, we consider edit operations between segments of s_i and t_i of length 0–2, referred to as a and b, respectively. If a aligns with phonemes in s_i, we also consider those phonemes, p. In our lexicon, the graphemes and phonemes of each word are aligned according to the method of Jiampojamarn et al. (2007). For example, the alignment for *without* is given in Table 2. The probability of each edit operation is then determined by three properties—the length of a, whether a aligns with any phonemes in s_i, and if so, p—as shown below:

$|a|$= 0 or 1, not aligned w/ s_i phonemes: $P(b|a, pos)$

$|a|$= 2, not aligned w/ s_i phonemes: 0

$|a|$= 1 or 2, aligned w/ s_i phonemes: $P(b|p, a, pos)$

3.1.2 Subsequence Abbreviations

We model subsequence abbreviations according to the equation below:

$$P(t_i|s_i, \text{subseq abrv}) = \begin{cases} c & \text{if } t_i \text{ is a subseq of } s_i \\ 0 & \text{otherwise} \end{cases}$$

where c is a constant.

Note that this is similar to the error model for spelling correction presented by Mays et al. (1991), in which all words (in our terms, all s_i) within a specified edit-distance of the out-of-vocabulary word (t_i in our model) are given equal probability. The key difference is that in our formulation, we only consider standard forms for which the texting form is potentially a subsequence abbreviation.

In combination with the language model, $P(t_i|s_i, \text{subseq abbrev})$ assigns a non-zero probability to each standard form s_i for which t_i is a subsequence, according to the likelihood of s_i (under the language model). The models interact in this way since we expect a standard form to be recognizable relative to the other words for which t_i could be a subsequence abbreviation

3.1.3 Prefix Clippings

We model prefix clippings similarly to subsequence abbreviations.

$$P(t_i|s_i, \text{prefix clipping}) = \begin{cases} c & \text{if } t_i \text{ is possible} \\ & \text{pre. clip. of } s_i \\ 0 & \text{otherwise} \end{cases}$$

Kreidler (1979) observes that clippings tend to be mono-syllabic and end in a consonant. Furthermore, when they do end in a vowel, it is often of a regular form, such as *telly* for *television* and *breaky* for *breakfast*. We therefore only consider $P(t_i|s_i, \text{prefix clipping})$ if t_i is a prefix clipping according to the following heuristics: t_i is monosyllabic after stripping any word-final vowels, and subsequently removing duplicated word-final consonants (e.g, *telly* becomes *tel*, which is a candidate prefix clipping). If t_i is not a prefix clipping according to these criteria, $P(t_i|s_i)$ simply sums over all models except prefix clipping.

3.2 Word Formation Prior

Keeping with our goal of an unsupervised method, we estimate $P(wf)$ with a uniform distribution. We also consider estimating $P(wf)$ using maximum likelihood estimates (MLEs) from our observations in Section 2. This gives a model that is not fully unsupervised, since it relies on labelled training data. However, we consider this a lightly-supervised method, since it only requires an estimate of the frequency of the relevant word formation types, and not labelled texting form–standard form pairs.

3.3 Language Model

Choudhury et al. (2007) find that using a bigram language model estimated over a balanced corpus of English had a negative effect on their results compared with a unigram language model, which they attribute to the unique characteristics of text messaging that were not reflected in the corpus. We therefore use a unigram language model for $P(s_i)$, which also enables comparison with their results. Nevertheless, alternative language models, such as higher order ngram models, could easily be used in place of our unigram language model.

4 Materials and Methods

4.1 Datasets

We use the data provided by Choudhury et al. (2007) which consists of texting forms—extracted from a collection of 900 text messages—and their manually determined standard forms. Our development data—used for model development and discussed in Section 2—consists of the 400 texting form types that are not in Choudhury et al.'s held-out test set, and that are not the same as one of their standard forms. The test data consists of 1213 texting forms and their corresponding standard forms. A subset of 303 of these texting forms differ from their standard form.[7] This subset is the focus of this study, but we also report results on the full dataset.

4.2 Lexicon

We construct a lexicon of potential standard forms such that it contains most words that we expect to encounter in text messages, yet is not so large as to make it difficult to identify the correct standard form. Our subjective analysis of the standard forms in the development data is that they are frequent, non-specialized, words. To reflect this observation, we create a lexicon consisting of all single-word entries containing only alphabetic characters found in both the CELEX Lexical Database (Baayen et al., 1995) and the CMU Pronouncing Dictionary.[8] We remove all words of length one (except *a* and *I*) to avoid choosing, e.g., the letter *r* as the standard form for the texting form *r*. We further limit the lexicon to words in the 20K most frequent alphabetic unigrams, ignoring case, in the Web 1T 5-gram Corpus (Brants and Franz, 2006). The resulting lexicon contains approximately 14K words, and excludes only three of the standard forms—*cannot*, *email*, and *online*—for the 400 development texting forms.

4.3 Model Parameter Estimation

MLEs for $P(g_t|g_s, pos)$—needed to estimate $P(t_i|s_i, \text{stylistic variation})$—could be estimated from texting form–standard form pairs. However, since our system is unsupervised, no such data is available. We therefore assume that many texting forms, and other similar creative shortenings, occur on the web. We develop a number of character substitution rules, e.g., $s \Rightarrow z$, and use them to create hypothetical texting forms from standard words. We then compute MLEs for $P(g_t|g_s, pos)$ using the frequencies of these derived forms on the web.

We create the substitution rules by examining examples in the development data, considering fast speech variants and dialectal differences (e.g., voicing), and drawing on our intuition. The derived forms are produced by applying the substitution rules to the words in our lexicon. To avoid considering forms that are themselves words, we eliminate any form found in a list of approximately 480K words taken from SOWPODS[9] and the Moby Word Lists.[10] Finally, we obtain the frequency of the derived forms from the Web 1T 5-gram Corpus.

To estimate $P(h_t|p_s, h_s, pos)$, we first estimate two simpler distributions: $P(h_t|h_s, pos)$ and $P(h_t|p_s, pos)$. $P(h_t|h_s, pos)$ is estimated in the same manner as $P(g_t|g_s, pos)$, except that two character substitutions are allowed. $P(h_t|p_s, pos)$ is estimated from the frequency of p_s, and its alignment with h_t, in a version of CELEX in which the graphemic and phonemic representation of each word is many–many aligned using the method of Jiampojamarn et al. (2007).[11] $P(h_t|p_s, h_s, pos)$ is then an evenly-weighted linear combination of $P(h_t|h_s, pos)$ and $P(h_t|p_s, pos)$. Finally, we smooth each of $P(g_t|g_s, pos)$ and $P(h_t|p_s, h_s, pos)$ using add-alpha smoothing.

We set the constant c in our word models for subsequence abbreviations and prefix clippings such that $\sum_{s_i} P(t_i|s_i, wf)P(s_i) = 1$. We similarly normalize $P(t_i|s_i, \text{stylistic variation})P(s_i)$.

We use the frequency of unigrams (ignoring case) in the Web 1T 5-gram Corpus to estimate our language model. We expect the language of text messaging to be more similar to that found on the web than that in a balanced corpus of English.

4.4 Evaluation Metrics

To evaluate our system, we consider three accuracy metrics: in-top-1, in-top-10, and in-top-20.[12] In-top-n considers the system correct if a correct standard form is in the n most probable standard forms. The in-top-1 accuracy shows how well the system determines the correct standard form; the in-top-10

[7] Choudhury et al. report that this dataset contains 1228 texting forms. We found it to contain 1213 texting forms corresponding to 1228 standard forms (recall that a texting form may have multiple standard forms). There were similar inconsistencies with the subset of texting forms that differ from their standard forms. Nevertheless, we do not expect these small differences to have an appreciable effect on the results.

[8] `http://www.speech.cs.cmu.edu/cgi-bin/cmudict`

[9] `http://en.wikipedia.org/wiki/SOWPODS`

[10] `http://icon.shef.ac.uk/Moby/`

[11] We are very grateful to Sittichai Jiampojamarn for providing this alignment.

[12] These are the same metrics used by Choudhury et al. (2007), although we refer to them by different names.

Model	% accuracy		
	Top-1	Top-10	Top-20
Uniform	59.4	83.8	87.8
MLE	55.4	84.2	86.5
Choudhury et al.	59.9	84.3	88.7

Table 3: % in-top-1, in-top-10, and in-top-20 accuracy on test data using both estimates for $P(wf)$. The results reported by Choudhury et al. (2007) are also shown.

and in-top-20 accuracies may be indicative of the usefulness of the output of our system in other tasks which could exploit a ranked list of standard forms, such as machine translation.

5 Results and Discussion

In Table 3 we report the results of our system using both the uniform estimate and the MLE of $P(wf)$. Note that there is no meaningful random baseline to compare against here; randomly ordering the 14K words in our lexicon gives very low accuracy. The results using the uniform estimate of $P(wf)$—a fully unsupervised system—are very similar to the supervised results of Choudhury et al. (2007). Surprisingly, when we estimate $P(wf)$ using MLEs from the development data—resulting in a lightly-supervised system—the results are slightly worse than when using the uniform estimate of this probability. Moreover, we observe the same trend on development data where we expect to have an accurate estimate of $P(wf)$ (results not shown). We hypothesize that the ambiguity of the categories of text forms (see Section 2) results in poor MLEs for $P(wf)$, thus making a uniform distribution, and hence fully-unsupervised approach, more appropriate.

Results by Formation Type We now consider in-top-1 accuracy for each word formation type, in Table 4. We show results for the same word formation processes as in Table 1, except for h-clippings and punctuation, as no words of these categories are present in the test data. We present results using the same experimental setup as before with a uniform estimate of $P(wf)$ (All), and using just the model corresponding to the word formation process (Specific), where applicable.[13]

[13]In this case our model then becomes, for each word formation process wf, $\text{argmax}_{s_i} P(t_i|s_i, wf)P(s_i)$.

Formation type	Freq.	% in-top-1 acc.	
	$n = 303$	Specific	All
Stylistic variation	121	62.8	67.8
Subseq. abbrev.	65	56.9	46.2
Prefix clipping	25	44.0	20.0
G-clipping	56	-	91.1
Syll. letter/digit	16	-	50.0
Unclear	12	-	0.0
Spelling error	5	-	80.0
Suffix clipping	1	-	0.0
Phonetic abbrev.	1	-	0.0
Error	1	-	0.0

Table 4: Frequency (Freq.), and % in-top-1 accuracy using the formation-specific model where applicable (Specific) and all models (All) with a uniform estimate for $P(wf)$, presented by formation type.

We first examine the top panel of Table 3 where we compare the performance on each word formation type for both experimental conditions (Specific and All). We first note that the performance using the formation-specific model on subsequence abbreviations and prefix clippings is better than that of the overall model. This is unsurprising since we expect that when we know a texting form's formation process, and invoke a corresponding specific model, our system should outperform a model designed to handle a range of formation types. However, this is not the case for stylistic variations; here the overall model performs better than the specific model. We observed in Section 2 that some texting forms do not fit neatly into our categorization scheme; indeed, many stylistic variations are also analyzable as subsequence abbreviations. Therefore, the subsequence abbreviation model may benefit normalization of stylistic variations. This model, used in isolation on stylistic variations, gives an in-top-1 accuracy of 33.1%, indicating that this may be the case.

Comparing the performance of the individual word models on only word types that they were designed for (column Specific in Table 4), we see that the prefix clipping model is by far the lowest, indicating that in the future we should consider ways of improving this word model. One possibility is to incorporate phonemic knowledge. For example, both *friday* and *friend* have the same probability under $P(t_i|s_i, \text{prefix clipping})$ for the texting form *fri*, which has the standard form *friday* in our data. (The language model, however, does distinguish between these forms.) However, if we consider the phonemic representations of these words, *friday* might emerge as more likely. Syllable structure information may also be useful, as we hypothesize that clippings will tend to be formed by truncating a word at a syllable boundary. We may similarly be able to improve our estimate of $P(t_i|s_i, \text{subseq. abrrev.})$. For example, both *text* and *taxation* have the same probability under this distribution, but intuitively *text*, the correct standard form in our data, seems more likely. We could incorporate knowledge about the likelihood of omitting specific characters, as in Choudhury et al. (2007), to improve this estimate.

We now examine the lower panel of Table 4, in which we consider the performance of the overall model on the word formation types that are not explicitly modeled. The very high accuracy on g-clippings indicates that since these forms are also a type of subsequence abbreviation, we do not need to construct a separate model for them. We in fact also conducted experiments in which g-clippings and h-clippings were modeled explicitly, but found these extra models to have little effect on the results.

Recall from Section 3.1 our hypothesis that suffix clippings, spelling errors, and phonetic abbreviations have common properties with formation types that we do model, and therefore the system will perform reasonably well on them. Here we find preliminary evidence to support this hypothesis as the accuracy on these three word formation types (combined) is 57.1%. However, we must interpret this result cautiously as it only considers seven expressions. On the syllabic letter and digit texting forms the accuracy is 50.0%, indicating that our heuristic to replace digits in texting forms with an orthographic representation is reasonable.

The performance on types of expressions that we did not consider when designing the system—unclear and error—is very poor. However, this has little impact on the overall performance as these expressions are rather infrequent.

Results by Model We now consider in-top-1 accuracy using each model on the 303 test expressions; results are shown in Table 5. No model on its own gives results comparable to those of the overall model (59.4%, see Table 3). This indicates that the overall model successfully combines information from the specific word formation models.

Model	% in-top-1 accuracy
Stylistic variation	51.8
Subseq. Abbrev.	44.2
Prefix clipping	10.6

Table 5: % in-top-1 accuracy on the 303 test expressions using each model individually.

Each model used on its own gives an accuracy greater than the proportion of expressions of the word formation type for which the model was designed (compare accuracies in Table 5 to the number of expressions of the corresponding word formation type in the test data in Table 4). As we note in Section 2, the distinctions between the word formation types are not sharp; these results show that the shared properties of word formation types enable a model for a specific formation type to infer the standard form of texting forms of other formation types.

All Unseen Data Until now we have discussed results on our test data of 303 texting forms which differ from their standard forms. We now consider the performance of our system on all 1213 unseen texting forms, 910 of which are identical to their standard form. Since our model was not designed with such expressions in mind, we slightly adapt it for this new task; if t_i is in our lexicon, we return that form as s_i, otherwise we apply our model as usual, using the uniform estimate of $P(wf)$. This gives an in-top-1 accuracy of 88.2%, which is very similar to the results of Choudhury et al. (2007) on this data of 89.1%. Note, however, that Choudhury et al. only report results on this dataset using a uniform language model;[14] since we use a unigram language model, it is difficult to draw firm conclusions about the performance of our system relative to theirs.

6 Related Work

Aw et al. (2006) model text message normalization as translation from the texting language into the

[14]Choudhury et al. do use a unigram language model for their experiments on the 303 texting forms which differ from their standard forms (see Section 3.3).

standard language. Kobus et al. (2008) incorporate ideas from both machine translation and automatic speech recognition for text message normalization. However, both of these approaches are supervised, and have only limited means for normalizing texting forms that do not occur in the training data.

Our work, like that of Choudhury et al. (2007), can be viewed as a noisy-channel model for spelling error correction (e.g., Mays et al., 1991; Brill and Moore, 2000), in which texting forms are seen as a kind of spelling error. Furthermore, like our approach to text message normalization, approaches to spelling correction have incorporated phonemic information (Toutanova and Moore, 2002).

The word model of the supervised approach of Choudhury et al. consists of hidden Markov models, which capture properties of texting language similar to those of our stylistic variation model. We propose multiple word models—corresponding to frequent texting language formation processes—and an unsupervised method for parameter estimation.

7 Conclusions

We analyze a sample of texting forms to determine frequent word formation processes in creative texting language. Drawing on these observations, we construct an unsupervised noisy-channel model for text message normalization. On an unseen test set of 303 texting forms that differ from their standard form, our model achieves 59% accuracy, which is on par with that obtained by the supervised approach of Choudhury et al. (2007) on the same data.

More research is required to determine the impact of our normalization method on the performance of a system that further processes the resulting text. In the future, we intend to improve our word models by incorporating additional linguistic knowledge, such as information about syllable structure. Since context likely plays a role in human interpretation of texting forms, we also intend to examine the performance of higher order ngram language models.

Acknowledgements

This work is financially supported by the Natural Sciences and Engineering Research Council of Canada, the University of Toronto, and the Dictionary Society of North America.

References

John Algeo, editor. 1991. *Fifty Years Among the New Words*. Cambridge University Press, Cambridge.

AiTi Aw, Min Zhang, Juan Xiao, and Jian Su. 2006. A phrase-based statistical model for SMS text normalization. In *Proc. of the COLING/ACL 2006 Main Conference Poster Sessions*, pages 33–40. Sydney.

R.H. Baayen, R. Piepenbrock, and L. Gulikers. 1995. The CELEX Lexical Database (release 2). Linguistic Data Consortium, University of Pennsylvania.

Thorsten Brants and Alex Franz. 2006. Web 1T 5-gram Corpus version 1.1.

Eric Brill and Robert C. Moore. 2000. An improved error model for noisy channel spelling correction. In *Proceedings of ACL 2000*, pages 286–293. Hong Kong.

Monojit Choudhury, Rahul Saraf, Vijit Jain, Animesh Mukherjee, Sudeshna Sarkar, and Anupam Basu. 2007. Investigation and modeling of the structure of texting language. *International Journal of Document Analysis and Recognition*, 10(3/4):157–174.

Cédrick Fairon and Sébastien Paumier. 2006. A translated corpus of 30,000 French SMS. In *Proceedings of LREC 2006*. Genoa, Italy.

Rebecca E. Grinter and Margery A. Eldridge. 2001. y do tngrs luv 2 txt msg. In *Proceedings of the 7th European Conf. on Computer-Supported Cooperative Work (ECSCW '01)*, pages 219–238. Bonn, Germany.

Sittichai Jiampojamarn, Gregorz Kondrak, and Tarek Sherif. 2007. Applying many-to-many alignments and hidden markov models to letter-to-phoneme conversion. In *Proc. of NAACL-HLT 2007*, pages 372–379. Rochester, NY.

Catherine Kobus, François Yvon, and Géraldine Damnati. 2008. Normalizing SMS: are two metaphors better than one? In *Proc. of the 22nd Int. Conf. on Computational Linguistics*, pp. 441–448. Manchester.

Charles W. Kreidler. 1979. Creating new words by shortening. *English Linguistics*, 13:24–36.

Rich Ling and Naomi S. Baron. 2007. Text messaging and IM: Linguistic comparison of American college data. *Journal of Language and Social Psychology*, 26:291–98.

Eric Mays, Fred J. Damerau, and Robert L. Mercer. 1991. Context based spelling correction. *Information Processing and Management*, 27(5):517–522.

Richard Sproat, Alan W. Black, Stanley Chen, Shankar Kumar, Mari Ostendorf, and Christopher Richards. 2001. Normalization of non-standard words. *Computer Speech and Language*, 15:287–333.

Crispin Thurlow. 2003. Generation txt? The sociolinguistics of young people's text-messaging. *Discourse Analysis Online*, 1(1).

Kristina Toutanova and Robert C. Moore. 2002. Pronunciation modeling for improved spelling correction. In *Proc. of ACL 2002*, pages 144–151. Philadelphia.

Morphological Productivity Rankings of Complex Adjectives

Stefano Vegnaduzzo
Ask.com
Oakland, CA 94607, USA
svegnaduzzo@ask.com

Abstract

This paper investigates a little-studied class of adjectives that we refer to as 'complex adjectives', i.e., operationally, adjectives constituted of at least two word tokens separated by a hyphen. We study the properties of these adjectives using two very large text collections: a portion of Wikipedia and a Web corpus. We consider three corpus-based measures of morphological productivity, and we investigate how productivity rankings based on them correlate with each other under different conditions, thus providing different angles both on the morphological productivity of complex adjectives, and on the productivity measures themselves.

1 Introduction

Adjectives as a syntactic category have received relatively scarce attention in theoretical and computational linguistics, at least when compared to noun and verbs. Within the class of adjectives there is a particular group that has not received much specific attention. These are the adjectives that can be operationally defined by the fact that in the orthography they are constituted by at least two tokens separated by a hyphen. Examples include: *left-wing politician*, *best-selling book*, *part-time job*, *large-scale experiment*. In this paper we will focus the analysis on 2-item adjectives; however the class includes several examples with more than two items: *day-to-day, tongue-in-cheek, up-and-coming, state-of-the-art, pay-as-you-go, all-you-can-eat,* etc.

We refer to these adjectives as 'complex adjectives'. They allow several mechanisms for the generation of new linguistic expressions which are spread along a continuum that goes from full productivity to lexicalized forms. Treating complex adjective formation as a morphological process allows us to characterize them in the light of the notion of morphological productivity.

Morphological productivity falls within the domain of how the broad notion of creativity is realized in language, by providing mechanisms for generating new words that are *unintentional*, *unlimited* and *regular* (Evert and Lüdeling 2001).

Previous work has typically considered complex adjectives only in the context of tokenization and generally low-level text processing, without specific focus on the class *per se*. Moilanen and Pulman (2008) identify polarity markers in certain complex adjectives for the purpose for assigning sentiment polarities to unknown words (*well-built* is positive, *rat-infested* is negative).

Highly productive classes like complex adjectives are problematic for computational lexicons in that they bring about a large number of unknown words. A typology of complex adjectives is important to support computational lexicons and the NLP applications based on them, for example by listing out the patterns (as defined in section 3) that complex adjectives are based on.

2 Data

The analysis presented here is based on two large text collections. The first is a portion of Wikipedia, consisting of about 250 million tokens. The second collection is a Web corpus specifically built for NLP applications targeted at adjectives, consisting of about 290 million tokens (after some reasonable clean-up process). The list of all adjectives in WordNet[1] was used as a seed list. Each seed adjective was sent as a query to the Yahoo search engine

[1] http://wordnet.princeton.edu.

Proceedings of the NAACL HLT Workshop on Computational Approaches to Linguistic Creativity, pages 79–86,
Boulder, Colorado, June 2009.

BOSS API[2]. For all the 1000 (the maximum allowed by the API) returned web results, each URL was used to fetch the corresponding web page, and the full text of the web page was processed for addition to the corpus. Both corpora were POS-tagged using the Stanford POS tagger[3] (reported accuracy is about 97%). Using such tagger that was trained on the Penn Treebank makes it easy to identify complex adjectives, since the Penn Treebank tagging guidelines explicitly prescribe that hyphenated compounds used as modifiers should be tagged as adjectives (JJ).

The two corpora give a slightly different view on the linguistic behavior of adjectives. The Wikipedia corpus is intended to provide a picture of adjective distribution in a large and relatively homogenous collection of current English text. The Web corpus is intended to bias the collection in the direction of making sure that at least for the WordNet seed adjectives a large number of instances are present even for adjectives that would have otherwise a very low frequency in a properly balanced corpus.

Throughout the paper we will use the Wikipedia corpus as the main data collection for the presentation of the analysis, and we will use the Web corpus as a validation set, to assess the stability and reliability of the results obtained on the Wikipedia corpus.

3 Theoretical background

We partition the orthographically defined class of complex adjectives in morphological categories defined by a variable part and a base generator. For example 'X-free' is a morphological category that specifies that the base generator *-free* can be combined with other words to form complex adjectives such as *risk-free*, *toll-free*, *gluten-free*, etc. The two corpora are used to analyze and quantify how different degrees of linguistic creativity are exhibited by different classes of complex adjectives. We will show that this yields a ranking of complex adjective types along a continuum going from high productivity to lexicalized forms. Specifically, we characterize the linguistic creativity of complex adjectives through three distinct and complementary measures of morphological productivity, following Baayen (1993, 2006) and his notation: realized productivity, expanding productivity, and potential productivity. Now, Evert and Lüdeling (2001) show that, in the general case, automatic pre-processing of text corpora with current morphological analyzers yields results that are too noisy for Baayen's measure of productivity to be reliable. The fact that complex adjectives are orthographically defined by the presence of the hyphen and the components are easy to separate eliminates some of those text-processing problems. By choice, we take at face value the morphological parse provided by the hyphen, and therefore we do not run into situations where the phonotactics obscures the morphological analysis (e.g., *lady* vs. *ladies*), affix ordering (*undoable*), accidental string identity (*restaurant* does not instantiate the prefix *re-*), and words generated by creative rather then morphological productive processes (*youtube*). Relying on the orthographical hyphen eases the problems of automatic morphological pre-processing and makes this a particularly good domain for using Baayen's measures.

Realized productivity is defined as V=V(C,N), the number of word types (as opposed to word tokens) of morphological category C in a corpus of N tokens. The intuition behind this measure is that it expresses the sheer size of a morphological category within a particular corpus.

Expanding productivity is defined as P* = V(1,C,N)/V(1,N), where V(1,C,N) is the number of words of category C that occur only once in a corpus of N tokens, and V(1,N) is the number of words of *any* category that occur only once in a corpus of N tokens. This measure expresses the contribution of the morphological category C to the growth rate of the total vocabulary. The underlying intuition is that a morphologically productive category contributes to the growth rate of the vocabulary of a language, and vocabulary growth rate can be estimated by the number of *hapax legomena* (words with frequency 1) in a sufficiently large corpus. *Hapax legomena* in turn are taken to be good estimators of novel linguistic forms.

Potential productivity is defined as P = V(1,C,N)/N(C), where N(C) is the total number of tokens in the corpus for a given category C. This measure expresses the growth rate of the vocabulary of the category C itself. In other words, it expresses the ease with which a category can be applied to new words.

[2] http://developer.yahoo.com/search/boss.

[3] http://nlp.stanford.edu/software/tagger.shtml.

These three measures are complementary, in that they capture different aspects of morphological productivity that can possibly be at odds with each other (Baayen 2006).

4 Analysis

At the highest level the two POS-tagged corpora allow us to compare the distribution of complex adjectives with respect to other major syntactic categories. In the context of morphological productivity, the *vocabulary* of a morphological process is the number of types that the process can potentially generate. If we understand complex adjective formation as a morphological process, we can obtain their general vocabulary growth curve by plotting the number of types against the number of tokens in a corpus. Figure 1 shows vocabulary growth curves for nouns, verbs, adjectives and their hyphenated counterparts for the Wikipedia corpus.

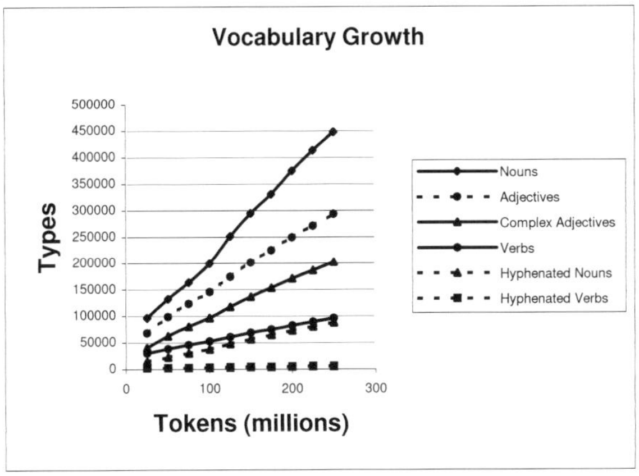

Figure 1. Wikipedia vocabulary growth.

Complex adjectives exhibit a surprisingly high growth rate, which at 250M tokens still doesn't tend to converge. The number of types corresponding to the final corpus size can be interpreted as an estimate of the realized productivity of complex adjectives as a whole class.

We focus the analysis on two-item adjectives, i.e., those of the form 'A-B' such as *cat-like*.

We describe first the data collection process. We process each POS-tagged corpus from beginning to end, and for each complex adjective (defined by the tag JJ and the presence of a hyphen), we generate all the possible categories by replacing in turn each item with a variable. So *cat-like* yields the two possible categories 'cat-X' and 'X-like'; *day-to-day* yields 'X-to-day', 'day-X-day', 'day-to-X' and the special case 'X-to-X', where the two side items are identical. Then for each category we count the number of types in that category and the number of tokens for each type, including *hapax legomena*. So the category 'X-like' includes the types *dog-like, cat-like, mouse-like,* etc., and each type is instantiated by a certain number of tokens (including types instantiated by exactly 1 token). In this way we obtain the basic counts that are needed to compute the three measures of productivity introduced above. Once these measures are obtained, all morphological categories (such as 'X-like') can be sorted into three productivity rankings corresponding to the three measures.

Of the three measures, realized and expanding productivity are by design directly dependent on corpus size, whereas potential productivity is dependent on the relative ratio of morphological categories but not directly on corpus size. This entails that, especially for the first two measures, productivity rankings obtained on a corpus of a particular size are not necessarily significant, in that productivity rankings obtained on corpora of different sizes could be different.

Realized and expanding productivity are affected in different ways by corpus size. Everything else being equal, realized productivity estimates will be more reliable with larger corpora. Expanding productivity is based on the assumption that *hapax legomena* (i.e., rare words with the lowest frequency in a corpus) are good estimators of morphological productivity. Rare words include various subtypes: misspellings, proper names, foreign words, words from different registers or genres than those represented in the corpus, new words generated by non-regular creative processes, and new words generated by morphologically productive processes. In a 'small' corpus, *hapax legomena* will include many words that do not fall in any of categories above, but just happen to be relatively uncommon words. As corpus size increases, uncommon words have a chance to occur more often, and the proportion of true morphological neologisms among hapaxes increases.

Given the dependency on corpus size, the question arises of how reliable productivity rankings are that haven been obtained for a specific corpus. In order to assess rankings reliability, we divided both the Wikipedia and Web corpus into 20 chunks of the same size, and then we added them up one after the other, essentially obtaining 20 corpora of increasing size for each of the two original text collections. Finally for each intermediate corpus we recomputed the productivity measures and rankings based on them. At this point we can measure the stability of the final productivity ranking for a given corpus by comparing it with each of the intermediate rankings using Spearman's rank correlation coefficient.

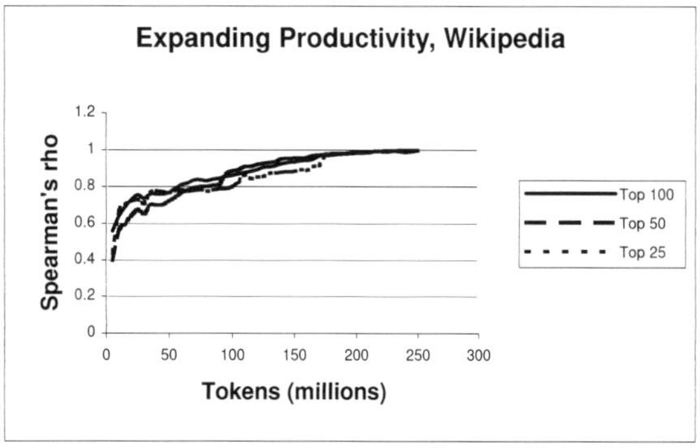

Figure 2. Expanding productivity stability, Wikipedia

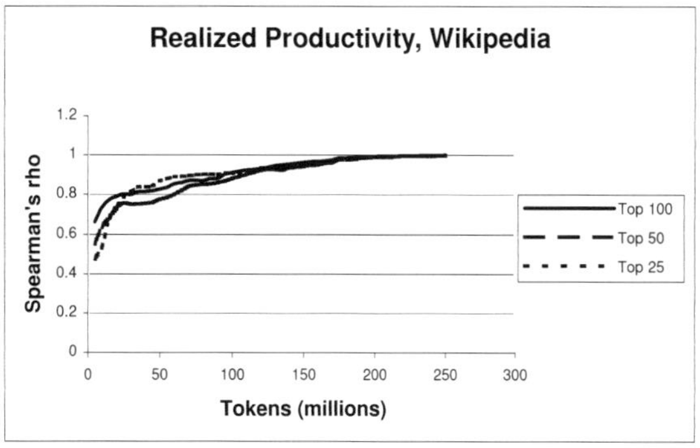

Figure 3. Realized productivity stability, Wikipedia

Plotting corpus size against Spearman's ρ coefficient reveals that rankings for realized and expanding productivity in both the Wikipedia corpus and the Web corpus are very stable. For example, for expanding productivity in the Wikipedia corpus the ranking of the top 20 complex adjectives does not change any more after the first 5M corpus chunk. Figures 2 and 3 show how Spearman's coefficient between the full Wikipedia corpus and each of the 19 sub-corpora varies as a function of corpus size for the top 25, 50 and 100 adjectives. Curves for the Web corpus are similar.

As corpus size continues to increase, a larger and larger portion of the rankings stabilizes, suggesting that realized and expanding productivity capture substantial properties of the language of which the Wikipedia corpus and the Web corpus are respectively representative.

The dependency of productivity rankings on a specific corpus is a reminder that another important factor that has been observed to affect linguistic creativity as expressed by morphological productivity is register and genre variation. In this context we are using two corpora that are representative of different types of language, and could therefore have substantially different rankings. However, it turns out that Spearman's rank correlation between the full size of the Wikipedia and Web corpus for both realized and expanding productivity rankings is quite strong (see Table 1).

Rankings	Realized	Expanding
Top 5	1	0.9
Top 10	0.91515	0.94545
Top 20	0.85939	0.70601
Top 25	0.80346	0.665
Top 50	0.64998	0.58909
Top 100	0.64309	0.62732

Table 1: Spearman's correlation between productivity rankings for Wikipedia and Web corpus

The high Spearman's correlation values confirm the stability of reliability of realized and expanding productivity rankings across different corpora.

The next question is to what extent productivity rankings based on different measures correlate with each other. We consider first the relationship between realized and expanding productivity. The two notions focus by design on different aspects of morphological productivity: realized productivity is oriented towards the 'present': a morphological process may be common to many existing word types, but might have no ability to be applied to generate new words. Baayen (1993) also refers to it as 'extent of use'. Expanding productivity is intended to assess the rate at which a morphological process is expanding in the language. A morphological process may be able to spread quickly in terms of its ability to generate new words, and yet not be very common in the general language.

In order to quantify the degree of agreement between realized and expanding productivity for complex adjectives we computed Spearman's rank correlation coefficient between pairs of productivity rankings (for the top 100 adjectives) at each of the intermediate corpus sizes described above, for both the Wikipedia and Web corpus.

Figure 4 shows that for complex adjectives in the Wikipedia corpus (the graph is similar for the

Web corpus) the correlation between realized and expanding productivity is very strong, the value of ρ being constantly around 0.9 from the very beginning, therefore independently of corpus size. We can interpret this fact as suggesting that the class of complex adjectives is overall a dynamic class, in the sense that its members, even the most established (i.e., those with high realized productivity), continue to expand in the language and to allow speakers to easily create new words. Table 2 shows the top 20 complex adjectives for both realized and expanding productivity.

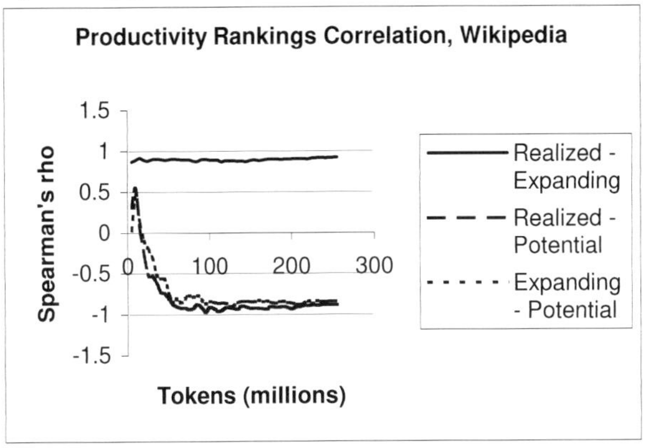

Figure 4: Productivity Rankings Correlation for the Wikipedia corpus, top 100 complex adjectives.

Figure 4 also shows that Spearman's correlation of both realized and expanding productivity with respect to potential productivity is significantly weaker. It is important to note that in the case of potential productivity we arbitrarily chose to require that the total number of tokens in the corpus for a given morphological category (the denominator of the potential productivity formula) be at least 100. We will show later that choosing a high value, (such as 100) for this factor indeed increases the strength of the correlation between potential productivity and the other two types. With low values the correlation coefficient is closer or equal to –1.

We are now going to discuss how rankings for potential productivity (and, consequently, their degree of correlation with realized and expanding productivity) vary with the choice of the minimum threshold for the denominator value of the formula $P = V(1,C,N)/N(C)$.

In general the situation for potential productivity is quite a different. On one hand it doesn't depend directly on corpus size like the other two measures. On the other hand, its definition as the ratio of *hapax legomena* of a morphological category with respect to all tokens of that category makes it susceptible to frequency effects. If a corpus is too small or a morphological category is fairly rare this measure will overestimate the productivity of low frequency items. In the extreme case, a morphological category instantiated by exactly one type that occurs exactly once in the corpus will get a potential productivity value of 1, the highest possible.

Wikipedia productivity rankings			
Realized		Expanding	
1.non-X	2.53E-05	1.non-X	0.014388
2.X-based	1.63E-05	2.X-based	0.009694
3.X-like	1.49E-05	3.X-like	0.00943
4.anti-X	9.59E-06	4.anti-X	0.005875
5.pre-X	8.00E-06	5.pre-X	0.005001
6.X-style	6.58E-06	6.X-style	0.004809
7.X-related	6.38E-06	7.X-related	0.004395
8.X-type	5.36E-06	8.X-type	0.004386
9.post-X	5.35E-06	9.post-X	0.003443
10.self-X	4.23E-06	10.then-X	0.002381
11.semi-X	3.78E-06	11.semi-X	0.00224
12.multi-X	3.73E-06	12.self-X	0.002197
13.re-X	3.64E-06	13.ex-X	0.002116
14.then-X	3.42E-06	14.X-oriented	0.002082
15.pro-X	3.41E-06	15.re-X	0.002078
16.X-oriented	3.22E-06	16.pro-X	0.002022
17.ex-X	2.97E-06	17.un-X	0.001937
18.single-X	2.95E-06	18.multi-X	0.001852
19.two-X	2.90E-06	19.X-only	0.001813
20.high-X	2.78E-06	20.half-X	0.001604

Table 2: Wikipedia rankings for realized and expanding productivity.

The notion of potential productivity is often used, especially in Baayen's work, in a deductive setting: typically a relatively small number of derivational morphemes is selected, and an in-depth analysis is carried out, for example assessing intuitive productivity rankings against those obtained from corpus statistics. The goal is often to achieve high explanatory depth, integrating for example mental processing and socio-linguistic factors. In this context the target morphemes are typically fairly common in the language, and a sufficiently large corpus will provide a sufficiently large sample of each morphological category so that the frequency effects mentioned above are negligible.

On the other hand, the setting of the work presented in this paper is inductive in nature, in that, by capitalizing on the easy identification of complex adjectives thanks to the orthography, we aim at an exploratory characterization of a large class of morphological categories.

In practice, in the large-scale scale setting of the present work, frequency effects have a significant consequence on how potential productivity values are computed, and on the rankings that derive from them. For the Wikipedia corpus 49.36% (40223 out of 81481) of the complex adjective morphological categories have only 1 type with 1 token. For example the category 'X-distracted' (based on a past participle like the much more common category 'X-controlled', which has types such as *computer-controlled*, *electronically-controlled*, etc.) has only the type *easily-distracted*, which occurs only once in the corpus. By blindly applying the formula V(1,C,N)/N(C), we would conclude that complex adjectives that occur only once have the highest potential productivity (1/1=1), which runs counter to intuition.

One option here would be to try to extrapolate the value of the potential productivity measure with respect to larger corpus sizes, using statistical models (LNRE models, for 'Large Number of Rare Events' models) that are appropriate for the Zipfian properties of word frequency distributions, as done in Baayen (2001). However, Evert and Lüdeling (2001) provide a detailed analysis of the specific problems encountered in automatic preprocessing of large amounts of textual data, and conclude that in the general case automatic tools deliver results that are too noisy to yield reliable extrapolations of potential productivity measures.

For this reason we choose instead to focus on the two existing corpora and explore how potential productivity measures vary when constraints are imposed on the minimum number of tokens that instantiate the morphological category whose potential productivity we want to measure.

We compute potential productivity measures for the full Wikipedia corpus by setting a minimum threshold for the number of tokens that instantiate morphological categories, starting from 0 (no constraint) and proceeding in increments of 5 up to 100. For each threshold level we derive productivity rankings.

We consider first a variant on the notion of stability of the productivity ranking by computing Spearman's rank correlation between the ranking obtained when setting the minimum threshold value to 100 and each of the rankings obtained at the 5-increment interval, shown in Figure 5.

Figure 5 visualizes how frequency effects impact the stability of potential productivity rankings. When the minimum threshold is very low (0 or the first few increments above 0), productivity rankings are extremely unstable, to the point that the correlation is negative with respect to the final ranking based on the highest threshold value (100). This is due to the fact that at low thresholds many categories have productivity 1, since all the types for those categories are instantiated by exactly 1 token. Because no attempt is made to add a second sort order (which could be for example the number of types) to the productivity value, the top portion of the ranking is basically random, since there can be hundreds of categories with productivity 1. However, as the constraint on the minimum threshold becomes increasingly stronger, rankings tend to stabilize. For the last few thresholds values the rankings at the highest positions are very similar. For the threshold value 100 the ranking is shown in Table 3.

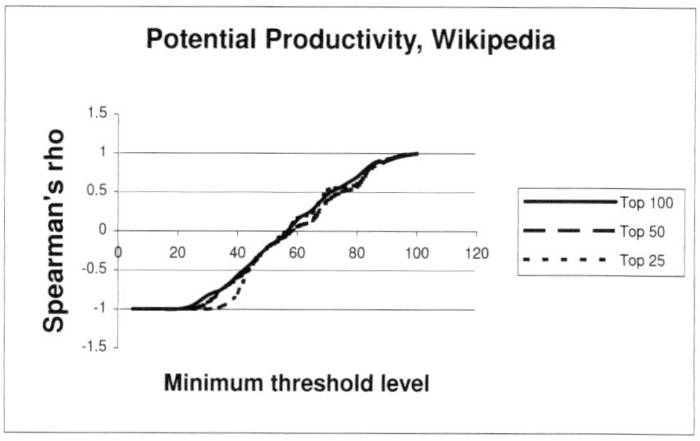

Figure 5: Potential productivity stability as a function of threshold level, on the Wikipedia corpus.

A simple visual comparison between Table 3 and Table 2 shows that complex adjectives with the highest potential productivity are very different from those with the highest realized and expanding productivity.

The main qualitative impression is that adjectives with high potential productivity seem to exemplify patterns that are grammatically and compositionally very transparent. There are many categories based on adverbs ('partially-X') and past participles ('X-obsessed'). These patterns could indeed be written out as two separate words (with a space instead of the hyphen) forming a syntactic adjective phrase. On the other hand, adjectives with high realized and expanding productivity seem to exemplify patterns that tend towards lexicalization. Patterns like 'anti-X', 'pre-X', 'post-X', 're-X', 'semi-X', 'multi-X' could be indeed written out as a single word that is syntactically an adjective[4]. In other words, we could suggest that potential productivity might correlate with the early stages of a lexicalization process, and realized and expanding productivity might correlate with the more advanced ones. In this paper we will not elaborate this suggestion any further, and leave it for future work.

Wikipedia potential productivity rankings			
1.X-ish	0.735849	11.X-wearing	0.47619
2.almost-X	0.649123	12.X-penned	0.451327
3.easily-X	0.613208	13.un-X	0.451001
4.already-X	0.581522	14.X-centric	0.443662
5.X-obsessed	0.529412	15.nearly-X	0.442308
6.partially-X	0.526786	16.X-kilometer	0.441176
7.X-focused	0.508197	17.X-associated	0.437229
8.X-less	0.48913	18.X-capable	0.434066
9.X-inspired	0.48537	19.previously-X	0.427907
10.micro-X	0.481081	20.mini-X	0.42449

Table 3: Potential productivity rankings for the Wikipedia corpus, based the threshold value 100.

We consider now another angle of the relationship between potential productivity on one hand and realized and expanding productivity on the other. Using the same rankings obtained by varying minimum threshold for the number of tokens that instantiate morphological categories, we calculate the Spearman's rank correlation of each potential productivity ranking at every increment interval with respect to correspondent rankings for realized and expanding productivity on the full Wikipedia corpus.

Figure 6 shows that no matter how we set the minimum threshold level, rankings for potential productivity appear to be significantly different with respect to the rankings for realized and expanding productivity, and at least for the size of the Wikipedia corpus the correlation remains strongly negative.

A slight upward trend is detectable though, and this corresponds to the fact that setting the minimum threshold value to 100 increases somewhat the strength of the correlation between potential productivity and the other two types as corpus size increases (as we discussed in regard to Figure 4). Indeed, the values of ρ at the rightmost edge of the respective curves in Figures 4 and 6 are the same, since they corresponds to the rank correlation among productivity rankings for the full Wikipedia corpus with minimum threshold value set to 100. We can interpret this slight upward trend as a consequence of the mitigation of frequency effects (which typically affect potential productivity rankings, as discussed above) brought about by the raising of the minimum threshold level.

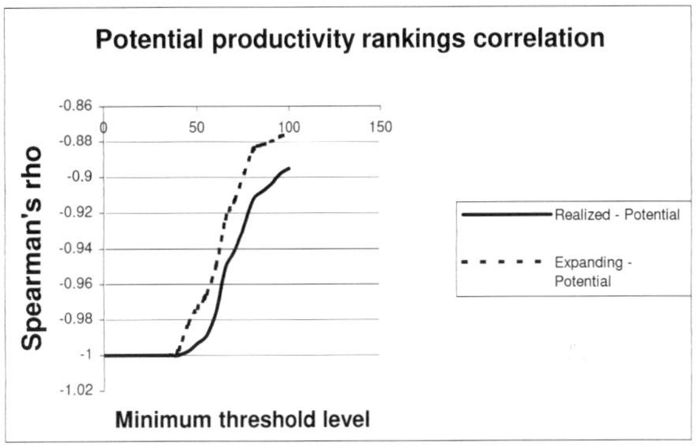

Figure 6. Potential productivity rankings correlation as a function of minimum threshold level in Wikipedia

This behavior highlights the fact that, compared to the other two measures, potential productivity focuses by design on a significantly different facet of the notion of morphological productivity. Potential productivity attempts to capture in a simple formula the ability of a morphological category to *continue* to enable speakers to generate new words. It is intended to characterize a morphological category in terms of the number of potential words that can still be created in that category. Thus it could be the case that a morphological category is well established in the language (realized productivity) and is expanding (expanding productivity), but does not have much potential for further expansion (potential productivity).

In order to explore these scenarios, we compare the three measures for the specific morphological pattern 'non-X', which has both the highest realized and expanding productivity for all the 19 intermediate corpus slices, and for the full corpus size (both for the Wikipedia corpus and for the Web corpus). On the Wikipedia full corpus this category yields 6444 distinct types for a total of 47489 tokens (including 4496 *hapax legomena*), ranging from very frequent types such as *non-profit* (2268 tokens), *non-existent* (619 tokens),

[4] The occurrence of single orthographic word variant can be construed as a signal of lexicalization for complex adjectives, but not in the general case, as demonstrated by the the orthographic integrity of words within idioms.

non-standard (501 tokens) to *hapax legomena* such as *non-ratified* (1 token), *non-amphibious* (1 token), etc. Specifically, the fact that 'non-X' has the highest expanding productivity means that it has more *hapax legomena* than any other morphological pattern. This notwithstanding, the fact that its different types yield a very large number of tokens results in a very low potential productivity value of 'non-X' (on the full corpus). Setting the minimum threshold value at 50, the average potential productivity rank for 'non-X' steadily gets worse as corpus size increases from rank 24 for the first intermediate corpus to rank 2404 for the full size corpus, in stark contrast to the rank position 1 it has for realized and expanding productivity (we use ranks since absolute productivity values for different measures cannot be compared to each other).

On the other hand, the pattern 'X-ish' which has the highest potential productivity when the minimum threshold is set to 100 exhibits radically different behavior. On the Wikipedia corpus this category yields 99 distinct types for a total of only 112 tokens, but including 87 *hapax legomena*. The most productive types are *cartoon-ish* and *blue-ish* (with 3 tokens each) and *40-ish*, *blues-ish*, *vanity-ish*, *place-ish*, *bully-ish*, *punk-ish*, *tree-ish*, *white-ish*, *noir-ish* (with 2 tokens each). All other types have 1 token each. The high proportion of *hapax legomena* pushes 'X-ish' at the very top of the potential productivity ranking. As is expected, the realized and expanding productivity ranks are much lower. However, they do increase steadily from rank 5204 and 3990 respectively for the first intermediate corpus to rank 403 and 242 for the full size corpus. We can interpret this trend as a consequence of the fact that for the category 'X-ish' almost every new token is also both a new type and a new *hapax legomena*. The effect of this is that it slows down the rate of decrease of the realized and expanding productivity measures (which always decrease inversely to corpus size), thus lifting the rank of 'X-ish' above that of competitors as corpus size increases.

Note that from a linguistic point of view, the hyphen in potential productivity patterns seems to signal the awareness of the writer/speaker regarding the 'novelty' of the complex adjective, along a continuum from compounding ('almost-X', 'X-capable') to more established derivational morphemes ('X-ish', 'un-X').

5 Conclusions and future work.

A general trend has consistently emerged throughout the analysis, as illustrated by the opposite properties of the categories 'non-X' and 'X-ish'. We have shown from a variety of angles how realized and expanding productivity measures tend to capture closely related aspects of morphological productivity, both in terms of the specific words and global correlation between productivity rankings. On the other hand, potential productivity consistently exhibits clearly different and indeed opposite properties compared to the other two, again both in terms of the specific words that score the highest values and in terms of productivity ranking correlation patterns.

The most significant question to be addressed next is the extent to which the above-mentioned conclusions about the relationships among different types of morphological productivity carry over to other segments of language.

Regarding complex adjectives, future work will focus in more detail on their internal typology, specifically considering the extent to which they impose selectional restrictions (whether morphosyntactic or semantic in nature) on the component associated with the base generator of a category, and the correlation patterns between such constraints and the three types of morphological productivity.

References

R. Harald Baayen. 1993. On Frequency, Transparency, and Productivity. In: Geert E. Booij and Jaap van Marle (eds). Yearbook of Morphology. Dordrecht: Kluwer Academic Publishers, 181-208.

R. Harald Baayen. 2001. *Word Frequency Distributions*. Dordrecht: Kluwer Academic Publishers.

R. Harald Baayen. 2006. Corpus Linguistics in Morphology: Morphological Productivity. In: Lüdeling, A. and M. Kytö (eds). Corpus Linguistics. An International Handbook. New York: Mouton De Gruyter.

Stefan Evert and Anke Lüdeling. 2001. Measuring Morphological Productivity: Is Automatic Preprocessing Sufficient? In: *Proceedings of the Corpus Linguistics 2001 Conference*, 167-175.

Karo Moilanen and Stephen Pulman. 2008. The Good, the Bad, and the Unknown: Morphosyllabic Sentiment Tagging of Unseen Words. In: *Proceedings of ACL 2008*.

How Creative is Your Writing? A Linguistic Creativity Measure from Computer Science and Cognitive Psychology Perspectives

Xiaojin Zhu, Zhiting Xu and Tushar Khot
Department of Computer Sciences
University of Wisconsin-Madison
Madison, WI, USA 53706
{jerryzhu, zhiting, tushar}@cs.wisc.edu

Abstract

We demonstrate that subjective creativity in sentence-writing can in part be predicted using computable quantities studied in Computer Science and Cognitive Psychology. We introduce a task in which a writer is asked to compose a sentence given a keyword. The sentence is then assigned a subjective creativity score by human judges. We build a linear regression model which, given the keyword and the sentence, predicts the creativity score. The model employs features on statistical language models from a large corpus, psychological word norms, and WordNet.

1 Introduction

One definition of *creativity* is "the ability to transcend traditional ideas, rules, patterns, relationships, or the like, and to create meaningful new ideas, forms, methods, interpretations, etc." Therefore, any computational measure of creativity needs to address two aspects simultaneously:

1. The item to be measured has to be different from other existing items. If one can model existing items with a statistical model, the new item should be an "outlier".

2. The item has to be meaningful. An item consists of random noise might well be an outlier, but it is not of interest.

In this paper, we consider the task of *measuring human creativity in composing a single sentence, when the sentence is constrained by a given keyword*. This simple task is a first step towards automatically measuring creativity in more complex natural language text. To further simplify the task, we will focus on the first aspect of creativity, i.e., quantifying how *novel* the sentence is. The second aspect, how *meaningful* the sentence is, requires the full power of Natural Language Processing, and is beyond the scope of this initial work. This, of course, raises the concern that we may regard a nonsense sentence as highly creative. This is a valid concern. However, in many applications where a creativity measure is needed, the input sentences are indeed well-formed. In such applications, our approach will be useful. We will leave this issue to future work. The present paper uses a data set (see the next section) in which all sentences are well-formed.

A major difficulty in studying creativity is the lack of an objective definition of creativity. Because creative writing is highly subjective ("I don't know what is creativity, but I recognize it when I see one"), we circumvent this problem by using human judgment as the ground truth. Our experiment procedure is the following. First, we give a keyword z to a human writer, and ask her to compose a sentence $\mathbf{x}$ about z. Then, the sentence $\mathbf{x}$ is evaluated by a group of human judges who assign it a subjective "creativity score" y. Finally, given a dataset consisting of many such keyword-sentence-score triples $(z, \mathbf{x}, y)$, we develop a statistical predictor $f(\mathbf{x}, z)$ that predicts the score y from the sentence $\mathbf{x}$ and keyword z.

There has been some prior attempts on characterizing creativity from a computational perspective, for examples see (Ritchie, 2001; Ritchie, 2007;

Proceedings of the NAACL HLT Workshop on Computational Approaches to Linguistic Creativity, pages 87–93,
Boulder, Colorado, June 2009.

Pease et al., 2001). The present work distinguishes itself in the use of a statistical machine learning framework, the design of candidate features, and its empirical study.

2 The Creativity Data Set

We select 105 keywords from the English version of the Leuven norms dataset (De Deyne and Storms, 2008b; De Deyne and Storms, 2008a). This ensures that each keyword has their norms feature defined, see Section 3.2. These are common English words.

The keywords are randomly distributed to 21 writers, each writer receives 5 keywords. Each writer composes one sentence per keyword. These 5 keywords are further randomly split into two groups:

1. The first group consists of 1 keyword. The writers are instructed to "write a not-so-creative sentence" about the keyword. Two examples are given: "Iguana has legs" for "Iguana", and "Anvil can get rusty" for "Anvil." The purpose of this group is to establish a non-creative baseline for the writers, so that they have a sense what does not count as creative.

2. The second group consists of 4 keywords. The writers are instructed to "try to write a creative sentence" about each keyword. They are also told to write a sentence no matter what, even if they cannot come up with a creative one. No example is given to avoid biasing their creative thinking.

In the next stage, all sentences are given to four human judges, who are native English speakers. The judges are not the writers nor the authors of this paper. The order of the sentences are randomized. The judges see the sentences and their corresponding keywords, but not the identity of the writers, nor which group the keywords are in. The judges work independently. For each keyword-sentence pair, each judge assigns a subjective creativity score between 0 and 10, with 0 being not creative at all (the judges are given the Iguana and Anvil examples for this), and 10 the most creative. The judges are encouraged to use the full scale when scoring. There is statistically significant ($p < 10^{-8}$) linear correlation among the four judges' scores, showing their general agreement on subjective creativity. Table 1 lists the pairwise linear correlation coefficient between all four judges.

Table 1: The pairwise linear correlation coefficient between four judges' creativity scores given to the 105 sentences. All correlations are statistically significant with $p < 10^{-8}$.

	judge 2	judge 3	judge 4
judge 1	0.68	0.61	0.74
judge 2		0.55	0.74
judge 3			0.61

The scores from four judges on each sentence are then averaged to produce a consensus score y. Table 2 shows the top and bottom three sentences as sorted by y.

As yet another sanity check, note that the judges have no information which sentences are from group 1 (where the writers are instructed to be non-creative), and which are from group 2. We would expect that if both the writers and the judges share some common notion of creativity, the mean score of group 1 should be smaller than the mean score of group 2. Figure 1 shows that this is indeed the case, with the mean score of group 1 being 1.5 ± 0.6, and that of group 2 being 5.1 ± 0.4 (95% confidence interval). A t-test shows that this difference is significant ($p < 10^{-11}$).

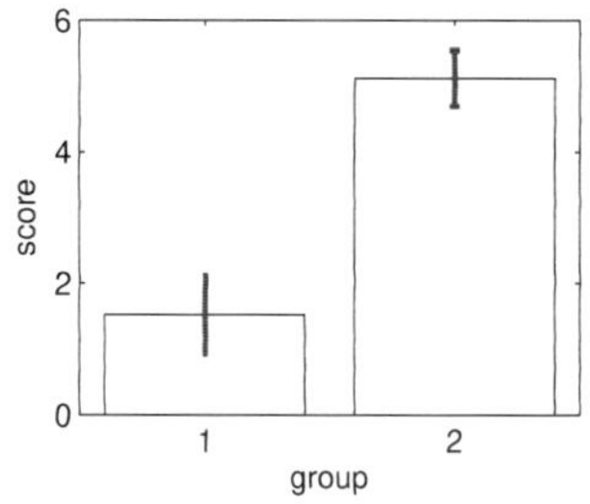

Figure 1: The mean creativity score for group 1 is significantly smaller than that for group 2. That is, the judges feel that sentences in group 2 are more creative.

To summarize, in the end our dataset consists of 105 keyword, sentence, creativity score tuples $\{(z_i, \mathbf{x}_i, y_i)\}$ for $i = 1, \ldots, 105$. The sentence group information is not included. This "Wisconsin Creative Writing" dataset is publicly available at `http:`

Table 2: Example sentences with the largest and smallest consensus creativity scores.

consensus score y	keyword z	sentence $\mathbf{x}$
9.25	hamster	She asked if I had any pets, so I told her I once did until I discovered that I liked taste of hamster.
9.0	wasp	The wasp is a dinosaur in the ant world.
8.5	dove	Dove can still bring war by the information it carries.
		...
0.25	guitar	A Guitar has strings.
0.25	leech	Leech lives in the water.
0.25	elephant	Elephant is a mammal.

//pages.cs.wisc.edu/~jerryzhu/pub/WisconsinCreativeWriting.txt.

3 Candidate Features for Predicting Creativity

In this section, we discuss two families of candidate features we use in a statistical model to predict the creativity of a sentence. One family comes from a Computer Science perspective, using large-corpus statistics (how people *write*). The other family comes from a Cognitive Psychology perspective, specifically the word norms data and WordNet (how people *think*).

3.1 The Computer Science Perspective: Language Modeling

We start from the following hypothesis: if the words in the sentence $\mathbf{x}$ frequently co-occur with the keyword z, then $\mathbf{x}$ is probably not creative. This is of course an over-simplification, as many creative sentences are about novel usage of common words[1]. Nonetheless, this hypothesis inspires some candidate features that can be computed from a large corpus.

In this study, we use the Google Web 1T 5-gram Corpus (Brants et al., 2007). This corpus was generated from about 10^{12} word tokens from Web pages. It consists of counts of N-gram for $N = 1, \ldots, 5$. We denote the words in a sentence by $\mathbf{x} = x_1, \ldots, x_n$, where $x_1 = \langle s \rangle$ and $x_n = \langle /s \rangle$ are special start- and end-of-sentence symbols. We design the following candidate features:

[f_1: Zero N-gram Fraction] Let $c(x_i^{i+N-1})$ be the count of the N-gram $x_i \ldots x_{i+N-1}$ in the corpus. Let $\delta(A)$ be the indicator function with value 1 if the predicate A is true, and 0 otherwise. A "Zero N-gram Fraction" feature is the fraction of zero N-gram counts in the sentence:

$$f_{1,N}(\mathbf{x}) = \frac{\sum_{i=1}^{n-N+1} \delta(c(x_i^{i+N-1}) = 0)}{n - N + 1}. \quad (1)$$

This provided us with 5 features, namely N-gram zero count fractions for each value of N. These features are a crude measure of how surprising the sentence $\mathbf{x}$ is. A feature value of 1 indicates that none of the N-grams in the sentence appeared in the Google corpus, a rather surprising situation.

[f_2: Per-Word Sentence Probability] This feature is the per-word log likelihood of the sentence, to normalize for sentence length:

$$f_2(\mathbf{x}) = \frac{1}{n} \log p(\mathbf{x}). \quad (2)$$

We use a 5-gram language model to estimate $p(\mathbf{x})$, with "naive Jelinek-Mercer" smoothing. As in Jelinek-Mercer smoothing (Jelinek and Mercer, 1980), it is a linear interpolation of N-gram language models for $N = 1 \ldots 5$. Let the Maximum Likelihood (ML) estimate of a N-gram language model be

$$p_{ML}^N(x_i | x_{i-N+1}^{i-1}) = \frac{c(x_{i-N+1}^i)}{c(x_{i-N+1}^{i-1})}, \quad (3)$$

which is the familiar frequency estimate of probability. The denominator is the count of the history of length $N - 1$, and the numerator is the count of the history plus the word to be predicted. A 5-gram

[1]For example, one might argue that Lincoln's famous sentence on government: "of the people, by the people, for the people" is creative, even though the keyword "government" frequently co-occurs with all the words in that sentence.

Jelinek-Mercer smoothing language model on sentence $\mathbf{x}$ is

$$p(\mathbf{x}) = \prod_{i=1}^{n} p(x_i|x_{i-5+1}^{i-1}) \quad (4)$$

$$p(x_i|x_{i-5+1}^{i-1}) = \sum_{N=1}^{5} \lambda_N P_{ML}^{N}(x_i|x_{i-N+1}^{i-1}), (5)$$

where the linear interpolation weights $\lambda_1 + \ldots + \lambda_5 = 1$. The optimal values of λ's are a function of history counts (binned into "buckets") $c(x_{i-N+1}^{i-1})$, and should be optimized with convex optimization from corpus. However, because our corpus is large, and because we do not require precise language modeling, we instead set the λ's in a heuristic manner. Starting from N=5 to 1, λ_N is set to zero until the N where we have enough history count for reliable estimate. Specifically, we require $c(x_{i-N+1}^{i-1}) > 1000$. The first N that this happens receives $\lambda_N = 0.9$. The next lower order model receives 0.9 fraction of the remaining weight, i.e., $\lambda_{N-1} = 0.9 \times (1 - 0.9)$, and so on. Finally, λ_1 receives all remaining weight to ensure $\lambda_1 + \ldots + \lambda_5 = 1$. This heuristic captures the essence of Jelinek-Mercer smoothing and is highly efficient, at the price of suboptimal interpolation weights.

[f_3: **Per-Word Context Probability**] The previous feature f_2 ignores the fact that our sentence $\mathbf{x}$ is composed around a given keyword z. Given that the writer was prompted with the keyword z, we are interested in the novelty of the sentence surrounding the keyword. Let x_k be the first occurrence of z in the sentence, and let $\mathbf{x}_{-k}$ be the *context* of the keyword, i.e., the sentence with the k-th word (the keyword) removed. This notion of context novelty can be captured by

$$p(\mathbf{x}_{-k}|x_k = z) = \frac{p(\mathbf{x}_{-k}, x_k = z)}{p(x_k = z)} = \frac{p(\mathbf{x})}{p(z)}, \quad (6)$$

where $p(\mathbf{x})$ is estimated from the naive Jelinek-Mercer 5-gram language model above, and $p(z)$ is estimated from a unigram language model. Our third feature is the length-normalized log likelihood of the context:

$$f_3(\mathbf{x}, z) = \frac{1}{n-1}\left(\log p(\mathbf{x}) - \log p(z)\right). \quad (7)$$

3.2 The Cognitive Psychology Perspective: Word Norms and WordNet

A text corpus like the one above captures how people *write* sentences related to a keyword. However, this can be different from how people *think about related concepts* in their head for the same keyword. In fact, common sense knowledge is often underrepresented in a corpus – for example, why bother repeating "A duck has a long neck" over and over again? However, this lack of co-occurrence does not necessarily make the duck sentence creative.

The way people think about concepts can in part be captured by *word norms* experiments in psychology. In such experiments, a human subject is provided with a keyword z, and is asked to write down the first (or a few) word x that comes to mind. When aggregated over multiple subjects on the same keyword, the experiment provides an estimate of the concept transition probability $p(x|z)$. Given enough keywords, one can construct a concept network where the nodes are the keywords, and the edges describe the transitions (Steyvers and Tenenbaum, 2005). For our purpose, we posit that a sentence $\mathbf{x}$ may not be creative with respect to a keyword z, if many words in $\mathbf{x}$ can be readily retrieved as the norms of keyword z. In a sense, the writer was thinking the obvious.

[f_4: **Word Norms Fraction**] We use the Leuven dataset, which consists of norms for 1,424 keywords (De Deyne and Storms, 2008b; De Deyne and Storms, 2008a). The original Leuven dataset is in Dutch, we use a version that is translated into English. For each sentence $\mathbf{x}$, we first exclude the keyword z from the sentence. We also remove punctuations, and map all words to lower case. We further remove all stopwords using the Snowball stopword list (Porter, 2001), and stem all words in the sentence and the norm word list using NLTK (Loper and Bird, 2002). We then count the number of words x_i that appear in the norm list of the keyword z in the Leuven data. Let this count be $c_{norm}(\mathbf{x}, z)$. The feature is the fraction of such norm words in the original sentence:

$$f_4(\mathbf{x}, z) = \frac{c_{norm}(\mathbf{x}, z)}{n}. \quad (8)$$

It is worth noting that the Leuven dataset is relatively small, with less than two thousand keywords. This is a common issue with psychology norms datasets, as massive number of human subjects are difficult to obtain. To scale our method up to handle large vocabulary in the future, one possible method is to automatically infer the norms of novel keywords using corpus statistics (e.g., distributional similarity).

[$f_5 - f_{13}$: **WordNet Similarity]** WordNet is another linguistic resource motivated by cognitive psychology. For each sentence $\mathbf{x}$, we compute WordNet 3.0 similarity between the keyword z and each word x_i in the sentence. Specifically, we use the "path similarity" provided by NLTK (Loper and Bird, 2002). Path similarity returns a score denoting how similar two word senses are, based on the shortest path that connects the senses in the hypernym/hyponym taxonomy. The score is in the range 0 to 1, except in those cases where a path cannot be found, in which case -1 is returned. A score of 1 represents identity, i.e., comparing a sense with itself. Let the similarities be $s_1 \ldots s_n$. We experiment with the following features: The mean, median, and variance of similarities:

$$f_5(\mathbf{x}, z) = \text{mean}(s_1 \ldots s_n) \quad (9)$$

$$f_6(\mathbf{x}, z) = \text{median}(s_1 \ldots s_n) \quad (10)$$

$$f_7(\mathbf{x}, z) = \text{var}(s_1 \ldots s_n). \quad (11)$$

Features $f_8, \ldots, f_{12}$ are the top five similarities. When the length of the sentence is shorter than five, we fill the remaining features with -1. Finally, feature f_{13} is the fraction of positive similarity:

$$f_{13}(\mathbf{x}, z) = \frac{\sum_{i=1}^{n} \delta(s_i > 0)}{n}. \quad (12)$$

4 Regression Analysis on Creativity

With the candidate features introduced in Section 3, we construct a linear regression model to predict the creativity scores given a sentence and its keyword.

The first question one asks in regression analysis is whether the features have a (linear) correlation with the creativity score y. We compute the correlation coefficient

$$\rho_i = \frac{\text{Cov}(f_i, y)}{\sigma_{f_i} \sigma_y} \quad (13)$$

for each candidate feature f_i separately on the first row in Table 3. Some observations:

- The feature f_4 (Word Norms Fraction) has the largest correlation coefficient -0.48 in terms of magnitude. That is, the more words in the sentence that are also in the norms of the keyword, the less creative the sentence is.

- The feature f_{12} (the 5-th WordNet similarity in the sentence to the keyword) has a large positive coefficient 0.47. This is rather unexpected. A closer inspection reveals that f_{12} equals -1 for about half of the sentences, and is around 0.05 for the other half. Furthermore, the second half has on average higher creativity scores. Although we hypothesized earlier that more similar words means lower creativity, this (together with the positive ρ for f_{10}, f_{11}) suggests the other way around: more similar words are correlated with higher creativity.

- The feature f_5 (mean WordNet similarity) has a negative correlation with creativity. This feature is related to f_{12}, but in a different direction. We speculate that this feature measures the strength of similar words, while f_{12} indirectly measures the number of similar words.

- The feature f_3 (Per-Word Context Probability) has a negative correlation with creativity. The more predictable the sentence around the keyword using a language model, the lower the creativity.

Next, we build a linear regression model to predict creativity. We use stepwise regression, which is a technique for feature selection by iteratively including / excluding candidate features from the regression model based on statistical significance tests (Draper and Smith, 1998). The result is a linear regression model with a small number of salient features. For the creativity dataset, the features (and their regression coefficients) included by stepwise regression are shown on the second row in Table 3. The corresponding linear regression model is

$$\hat{y}(\mathbf{x}, z) = -5.06 \times f_4 + 1.80 \times f_{12} - 0.76 \times f_3 - 3.39 \times f_5 + 0.92. \quad (14)$$

A plot comparing $\hat{y}$ and y is given in Figure 2. The root mean squared error (RMSE) of this model is

Table 3: ρ: The linear correlation coefficients between a candidate feature and the creativity score y. β: The selected features and their regression coefficients in stepwise linear regression.

	$f_{1,1}$	$f_{1,2}$	$f_{1,3}$	$f_{1,4}$	$f_{1,5}$	f_2	f_3	f_4	f_5
ρ	0.09	0.09	0.17	0.06	-0.04	-0.07	-0.32	-0.48	-0.41
β							-0.76	-5.06	-3.39

	f_6	f_7	f_8	f_9	f_{10}	f_{11}	f_{12}	f_{13}
ρ	-0.19	-0.25	-0.02	0.06	0.23	0.30	0.47	-0.01
β							1.80	

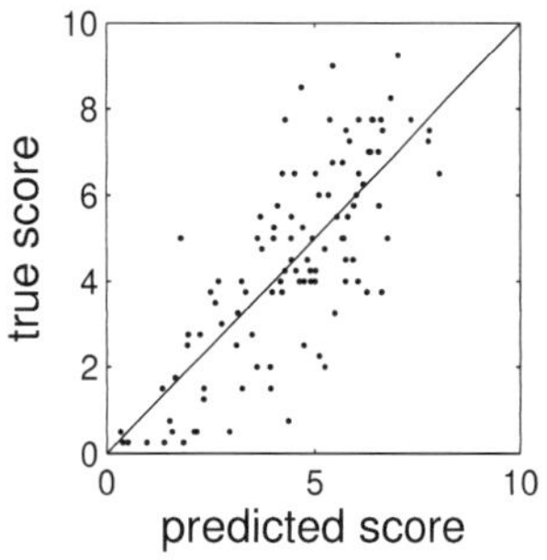

Figure 2: The creativity score $\hat{y}$ as predicted by the linear regression model in equation 14, compared to the true score y. Each dot is a sentence.

1.51. In contrast, the constant predictor would have RMSE 2.37 (i.e., the standard deviation of y).

We make two comments:

1. It is interesting to note that our intuitive features are able to partially predict subjective creativity scores. On the other hand, we certainly do not claim that our features or model solved this difficult problem.

2. All three kinds of knowledge: corpus statistics (f_3), word norms (f_4), and WordNet (f_5, f_{12}) are included in the regression model. Coincidentally, these features have the largest correlation coefficients with the creativity score. The fact that they are all included suggests that these are not redundant features, and each captures some aspect of creativity.

5 Conclusions and Future Work

We presented a simplified creativity prediction task, and showed that features derived from statistical language modeling, word norms, and WordNet can partially predict human judges' subjective creativity scores.

Our problem setting is artificial, in that the creativity of the sentences are judged with respect to their respective keywords, which are assumed to be known beforehand. This allows us to design features centered around the keywords. We hope our analysis can be extended to the setting where the only input is the sentence, without the keyword. This can potentially be achieved by performing keyword extraction on the sentence first, and apply our analysis on the extracted keyword.

As discussed in the introduction, our analysis is susceptible to nonsense input sentences, which could be predicted as highly creative. Combining our analysis with a "sensibility analysis" is an important future direction.

Finally, our model might be adapted to explain why a sentence is deemed creative, by analyzing the contribution of individual features in the model.

6 Acknowledgments

We thank the anonymous reviewers for suggestions on related work and other helpful comments, and Chuck Dyer, Andrew Goldberg, Jake Rosin, and Steve Yazicioglu for assisting the project. This work is supported in part by the Wisconsin Alumni Research Foundation.

References

Thorsten Brants, Ashok C. Popat, Peng Xu, Franz J. Och, and Jeffrey Dean. 2007. Large language models in machine translation. In *EMNLP*.

S. De Deyne and G Storms. 2008a. Word associations: Network and semantic properties. *Behavior Research Methods*, 40:213–231.

S. De Deyne and G Storms. 2008b. Word associations: Norms for 1,424 Dutch words in a continuous task. *Behavior Research Methods*, 40:198–205.

Norman R. Draper and Harry Smith. 1998. *Applied Regression Analysis (Wiley Series in Probability and Statistics)*. John Wiley & Sons Inc, third edition.

Frederick Jelinek and Robert L. Mercer. 1980. Interpolated estimation of Markov source parameters from sparse data. In *Workshop on Pattern Recognition in Practice*.

Edward Loper and Steven Bird. 2002. NLTK: The natural language toolkit. In *The ACL Workshop on Effective Tools and Methodologies for Teaching Natural Language Processing and Computational Linguistics*, pages 62–69.

Alison Pease, Daniel Winterstein, and Simon Colton. 2001. Evaluating machine creativity. In *Workshop on Creative Systems, 4th International Conference on Case Based Reasoning*, pages 129–137.

Martin F. Porter. 2001. Snowball: A language for stemming algorithms. Published online.

Graeme Ritchie. 2001. Assessing creativity. In *Proceedings of the AISB01 Symposium on Artificial Intelligence and Creativity in Arts and Science*, pages 3–11.

Graeme Ritchie. 2007. Some empirical criteria for attributing creativity to a computer program. *Minds and Machines*, 17(1):67–99.

Mark Steyvers and Joshua Tenenbaum. 2005. The large scale structure of semantic networks: Statistical analyses and a model of semantic growth. *Cognitive Science*, 29(1):41–78.

'Sorry' seems to be the hardest word

Allan Ramsay
School of Computer Science
Univ of Manchester
Manchester M60 1QD, UK

Debora Field
Dept of Computer Science
Univ of Sheffield
Sheffield S1 4DP, UK

Abstract

We are interested in the ways that language is used to achieve a variety of goals, where the same utterance may have vastly different consequences in different situations. This is closely related to the topic of creativity in language. The fact that the same utterance can be used to achieve a variety of goals opens up the possibility of using it to achieve new goals. The current paper concentrates largely on an implemented system for exploring how the effects of an utterance depend on the situation in which it is produced, but we will end with some speculations about how how utterances can come to have new kinds of uses.

1 Introduction

We are interested in the ways that language is used to achieve a variety of goals, where the same utterance may have vastly different consequences in different situations. We will take, as a running example, the use of the single word *'Sorry'*.

We will look at a number of situations in which this word may be uttered, and investigate the ways in which its consequences may be determined by considering the goals and belief states of the participants. The kinds of reasoning that lie behind the various uses of this word are, we believe, typical of the way that utterances can be used to achieve novel aims. *'Sorry'* is perhaps a fairly extreme case: very simple indeed on the surface, very complex indeed in terms of its uses. Any account of how this specific word gets used will have lessons for other kinds of novel action.

As with many common but slippery words, dictionary definitions are not much help when trying to work out what *'sorry'* means: Merriam-Webster, for instance, has 'feeling sorrow, regret, or penitence' as the primary definition, and the free dictionary (`www.thefreedictionary.com` has 'Feeling or expressing sympathy, pity, or regret'. These definitions are, as is common for words whose meanings are highly context dependent, essentially circular. How much do we gain from knowing that *'sorry'* is a word that is used to express sorrow, or from the free dictionary's definition of *'sympathy'* as a 'feeling or an expression of pity or sorrow for the distress of another'?

Perhaps, then, considering a set of examples of situations where someone utters this word is a better way of getting at what it means. The following is a rather long list, but then there are a very wide set of situations in which people say *'sorry'*. That is, after all, the problem:

(1) a. EXPRESSION OF DISAPPOINTMENT
I'm sorry I missed your talk. I forgot to set my alarm. I'd really been looking forward to seeing your demo.

b. APOLOGY FOR OWN ACTION WHILE NOT TAKING FULL PERSONAL RESPONSIBILITY
I'm sorry I missed your talk. My flight was delayed. [situation: S & H mutually knew that S was counting on H to help with a demo during the talk.]

Proceedings of the NAACL HLT Workshop on Computational Approaches to Linguistic Creativity, pages 94–101,
Boulder, Colorado, June 2009.

c. APOLOGY FOR OWN ACTION WHILE ALSO TAKING FULL PERSONAL RESPONSIBILITY
I'm sorry I missed your talk. I forgot to set my alarm. [situation: S & H mutually knew that S was counting on H to help with a demo during the talk.]

(2) a. EXPRESSION OF EMPATHY
I'm sorry that this situation is so awful for you. I would not be coping if I were in your shoes.

b. APOLOGY FOR A 3RD PARTY'S ACTION WHILE NOT TAKING FULL PERSONAL RESPONSIBILITY
I'm sorry that this situation is so awful for you. My parents have really excelled themselves this time [sarcasm].

c. APOLOGY FOR A 3RD PARTY'S ACTION WHILE ALSO TAKING FULL PERSONAL RESPONSIBILITY
I'm sorry that this situation is so awful for you. As head of the division I take full responsibility, and I am submitting my resignation.

d. APOLOGY FOR OWN ACTION WHILE ALSO TAKING FULL PERSONAL RESPONSIBILITY
I'm sorry that this situation is so awful for you. I should have been more careful.

e. EXPRESSION OF EMPATHY
I'm sorry that this situation is so awful for you. I'm not sorry for causing the situation, because I didn't cause it. But I am sorry it is so awful.

(3) a. EXPRESSION OF DISDAIN+PITY
I'm sorry they're not good enough. It's your loss.

b. APOLOGY FOR OWN ACTION WHILE ALSO TAKING FULL PERSONAL RESPONSIBILITY
I'm sorry they're not good enough. I tried very hard, but I couldn't get them quite right.

(4) a. EXPRESSION OF EMPATHY
I'm sorry, Dave, I'm afraid I can't do that. All the pod locks are jammed shut. I have tried everything I can think of, but I can't get them open.

b. APOLOGY FOR OWN ACTION WHILE ALSO TAKING FULL PERSONAL RESPONSIBILITY
I'm sorry, Dave, I'm afraid I can't do that. I have turned the tables and you are my prisoner now.

(5) a. EXPRESSION OF REGRET
I'm sorry I told him. Things would be much simpler for me now if I'd kept quiet.

b. APOLOGY FOR OWN ACTION WHILE ALSO TAKING FULL PERSONAL RESPONSIBILITY
I'm sorry I told him. I know I promised you I wouldn't but it just slipped out.

(6) a. EXPRESSION OF REGRET
I'm sorry I killed their daughter. She was in the wrong place at the wrong time. [Speaker feels no remorse for killing, only regret for killing the wrong person.]

b. APOLOGY FOR OWN ACTION WHILE ALSO TAKING FULL PERSONAL RESPONSIBILITY
I'm sorry I killed their daughter. It was a terrible thing I did.

If nothing else, these examples show how flexible the word *'sorry'* is. About all they have in common is that the speaker is referring to some action or state of affairs which is disadvantageous to someone (usually, but not necessarily, either the speaker or hearer: see (6) for a counter-example). The follow-up sentences then say something more about the speaker's attitude to this action or state of affairs (we will use the generic term 'event' to cover both of these). Just what the speaker's attitude to the event is varies wildly: the glosses in the examples use terms like 'empathy', 'apology', 'regret', but these are almost as slippery as *'sorry'* itself.

2 Literal uses of *'sorry'*

The idea that *'sorry'* is ambiguous, with fifteen different senses, is ludicrous. Apart from anything else, we have another dozen examples up our sleeves that do not fit any of the patterns above, and it would be easy to find yet further uses. It seems more plausible that it has a single meaning, which can be used as the trigger for a variety of ideas depending on the the nature of the event and the beliefs of the speaker and hearer. The task of determining what a speaker meant by using this word in a given utterance then devolves to epistemic inference. This does not actually make it very easy; but it does at least put it in the right place.

We will take it, then, that *'sorry'* is an adjective that takes a sentential complement, and that the interpretation of a sentence involving it is something like Fig. 1[1]. In other words, (1a) says that right now the relation *sorry* holds between me and the fact that I missed your talk.

That seems fair enough, but it also seems rather weak. We cannot do anything with it unless we know what follows from saying that the relation *sorry* holds between a person and a proposition. In other words, we need to start writing axioms (meaning postulates, rules, definitions, ...) to link this relation with other concepts.

The first thing we note is that any such axioms will be inherently intensional: *sorry* is a relationship between a person and a proposition (a description of a state of affairs). We will therefore have to use some kind of intensional logic for writing our axioms. We follow (Chierchia and Turner, 1987; Fox and Lappin, 2005) in using a variant on 'property theory' (Turner, 1987) for this purpose. Property theory has the required expressive power for writing rules that discuss propositions, and it has an axiomatisation which allows the implementation of a practical theorem prover (Ramsay, 2001).

So what do we want to say about *sorry*? The very first observation is that it is factive: if I am sorry about something, then it must have happened. I cannot (sensibly) say that I am sorry that the moon is made of green cheese, because it isn't. Our first axiom, then, says that anything that anyone is sorry about is indeed true (A1):

(A1)
$\forall B \forall C(sorry(B,C) \rightarrow C)$

The only other thing that all the examples above have in common is that the speaker wishes that the proposition she is sorry about were not true (A2):

(A2)
$\forall B \forall C(sorry(B,C) \rightarrow C \,\&\, wish(B, \neg(C)))$

There are, indeed, cases where absolutely nothing more follows from the use of *'Sorry'*:

(7) My dear Pandora, you're going to be sorry you opened that.

In (7), the speaker is simply telling their hearer that she is going to wish she hadn't opened it, whatever it is. No hint of apology or remorse or empathy. Just a plain a statement of fact: at some time in the future the hearer is going to wish that she'd left the box closed.

It is hard to find a distinction between the set of propositions that follow from every use of a term and its meaning. We will therefore take it that (A1) and (A2) characterise the meaning of *'sorry'*: that the proposition in question is true, and that the person who is sorry about it wishes that it wasn't.

[1] We use the 'restricted quantifiers' $\forall X :: \{P\}Q$ and $\exists X :: \{P\}Q$ as shorthand for $\forall X(P \rightarrow Q)$ and $\exists X(P\&Q)$

$$
\begin{array}{l}
\exists L at(L, \\
\quad sorry(ref(\lambda M(speaker(M))), \\
\qquad \exists N\text{: } \{past(now,N)\} \\
\qquad\quad \exists O event(miss,O,P,Q) \\
\qquad\qquad \&\theta(O,object,ref(\lambda R(own(ref(\lambda S(hearer(S))),R) \,\&\, sort(talk,R,T,U)))) \\
\qquad\qquad\; \&\theta(O,agent,ref(\lambda V(speaker(V)))) \,\&\, aspect(N,simplePast,O))) \\
\quad \&aspect(now,simple,L)
\end{array}
$$

Figure 1: Logical form for (1a)

How, then, do all the other examples get their force? The key is that once you have said that you wish something were not true, two questions arise: why do you wish it were not so, and *why are you telling me that you wish it were not so*. To answer these two questions you have to think harder about what the proposition in question is like.

There are two particularly interesting issues. Who, if anyone, was responsible for the proposition being true; and who, if anyone, is affected by it. In particular, if the speaker is the person who was responsible for it then wishing that it were not now true entails wishing that they had not earlier performed the action that led to it; and if the person who is affected by it is the hearer, and the effect is adverse, then the fact that the speaker wishes it were not true establishes some degree of empathy between the two.

Before we can start formalising these notions we need to introduce rules that specify responsibility and affectedness.

The simplest rules for these notions are centred around the roles that individuals play in events. What, for instance, is the difference between (8a) and (8b)?

(8) a. I saw him fall off a cliff.
b. I watched him fall off a cliff.

They both refer to the same set of events: he fell off a cliff, and I had my eyes open and looking in that direction at the time (and I was awake, and various other routine side-conditions). The difference is that (8b) implies a degree of control: that I was aware that he was falling, and I deliberately kept my attention on what I was seeing.

One way of capturing this distinction concisely is by using names for thematic roles which reflect the way that the individuals concerned are involved: if, for instance, we say that the speaker was the *patient* of the seeing event in (8a), but was the *agent* in (8b), then we can use rules like (A3) and (A4) to distinguish between cases where someone was just accidentally involved in an event from ones where they caused it or where they intentionally caused it.

(A3)
$\forall B \forall C$: $\{\theta(C,actor,B) \vee \theta(C,agent,B)\}$
$cause(B,C)$

(A4)
$\forall B \forall C$: $\{\theta(C,agent,B)\} intended(B,C)$

We can use (A3) and (A4) to pick out cases where the person who is sorry for some state of affairs is in fact the person who caused it to come about. We will not yet say much about what follows from recognising these cases. For the moment we will just label them as cases where the person regrets the event in question.

(A5)
$\forall B \forall C : \{wish(B, \neg(C))\}$
$\forall D : \{C \rightarrow cause(B,D)\}$
$regret(B,D))$

Note that what the person is sorry about is a proposition, but what they regret is an event (in a classical Davidsonian treatment of events (Davidson, 1980)). The key question here is whether the description of the state of affairs entails the existence of an event for which they are responsible. The rules in (A3) and (A4) provide the relevant support in very many cases: just using a verb whose set of thematic roles includes one with connotations of causality is a shorthand for making a statement about responsibility. There are, of course, other more complex cases, but in many such cases the key lies in spotting sequences of causally related events where the start of the sequence involves the person in a causal role.

Given these rules, we can distinguish between the cases in (9):

(9) a. I'm sorry I saw him fall off a cliff.
b. I'm sorry I watched him fall off a cliff.

If we assume that the hearer believes what the speaker tells them, then following (9)b we can ask who believes that someone regrets something:

| ?- *prove(bel(X, regret(A, B))).*
A = '#speaker',
B = '#166',
X = '#hearer' ?
yes

The hearer believes that the speaker regrets something, namely the action of watching someone fall of a cliff (represent here by a Skolem constant *#166*, introduced by the existential quantifier for the event in the logical form for (9b), shown in Fig. 2.

$$
\begin{array}{l}
\mathit{sorry}(\#\mathit{user}, \\
\quad \exists O\text{: } \{\mathit{past}(\mathit{now},O)\} \\
\quad \exists P\mathit{event}(\mathit{watch},P,Q,R) \\
\qquad \&\theta(P, \\
\qquad\quad \text{-}\mathit{event}, \\
\qquad\quad \exists S\text{: } \{\mathit{sort}(\mathit{cliff},S,T,U)\} \\
\qquad\quad \exists V\mathit{event}(\mathit{fall},V,W,X)\ \&\ \theta(V,\mathit{agent},\#171)\ \&\ \mathit{off}(V,S)\ \&\ \mathit{aspect}(\mathit{now},\mathit{simple},V)) \\
\quad \&\theta(P,\mathit{agent},\#\mathit{user})\ \&\ \mathit{aspect}(O,\mathit{simplePast},P))
\end{array}
$$

Figure 2: Logical form for (9b)

Although the speaker regrets watching this unfortunate event, he cannot be seen as apologising for it. An apology expresses regret that the speaker caused something unfortunate to happen *to the hearer*. We need the axiom A6 below to describe this situation:

(A6)

$$
\begin{array}{l}
\forall B\forall C\text{: } \{\mathit{regret}(B,C)\} \\
\quad \forall D\forall E\text{: } \{\mathit{want}(D, \neg(E)) \\
\qquad \&\ E \rightarrow \mathit{event}(F,C,G,H)\} \\
\qquad \mathit{apologise}(B,D,C)
\end{array}
$$

In other words, if B regrets performing the action C then if C is part of some situation which D regards as undesirable, the B can be seen as apologising to D.

We also need, of course, descriptions of situations which people might find undesirable. A typical rule might be as in (A7), which simply says that people do not want to be hurt (any individual B wants the proposition $\mathit{event}(\mathit{hurt},D,E,F)\&\theta(D,\mathit{object},B)$ to be false for all D, E and F):

(A7)

$$
\begin{array}{l}
\forall B\forall C\forall D\mathit{want}(B, \\
\qquad \neg(\mathit{event}(\mathit{hurt},D,E,F)\&\theta(D,\mathit{object},B)))
\end{array}
$$

Given A6 and A7, we can see that saying *'I am sorry I hurt you'* would be an apology: the speaker is saying that he wishes that *'I hurt you'* was not true, and since this is something which was under the speaker's control (so he regrets it), then since it also something that the hearer did not want then the speaker's utterance of this sentence is indeed an apology.

Clearly this approach to the problem requires a great deal of general knowledge. There is nothing esoteric about A7. On the contrary, it as about as obvious a fact of life as it is possible to imagine.

Collecting a large enough body of such rules to cope with everyday language is, indeed, a daunting task, but it is the sheer number of such rules that make it problematic, not the nature of the rules themselves.

Once we have this background knowledge, however, we can see that various rather subtle differences between the basic uses of *'Sorry'* emerge quite straightforwardly from rules like the ones above. Many of these rules are inherently intensional, as noted above, so for a program to be able to work out whether someone is actually apologising for some action it will have to have access to a theorem prover for an intensional logic. Fortunately such theorem provers exist (see e.g. (Ramsay, 2001) for an example).

3 Indirect uses

The axioms in Section 2 let us distinguish between some of the examples in (1)–(6). We are faced with two remaining questions. What do we gain by labelling some examples as instances of regret or apology, and what do we do about the less obvious cases?

The key to both these questions is that linguistic acts are inherently epistemic. They are concerned with conveying information about what the speaker S believes, including what she believes about the hearer H's beliefs, with the intention of changing H's beliefs.

We will consider, in particular, the cases that we have labelled as apologies. What is the point of an apology? What does S want to achieve by making an apology?

We have characterised apologising above as the act of saying that S wishes some proposition P were not true, in a situation where S is responsible for P being true and is something that H would like to be untrue. Note that all that S actually did was to say that she wished P were not true. There is nothing in the form of the utterance *'I am sorry that I didn't do the washing up'* that makes it obviously different from *'I am sorry that you didn't do the washing up'*. The two utterances do, of course, feel very different–one is an apology, the other is something more like a threat or an admonition–but their structural properties are very similar. They are both, essentially, simple declarative sentences.

To get a closer grip on why they convey such radically different underlying consequences, we will revisit the idea that linguistic actions are just actions, to be dealt with by specifying their preconditions and effects, to be linked together by some planning algorithm so that they lead to outcomes that are desirable for the speaker.

We have argued elsewhere for a very sparse treatment of speech acts (Field and Ramsay, 2004; Field and Ramsay, 2007; Ramsay and Field, 2008). The argument starts by considering the classical use of AI planning theory in domains such as the blocks world, where the preconditions of an action are a set of propositions that must hold before that action can be performed, and the effects are a set of actions that will definitely hold after it has been performed. If preconditions and effects were not entirely rigid in this way then planning algorithms, from the original means-end analysis of (Fikes and Nilsson, 1971) through more modern approaches that involve static analysis of the relationships between different types of action (Kambhampati, 1997; Nguyen and Kambhampati, 2001; Blum and Furst, 1997) would just not work.

Suppose, however, that we try to give this kind of description of the linguistic act of stating something. What should the preconditions and effects of the act of stating something be?

There seem to be very few limits on the situations in which you can state something. Consider (3) (repeated here).

(3) a. EXPRESSION OF DISDAIN+PITY
I'm sorry they're not good enough. It's your loss.

b. APOLOGY FOR OWN ACTION WHILE ALSO TAKING FULL PERSONAL RESPONSIBILITY
I'm sorry they're not good enough. I tried very hard, but I couldn't get them quite right.

It is very hard to say that the speaker is performing two different actions when she utters the words *'I'm sorry they're not good enough'* in these two examples. She is, clearly, intending to achieve different outcomes in the two cases, but they are, surely, the same action, in the same way that getting the milk out of the fridge in order to make custard and getting the milk out of the fridge in order to in order to make space for the orange juice are the same action. In both (3a) and (3b) S is claiming to be sorry that they (whatever they are) are not good enough. In (3a), of course, it is clear that she does not believe that this is true. Nonetheless, the form of the utterance makes it clear that she is making a statement.

This is typical of linguistic actions. It is possible to state things that you do not believe, or to ask questions where you already know the answer, or to issue commands which you do not want to have carried out. Unless we want to have as many sub-types of the action 'statement' as there are examples in (1)–(6) (and then the dozen other examples that we did not include, and then all the ones we haven't thought of) then we have to see whether we can make a single, rather simple, act cover all these cases.

What are the preconditions and effects of this act? The only completely essential precondition for making a statement is that you have the proposition in question in mind, and the only thing that you can be sure that your hearer will believe is that you had it in mind. When S states a proposition P, S may believe it (3a); or she may disbelieve it (3b); or she may be unsure about it (there are no examples of this in (1)–(6), but situations where a speaker makes a statement despite not having an opinion on whether it is true or not can occur). The situation for H is even less clear: H may or may not believe that S is being honest, and he may or may not believe that S is reliable. Hence, H may decide that although S has claimed P she does not actually believe it; and even if he does decide that she believes it, he may regard her being unreliable (on, at least, the topic of

P) so he may decide not to believe it anyway. And as for what S believes that H will believe after she has uttered P, the possibilities are almost boundless ...The only thing you can be reasonably sure of is that so long as H was paying attention and the utterance was not ambiguous then H will know that a claim was made, and *hence that its preconditions must have held* (because that is what preconditions are: a set of propositions that must held in order for the action to be performable).

The only safe characterisation of a claim seems to be as in Fig. 3

claim(S, H, P)
  pre: bel(S, P) or bel(S, ¬P) or bel(S, P or ¬P)
  effects:

Figure 3: Preconditions and effects of 'claim'

The preconditions will hold so long as S has thought about P (and so long as P is not something paradoxical like the Liar Paradox). They do not hold at all times for all speakers. Until you read the sentence *'Dan Holden hit some good first serves last night'* it was not the case that you believed that this sentence was either true or false, because you had never thought about it before. Thus the preconditions of this action are roughly equivalent to saying that S has the proposition P in her mind.

Given the extremely wide range of conclusions that H can come to, it seems safest not to say anything about the effects of a claim. It would be fairly pointless to say that the effects of a claim are either H believes S believes P or H believes that S does not believe P or H believes that S believes that P is false, and that either H believes P or H is agnostic about P or H believes P is false. What we can say is that if H realises that S has claimed P then he will be recognise that S deliberately raised the topic of P's truth value. In order to come to a conclusion about *why* S should do this, he will have to come to some view on S's opinion of P. In other words, a claim is an invitation to verify *bel(S, P) or bel(S, ¬P) or bel(S, P or ¬P)*.

This will, of course, always be verifiable unless P is a paradox, but the process of verification will typically have side-effects. In particular, *bel(S, P) or bel(S, ¬P) or bel(S, P or ¬P)* can be verified by showing that *bel(S, P)* holds, or by showing that *bel(S, ¬P)* holds. H's first move, then, will be to investigate *bel(S, P)*. S will know this, so if S does believe P then if she also thinks that H has a reasonable model of her beliefs then she will conclude that H will shortly have the proposition *bel(S, P)* available to him.

If, on the other hand, S believes that P is false then again assuming that H has a reasonable model of her beliefs she can assume that he will shortly have *bel(S, ¬P)* available to him. In other words, if S believes that H's picture of her beliefs is reasonably complete and reasonably accurate then by claiming P she can bring either P or $\neg P$ to H's attention.

Given that linguistic acts are public, in the sense that all the participants are aware that they have taken place and that all the other participants are aware of this, both S and H will be aware that H knows that one of $bel(S, P)$, $bel(S, \neg P)$ and $bel(S, Por\neg P)$ is true. However, this disjunction is so uninformative that it amounts to an invitation to H to try to work out which disjunct actually holds. Furthermore, S knows that it is tantamount to such an invitation, and H knows that S knows this. Thus the simple act of producing a highly uninformative utterance in a public situation will lead both S and H to expect that they will both believe that H will try find out which of the disjuncts actually holds.

This allows S to say *'I'm sorry they're not good enough'* in a situation where both parties know that S actually believes they are good enough. H will try to check the preconditions of S's act of claiming to be sorry about the situation. He will not manage to verify that S is sorry about, but he can show that she is not: the fact that she believes they are good enough will clash with (A1), which says that you can only actually be sorry about things that are true. Thus S has brought to the fact that she does not believe they are not good enough, whilst also raising the possibility that she might have been, but is not, sorry about something. She has done so in a way that has forced H to think about it, and to arrive at these conclusions for himself, which is likely to be more forceful and indeed more convincing than if she had just asserted it. In other words, by saying that she has sorry about something she has conveyed the complex message that the proposition in question is not true, and that she is not apologising for

H's disappointment with the situation.

4 Conclusions

In the first part of the paper we explored the way that the consequences of direct uses of a word like *'Sorry'* can vary, depending on aspects of the proposition under consideration. Saying that you wish some state of affairs for which you are responsible and which adversely affects your hearer did not hold has different consequences from saying that you wish that some more neutral proposition were true. The degree of (admitted) responsibility of the speaker for the situation affects these consequences – *'I'm sorry I shrank your favourite jumper'* carries a different message from *'I'm sorry your favourite jumper shrank when I did the washing yesterday'* because of the indirectness of the causal link between me and the shrinking in the second example. We have all the machinery for accounting for examples like these implemented, via a theorem prover which can handle intensionality and which can effectively ascribe beliefs to individuals. Clearly this relies on background knowledge about everyday facts such as the obsvervation that people generally dislike being hurt (A7). We do not have a massive repository of such general knowledge, and inspection of publicly available sources such as CYC and ConceptNet suggests that they generally omit such very basic facts, presumably because they are so self-evident that the are below the radar of the compilers. Nonetheless, there is nothing about such rules that makes them particularly difficult to express, and we have no doubt that if we had more general-knowledge of this kind then we would be able to determine the consequences of a wide range of literal uses of *'Sorry'*.

The later discussion of indirect uses of *'sorry'* is more speculative: we have an implementation of a planner which can use very underspecified actions descriptions of the kind in Fig. 3 by looking for instantiations of such an action which *entail* some proposition in a particular situation, rather than simply looking for actions whose effects match the user's goals, and we have used this to explore a number of examples of 'indirect speech acts'. There is more work to be done here, but the kind of analysis we are looking at has the potential for handling entirely novel uses of linguistic acts that approaches that enumerate a fixed set of acts (e.g. (Austin, 1962; Searle, 1969; Cohen and Perrault, 1979; Allen and Perrault, 1980; Cohen et al., 1990) with detailed preconditions and effects, would find more difficult. In the same way that having a very simple definition of *'sorry'* and allowing the different consequences to emerge in the light of other information that is available in the situation lets us treat an open-ended set of literal uses of this word, using a very simple notion of linguistic act and allowing the different consequences to emerge in different situations leads to the possibility of accounting for entirely novel uses.

References

J F Allen and C R Perrault. 1980. Analysing intention in utterances. *Artificial Intelligence*, 15:148–178.

J Austin. 1962. *How to Do Things with Words*. Oxford University Press, Oxford.

A Blum and M L Furst. 1997. Fast planning through planning graph analysis. *Artificial Intelligence*, 90(1-2).

G Chierchia and R Turner. 1987. Semantics and property theory. *Linguistics and Philosophy*, 11(3).

P R Cohen and C R Perrault. 1979. Elements of a plan-based theory of speech acts. *Cognitive Science*, 7(2):171–190.

P R Cohen, J Morgan, and M E Pollack. 1990. *Intentions in Communication*. Bradford Books, Cambridge, Mass.

D Davidson. 1980. *Essays on actions and events*. Clarendon Press, Oxford.

D G Field and A M Ramsay. 2004. Sarcasm, deception, and stating the obvious: Planning dialogue without speech acts. *Artificial Intelligence Review*, 22:149–171.

D G Field and A M Ramsay. 2007. Minimal sets of minimal speech acts. In *Recent Advances in Natural Language Processing (RANLP'07)*, pages 193–199, Borovets, Bulgaria.

R E Fikes and N J Nilsson. 1971. Strips: a new approach to the application of theorem proving to problem solving. *Artificial Intelligence*, 3(4):251–288.

C Fox and S Lappin. 2005. *Foundations of Intensional Semantics*. Blackwell.

S Kambhampati. 1997. Refinement planning as a unifiying framework for plan synthesis. *AI Magazine*, 18(2):67–97.

X Nguyen and S Kambhampati. 2001. Reviving partial order planning. In *IJCAI*, pages 459–466.

A M Ramsay and D G Field. 2008. Speech acts, epistemic planning and Grice's maxims. *Logic and Computation*, 18:431–457.

A M Ramsay. 2001. Theorem proving for untyped constructive λ-calculus: implementation and application. *Logic Journal of the Interest Group in Pure and Applied Logics*, 9(1):89–106.

J R Searle. 1969. *Speech Acts: an Essay in the Philosophy of Language*. Cambridge University Press, Cambridge.

R Turner. 1987. A theory of properties. *Journal of Symbolic Logic*, 52(2):455–472.